Rugby Portland Cement Transport

A story of vehicles and their drivers

Glen McBirnie

This book is dedicated to all former members of RPC Transport. It should not be regarded nor interpreted as any kind of technical reference. This is a story about people, characters and individuals, many of whose own personalities contributed wholeheartedly to the undisputed success of the Company over many years. If I have made errors or omissions in the names, dates or events recounted in this story - my sincere apologies; there has been no deliberate intention on my part to offend any person in the telling.

Glen McBirnie - Author

All rights reserved except for normal review purposes. No part of this book may be reproduced in any form or by any means without prior written consent of the author, Glen McBirnie, or the publisher, Silver Link Publishing, Kettering.

This book is intended for general interest. It has been published with financial support from The Rugby Group Benevolent Fund. We have used all reasonable endeavours to ensure the accuracy of the information in this publication. Much of the information in this book however, has been obtained from third parties and although we believe it to be correct it has not been verified. The Rugby Group Benevolent Fund does not guarantee or warrant the accuracy or completeness, factual correctness or reliability of any information contained and does not accept any liability for any errors or omissions including any inaccuracies or typographical errors.

Published by:
Silver Link Publishing Ltd
The Trundle
Ringstead Road
Great Addington
Kettering
Northamptonshire NN14 4BW

Tel/Fax 01536 330588
Email: sales@nostalgiacollection.com
www.nostalgiacollection.com
Copyright © Glen McBirnie 2015

Supported by:
The Rugby Group Benevolent Fund Ltd
www.rugbygroupbenevolentfund.org.uk

ISBN 978-1-85794-447-1

Cataloguing in Publication Data is available from The British Library

Designed by:
Oxygen Graphics, Rugby
www.oxygengraphics.co.uk

ABOUT THIS BOOK

Rugby Portland Cement Transport – A story about vehicles and their drivers

Part One of this story, launched in July 2002 is still selling mainly on recommendation from satisfied readers and the positive reaction of Rugby Cement employees and former driver colleagues alike. The impact of this book has been to urge many people from around the country to realise that photographs of Rugby Cement were wanted. Since 2005 onwards I have been extremely fortunate to acquire many of the original black and white photographs which I knew had existed but did not know where. I have also received very many more entirely new to me. What you, the reader, are about to see and enjoy therefore is my second time around interpretation of this new material which again includes colour photographs from my own collection plus that of others. This time transport of the product includes horse and cart, steam lorries, Thames barge, petrol/diesel lorries, canal boat operation and rail bulk transport to depots. In addition much new reference material is again supported by as yet unused photographs which show quarry extraction equipment alongside many photographs of drivers on whom this second publication is based.

The general format of this book follows the same pattern as Part One regarding the origins of Rugby Cement and Associate Companies all bound together within the Rugby Group. Most of the colour and black and white photographs have never been seen before as far as I know. I trust therefore that you will enjoy reading this 2nd publication and remember one of the best post war road transport companies which lasted for sixty one years before acquisition of the Rugby Group by RMC in 2000.

Glen McBirnie

(Author)

CONTENTS

Introduction & acknowledgements from within the company — 4

Chapter 1 - Rugby Cement and Associated Companies / Delivering Cement 1900s-1950s by various transport methods — 9

Chapter 2 - More Post-war Reorganisation / New People in Charge / Eastwoods Cement Acquisition / Pressure Bulk Deliveries — 31

Chapter 3 - Raw Material Extraction & Equipment / Barrington Light Railway & Works Characters / Rail Bulk Deliveries / Eastwoods Cement — 69

Chapter 4 - Chalk or Cement and There's a Foden Lorry for the Job — 85

Chapter 5 - RPC Transport 1950s & 1960s Commer / ERFs — 97

Chapter 6 - ERF & Fodens / Drivers and Garage Fitters' Memories — 135

Chapter 7 - Rugby Portland Cement Transport 1970s and early 1980s — 179

Chapter 8 - Fodens and ERFs / A Driver's Own Story / Crashes and Conversion – More Memories / RPC Transport in Miniature. — 205

Chapter 9 - The Simple Ideas Are Always the Best / New Chassis for Bags and Bulk / S/Atkinson ERF C Series / Artics Introduction / Sold Out of Service — 229

Chapter 10 - Cement Works, Depots and Crown House Remembered — 253

Chapter 11 - The Drivers, Supervisors and Reunions (And, the Final Chapter!) RoSPA Safe Driving Chicken Dinners / Medal Presentations — 271

Chapter 12 - The Conclusion - Crown Won't Let You Down — 296

RUGBY PORTLAND CEMENT TRANSPORT

Introduction

In 1982 I started to research the story of Rugby Portland Cement Transport and its associate companies. That research was destined to involve ten years of hard graft up until 1992. Right from the beginning it was always my intention to concentrate the basis of my story upon the individuals and characters within the company. Here I refer directly to my fellow drivers, garage staff and packers/loaders, together with the people who made the rules and gave the orders.

Putting all the facts together, sorting through the hundreds of photos and finally writing the basic story-line was to prove equally time consuming whilst still continuing to work full-time, and so consequently this was not finally completed until the latter part of 1999.

Much of the original material and general information, together with all of the photography in the Rugby book was really only the tip of the iceberg. Spending almost a quarter of my life putting this book together, and finding that for one reason or another, none of the established road transport publishers wanted to take it on board, was very dispiriting, but I became more determined than ever to get my story into print. In 2000 Rugby Cement was purchased by the RMC Group of Companies, and so in December of that year I sat down and wrote a letter to the Managing Director of RMC/Rugby Cement outlining the project of my book on Rugby Portland Cement Transport which had occupied so much of my life. Within the next year and three quarters, thanks to the combined efforts of RMC/Rugby Cement, together with the Rugby Group Benevolent Fund, the Rugby Portland Cement Transport book was launched on the 28th July 2002 at the High Street Rugby premises of Hunts Bookshop. Since that memorable day, well over 1,400 copies of my book have been sold within the United Kingdom and abroad. Many local people, both ex Rugby Cement employees and members of the general public alike, some with little or no contact with the company have supplied countless answers to questions which over the years had eluded me in the continuing search for additional information. Privately-owned photo collections, advertisement leaflets concerning products or parts used by RPC Transport during its halcyon 61 years of existence and operation have since come to light. Other material has been loaned to me indefinitely.

Following the takeover of Rugby Cement by the RMC Group, several major changes took place; Chinnor, Southam, Rochester and Barrington cement works have been closed for several years, also the Owner/Driver's scheme which replaced RPC Transport has ended, with remaining drivers, and vehicles now back operating in-house. Rugby Works itself underwent a massive rebuild to permit cement production equal to that of the three old works ie Rugby, Southam and Chinnor.

During the short-lived ownership of the RMC Group, the once familiar orange/black livery of the transport lorries remained, although various changes to both curtain sided trailers and by then

non-tip bulk tanker versions indicated that the new owners of Rugby were involved with much more than just cement.

In 2005 the RMC Group was the subject of a takeover by Cemex of Mexico, a global concern, who in 2006 celebrated their century of operations. Since then, more changes have taken place. Barrington Cement Works in Cambridgeshire was closed in late December 2008. The kiln was shut down a month before, with the consequent redundancy of all remaining employees. In early 2008 Chinnor cement works was completely dismantled. These two happenings finished almost one hundred years of cement making in both locations.

As far as the reader of this publication is concerned, Cemex oversees the making of cement at Rugby and South Ferriby manufacturing plants together with a new deep water port facility at Tilbury in Essex. The facility at Newport in South Wales has closed. Cemex transport lorries are now painted white overall with rear mounted red/blue Cemex liveried details on both bulk and curtainsider vehicles. Nothing lasts forever, but who would have thought that RPC Transport, a company which lasted for 61 years and was respected by everyone in road transport would one day disappear forever. I, as author, often wonder what the former Chairman/Managing Director of Rugby Cement, the late Sir Halford Reddish, would have thought of today's operation and more to the point, the disbanding of his beloved RPC Transport. Rugby Cement works has changed out of all proportion since the early part of this new century. The town itself is dominated by the enormous reconstruction of the cement works as the two photographs, taken by myself in the Autumn of 2002 show.

Now affectionately known by local people as "Cape Canaveral", the enormous towers and supporting construction break the Warwickshire sky-line visible from all of the surrounding motorways for many miles. Modern day cement works architecture bears absolutely no resemblance to the former single chimney which dominated the Rugby area for more than thirty years.

This second photo, taken directly opposite the works in Lawford Road, shows the once familiar reddish colours of years gone by on Rugby Cement lorries. Before not too many days passed, these two original bulk storage silos would be dismantled along with the loading weighbridges which were the bee's knees of time-saving bulk-loading operations in the early 1970s but had become seriously outdated in this new century.

Change happens. It is part of life, but people the world over do not take to sudden alteration in either change or alternatives.

Photo 1 was taken from the railway bridge in Parkfield Road behind the cement works. To the casual passer-by, the enormity of the rebuild cannot seriously be imagined until you visit the interior of these works. In photo 2, the combination of old/new structures brings the total concept in construction to the human eye. A complete new purpose-built and entirely automatic bag shed operation, includes provision of new conveyor belts and attendant buildings. These convey cement bags one per second, down to faster packing/distribution facilities, which in earlier years were pipe dreams away.

The enormity of the tonnages handled is mind-blowing with the faster turnaround of curtainsider trailer operations which, when demand is high, can be operated around the clock.

Acknowledgements

The author offers grateful thanks to the Rugby Group Benevolent Fund Limited which generously agreed to underwrite the costs of the preparation of this book. Without the support of the Fund, together with many former employees of Rugby Cement, the author would never have been able to share these stories.

The author would like to thank everyone who has helped him in the creation of this story of drivers and their vehicles. He is indebted to all these people who have recounted their memories and provided pictures, and would like to apologise if he has omitted mention of anyone who helped make this book a reality.

Company employees who have contributed to this story are listed below.

Rugby Works, Warwickshire

Isobel Watson	A former admin assistant to Sir Halford Reddish at Head Office, Crown House, started 1954, left 1964, returned 1979 – 2004. Currently Administrator for the Benevolent Fund
John Frearson	Formerly of Technical Services, Crown House, 1997 – 2002
Glen McBirnie	Driver (author), 1968 – 90

Southam Works, Warwickshire

Tim Griffin	Garage Fitter (Days), 1978 – 88
Tony Higgins	Garage Fitter (Nights), 1977 – 84

Chinnor Works, Oxfordshire

Terry Golder	Driver, 1970 – 88

Rochester Works, Kent

Jim Hastings	Driver, 1964 – 85

South Ferriby Works, North Lincolnshire

John Todd	Driver/Driving Assessor, 1967 – 09
Mick Lowe	Driver (Nights), 1973 – 87

Grateful thanks must be acknowledged by me as author to Brian Peeps, who drove in the early days for both Eastwoods and Rugby Cement and always carried his camera, for classic photos freely given. Also to Terry Clipston, a former works clerk/tour guide for all his assistance and help over many years.

Leeds Depot, Crossgreen, Leeds, Yorkshire

Tony Foster	Driver/Chargehand (Nights), 1972 – 88

Barrington Works, Cambridgeshire

Peter Dimes	Driver, Eastwoods Cement 1955 – 62, RPC Transport 1962 – 91
John Drayton MBE, Barrington Works	Yard/Production Supervisor, Caretaker/Quarry Guide, 1970 - present

Contributions from outside the Company

Members of the Fairground Society of Great Britain (FAGB) Dick Furniss, Stratford. Rod Jesson, Redditch and the late John Crumpton, Brierlely Hill, Staffs.

Jamie Goddard

WG Goddard & Sons Ltd were Rugby's premier road haulage company for many years. They were to be employed internally within Rugby works, as well as moving bulk cement in Bedford tippers. Later on they delivered cement in sacks on Leyland lorries. I am indebted to Jamie for allowing me to include his photographs which related to the anti-nationalisation protests in the 1950s.

Alan Moorey

Alan worked as a driver for EA Castle, delivering cement in sacks out of Rochester works for many years. With the ultimate disbandment of RPC Transport together with a run down of all Rochester operations after 2000, Alan saved hundreds of photographs which had been dumped in skips, for which I remain indebted to him. Some of these photos have been used within this second book.

Steve Hastings

Steve is the son of Jim Hastings, who was a driver at Rochester works in Kent. My ongoing friendship with both father and son has resulted in me obtaining concise details of most drivers based at these works. Additionally, Steve continues to find out more information concerning former RPC lorries based at these works which have appeared in 2nd ownership. Sincere thanks to both father and son for their time and energies.

Richard Storey of Kenilworth, Warwickshire

Our friendship of more than twenty five years standing derives from a mutual interest in local and national road transport. With his love of books and all transport publications, Richard from time to time continues to offer support, time and kindness in so many ways.

Jeff Isted of Lewes, Sussex

Jeff Isted is concerned with local history relating to cement companies of many years in and around Sussex. His assistance to me concerns Eastwoods Cement ownership of Lewes in pre-Rugby Cement days. I am indebted to him for supplying photos of drivers and lorries which relate to the years before 1962. I thank him sincerely.

Additional acknowledgements can be found within the text of this story where individuals have supplied material in later years. This includes locations of photographs, types of lorries used, and general notes.

Glen McBirnie - Author

CHAPTER 1

Rugby Cement and Associated Companies Delivering Cement 1900s-1950s by various transport methods

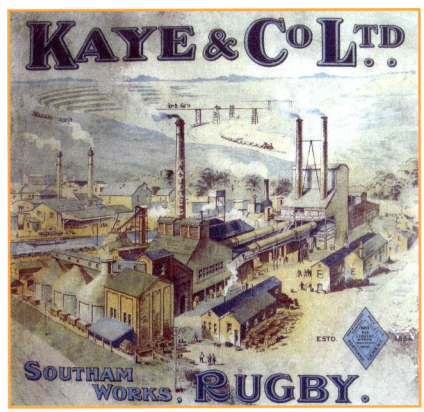

Kaye's Cement Works, Southam, near Rugby – 1915

The original works on the Southam site was established in about 1854. When Captain Arthur Lister-Kaye and LM Tatham took on the lease in 1870, little, if any, cement had been produced. Lister-Kaye became the main Partner of Kaye & Co in 1875. After his death in 1893, his son, Lister, and widow, Eugenia, inherited the business. She died in 1909, just after the start of the major expansion of the works in 1908. The business had difficulties in the recession of the 1930s, and the Rugby Portland Cement Company, already having business interests, bought the Company in 1934 for £27,000.

The image on this card is taken from a Calendar produced by the Kaye & Co Portland Cement Company in 1915. It shows the recently upgraded cement works with its quarry. This view includes the two "modern" rotary cement kilns and the three storage silos that were part of the 1908 expansion. On the far side of the Canal Arm is part of the older works. In the quarry, in the background, can be seen the plank "runs" used in the removal of waste clay by wheel-barrow - a notoriously dangerous operation.

The calendar was found in a carpenter's workshop in Staffordshire by Jack Brown (of Lichfield Morris Men and sometime member of the Abbotts Bromley Horn Dancers) who, knowing its interest, generously gave it to John Frearson.

Digital photographic editing has been used to "clean and repair" the image for this card. In due course, the original calendar will be deposited for safekeeping in the Warwickshire Record Office. It will be included with the collection of materials from the CEMEX / Rugby Cement Archive that is currently being catalogued and prepared for preservation by John Frearson Limited.

A splendid aerial view of the Southam cement works, looking east, with the office block (built in 1913) prominent in the foreground and the rotary kilns clearly discernible in the distance. The sidings at the lower left edge of the frame are part of the Southam & Long Itchington station goods yard. The narrow gauge line to the quarry can be seen in the distance on the right, heading off via the trees. Unfortunately the photograph is undated.

The building in the foreground was the company's main office block. This, together with the smaller building immediately behind, which was used initially in earlier years to store blasting equipment for use within the quarries, has survived to this day. Of the four chimneys in the photograph below, the nearest carried prominent white painted letters advertising Kaye & Company's name which could be seen for miles by the bystanders and local inhabitants of the period. From various sources, including the Sentinel Drivers Club, we now know that at least four Sentinels were operated by Kaye and Co. They had dropside bodies and towed four wheel trailers. Known registration/chassis numbers are: NX 7052 (34495), UE 602 (34821) and NX 7563 (34576). Each wagon carried six tons of bagged cement (120 bags) and each trailer four tons (80 bags), giving a multiple load of 10 tons. Shown above is an illustration taken from a printed calendar of 1915.

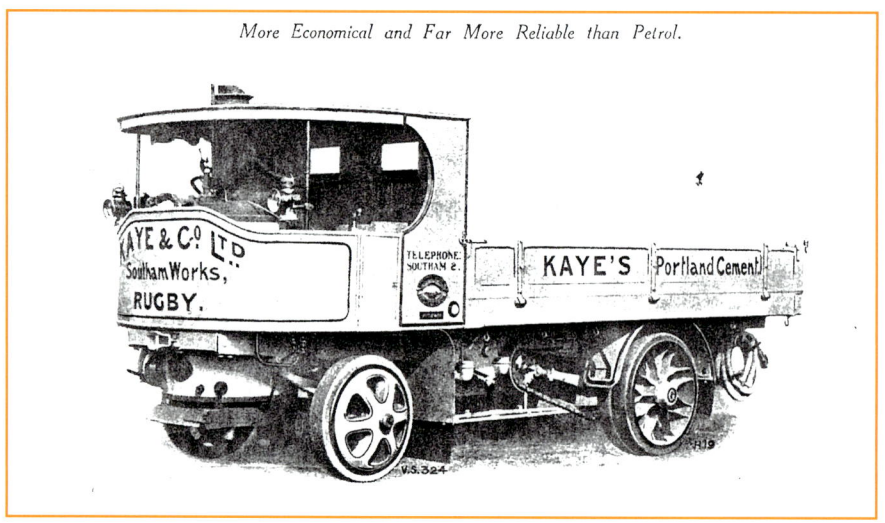

More Economical and Far More Reliable than Petrol.

The efforts of a driver and a mate required an extremely long working day starting with boiler cleaning / preparation before loading both lorry and trailer which ran on solid tyred wheels. The physical daily exertion from each crew must have been hard work in the extreme.

Shown below is a line-up of loaded Kaye & Co Sentinel steamers and trailers ready to depart. As a former bag driver with RPC Transport I can appreciate that the double stacked one hundredweight bags would have sorted the men from the boys.

Above is a view of the Ruston No.3 Railroad Shovel owned by Kaye & Company seen loading limestone into a hopper in the mid-1920s; the company was incorporated in 1880 and its cement works and quarries in the Stockton area were purchased from the Oldham family. A progressive and successful cement manufacturing company, Kaye & Co was taken over in 1934 by the Rugby Portland Cement Co Ltd.

The Peckett locomotives mentioned earlier are detailed to some extent in the press-cutting which shows one of possibly nine such machines used to haul small-wheeled, side-tipping trucks from the quarry face.

The excavated clay would be taken to the wash mill receiving areas and tipped on to conveyors at the start of the cement making-process. From information since received via a private source, it appears that at least one of these Pecketts has survived into preservation.

The Rugby Portland Cement works operated a 1ft 11 ½ in gauge system utilising four Peckett-built 0-6-0 STs. Illustrated here on 9th March 1958 is Mesozoic, works no 1327, built in 1913. The other three were Jurassic, Triassic and Liassic. Mesozoic is now preserved on the Bromyard & Linton Light Railway; Jurassic on the Lincolnshire Coast Light Railway at Burgh-le-Marsh and Triassic at the Bala Lake Light Railway at Llanuwchllyn. Liassic was shipped to Canada in 1959.

The photograph shown below is Mesozoic sitting just outside the covered "loco sheds" within the Southam Cement Works areas.

Southam and Long Itchington

Right: The Rugby Portland Cement works operated a 1ft 11½in gauge system utilising four Peckett-built 0-6-0STs. Illustrated here is *Mesozoic*, works no 1327, built in 1913. The other three were *Jurassic*, *Triassic* and *Liassic*. *Mesozoic* is now preserved on the Bromyard & Linton Light Railway; *Jurassic* on the Lincolnshire Coast Light Railway at Burgh-le-Marsh and *Triassic* at the Bala Lake Light Railway at Llanuwchllyn. *Liassic* was shipped to Canada in 1959. *9th March 1958*

Southam & Long Itchington

Part One of my book about Rugby Portland Cement Transport described the origin and subsequent growth of their original cement mills together with associate companies and other depots strategically placed around the country. These numbered seven overall. Since the book came out in July 2002, I have acquired many more photos, both black and white and colour. Some of the black and whites refer to the early post-war years, together with activities in a general sense much later. All cover a variety of transport within the cement works owned by Rugby Cement.

In the first half of the twentieth century, hundreds of privately owned barges carried mixed cargoes on the River Thames. Shown right is a typical example of how one appeared to the general public. As to whether it was employed on contract to RPC or indeed any of the cement makers of that period, I am unsure. Possibly a crew of seven would be required to man such a vessel as manual loading/unloading of cement in hessian sacks required hard physical labour, with the captain/owner in charge of the crew. Perhaps the actual sailing of the barge came as a blessed relief after the rigours of loading!! This striking photograph is so much a part of this second story. Under a magnifier, crew members can be seen preparing for sea when the tide rises and the barge refloats.

Industrial working practices in Great Britain in the 1900s, and well before, did not take too much account of health and safety. The industry and country as a whole then had to re-equip/rebuild completely between the two world wars. The vastness of any cement works, its quarry perimeters and surrounding enormous tracts of occupied land meant that individuals of years ago who opted to work outside in the open air were hardy people. The British workman has for centuries loved his cup of tea, and so down at Rochester cement works in Kent, the canteen staff, aided by engineering fitters, produced the pedal-powered trolley on a tricycle frame, on which an electrical unit heated a squared-off hot water boiler, which in turn was used to fill worker's billy-cans at break times.

The rider's seat was a basic saddle and a pivot under the cargo allowed for steering. As for stopping, I can't comment. This was a very basic, simple design at that time, which provided a welcome service to outside workers whose daily occupations kept them from canteen services. The ground area in terms of size and distance within the Rochester cement works and quarry/chalk lagoon was immense to say the least. Having seen this for myself in later years I can only suggest that the cyclist/attendant's job with this tea trolley would involve quite a few hours of pedalling there and back.

Many ordinary members of the public, some with little or no connection with Rugby Cement and Associate Companies, began to realise within months of my first book being launched, that any surviving material relating to Rugby Cement was indeed required. The book itself has brought back memories, not only for former Rugby Cement drivers, but it has also worked its magic on the ordinary person. To this end photographs, advertising material, calendars,

waybills etc hidden away for years in pockets and lofts have suddenly re-appeared. They represent in this second volume the simple horse and cart, canal barge traffic, steam wagon and early motor lorries. Shown left, this computer enhanced photograph illustrates its origins on the cart sides with the immortal wording "Rugby

Portland Cement Company New Bilton No1". The display of mounted ceramic products positioned on a double sided framework was done to celebrate the Coronation of George VI, both the horse and cart being suitably decorated for the occasion, together with the carter and his immediate superior. Horse and cart deliveries were used initially within a fifteen mile radius of the original Rugby Cement Works, which to local people is still remembered as Malpass Farm. When petrol and ultimately diesel powered lorries began to appear, the delivery radius from these works was extended to twenty five miles. Prior to cement being packed in paper sacks, which from memory began in earnest after the Second World War, hessian and/or jute produced bags were the norm for very many years, certainly from the 1900s onwards, and perhaps even earlier. Gangs of women were employed at Southam Works under both Kaye & Company's ownership and later still, Rugby Cement, to wash, clean and repair countless hundreds of these material based sacks. This was a dusty, horrible occupation, but it meant that numerous bags could be used over and over again. Impregnated cement powder over a period of time became hard and so each bag retained an element of unusable weight of neither use nor ornament to the manufacturer or indeed the customer. A levy was paid to customers who returned these bags for re-use / cleaning. Use of cloth bags ended when paper bags were introduced.

Copyright of the image of the Nelson canal barge drawing seen above is retained by Christopher M Jones of Birmingham who very kindly gave me permission to include his unique interpretation of exactly how things used to be in the days of manual loading and unloading of cement in bags in relation to canal barge operation. Both the drawing and the accompanying text speak for themselves, given that the immense physical effort involved in loading a barge manually would take perhaps the best part of a day.

As cement is being loaded into the steam barge "Jason", owned by Charles Nelson & Co Ltd of Stockton, a tally man on the wharf keeps a record of how many bags are taken aboard. This figure, coupled with the measured weight in each bag, was entered on a declaration certificate, which the captain presented to the toll clerk who then calculated the toll. The gauged weight measured at the toll stop should tally with this declared weight; if it did not, further inquiries had to be made. Often the returnable jute bags became so impregnated with cement that they could account for an extra quarter of a ton on a full boat load, above the declared weight. A day's wage for labourers would be calculated on how long the loading took. Often as not, both the motor and a butty (towed boat) constituted a full load. This is both a fantastic drawing in its own right together with a true representation of how things used to be. Christopher Jones has captured this scene exactly, and should be extremely proud of his efforts in presenting this scene.

Following an article in the *Waterways World* magazine in March 1998 by Alan Faulkener entitled Cement Carriers Part One – The Stocktons, I sought copyright permission from both Alan and the Waterways Archive at Ellesmere Port, Cheshire, to use certain photos relating to the former British Waterways operated canal boats. 'Banstead' and 'Tow' were two of the boats still working out of Southam cement works into the late 1960s, operated by a family of four comprising the boat-man, his wife and two strapping daughters. Being a regular visitor to Birmingham Depot with stock loads of bags I soon got to know the family: when the boats came in all waiting drivers "both bags or bulk" were required to assist with the unloading. The two daughters, both in their teens, had combined opinions on a variety of subjects as well as people alike, which did justice to the English language and a dictionary!! The boat people were grafters in the true sense of the word because two days would involve loading fifty tons of bags between both the lead boat and butty. Travelling up the canal took a further two days to get to Sampson Road Depot Wharf, plus a further two days for unloading. Twenty bags (one ton) were unloaded from each boat via a hoist, but manual unloading and stacking was done by RPC personnel and available drivers. Nothing happened on a Sunday because for most people then that was the day of rest and this was rigidly observed by many canal boat families.

Charles Nelson & Sons of Stockton originated the carrying of bagged materials in the early years of the last century. This then benefitted both the manufacturer and the customer alike. Because of the nature of the work invariably the boat-man and his family were paid for loaded journeys of material brought up for production purposes, plus finished products either to customers or for further manufacture elsewhere.

The Kayes Arm area of Southam works which ultimately after take-overs of both Nelson and Kayes by Rugby, would be transformed into the main canal boat loading areas where cement in sacks was brought down on a series of conveyor belts prior to loading in the boats. Imagine setting out on a frosty morning, moving at less than 4mph on the canals and faced with a 34 mile journey fully loaded.

Shown on the next page are two images from Alan Faulkener's article which themselves might portray to the reader the starkness of the job ahead, necessitating bodily strength for steering the boats and working the various locks along the way.

British Waterways boats 'Banstead' & 'Tow' leaving one of the Bascote locks on their way north with another cargo of Southam cement for Birmingham.

Journey's End. 'Banstead' & 'Tow' tied up at Sampson Road waiting to unload their cargo of cement from Southam Works.

These two pictures speak for themselves and show the beginning of a journey done in all weathers which only the very hardy boat families could manage. This they did for very many years. Canal boat transfer of bagged cement from Southam Cement Works to Birmingham Depot ended after 1969, however Birmingham Depot in its entirety and the Sampson Road Wharf remain in situ because of a clause during Charles Nelson's ownership which prevents the whole area from being demolished.

A photograph taken by Alan Faulkener on the 4th May 1975 in support of his article on cement-carrying canal boats shows Kayes Arm at the rear of the Southam Cement Works, some six years after the ending of sending cement in sacks by canal boats. This superb picture captures the entirety of a working cement works.

The then three working chimneys are reflected alongside other structures on the water surface in a magical view. A line of loaded coal wagons waits to be unloaded: such movements are now but distant memories for everyone who worked in or lived near the cement works. The old manual loading area for cement in sacks to be transferred into the boats is shown on the right-hand side. Here the bags would be brought

down to gangs of manual labourers by long conveyor belts, sheer hard, physical work for those concerned. This is a truly fantastic photograph of this well known area of the cement works and I am indebted to Alan Faulkener for allowing me to use it.

The red brick building shown upper right was the Dumper Shop from where repairs and general servicing of quarry equipment were carried out. This is another photograph supplied to me some twelve years after 1975 which shows the Kayes Arm area in a pitiful state of disrepair and disuse. The canal water has drained away as nature takes its toll, and whilst the cement works was still in operation, gradual decay is prominent in all areas. Kiln bricks in front of the Dumper Shop are stacked in readiness for repair work and one of the old Foden Dumptrucks is visible behind the Dumper Shop. Shown centre right is the triangular end shaped new clinker storage building built at Southam towards the middle 1980s. Some RPC Transport lorries are visible under the conveyor belts. The comparison of these two photographs, together with the period of years which have passed since they were taken, show the reader the decline and fall of the operation. Cement production ended at Southam Works shortly before the start of this new century. Southam remains open for quarry extraction of clay together with return transport of process dust from the new larger cement works at Rugby.

Some years were to pass after the ending of canal boat operations. The old loading area seen above was set aside for movement and manual loading of cement in sacks by conveyor down to the canal boats. These areas at the rear show deterioration along with the general run down of other areas over a long period of time.

Nelson Cement Works, Stockton

Shown below is a fantastic copy of a photo of the former Nelson cement works at Stockton near Southam, Warwickshire, which is of particular interest to the local people who remember these works. The railway bridge over the Grand Union canal shows a crowded anchorage of boats, with the left hand boat loaded with bricks or pipes. Canal boats of the period, thought to be the late 1920's or perhaps the early 1930's, delivered raw materials into the cement works and were loaded with cement in sacks for outward journeys. Bob Monroe, a resident of Birdingbury, remembers as a young lad playing in the later years long after Nelson had been demolished whereby he and his friends climbed all over the site. Bob informed me that the canal link into the cement works was excavated or dug by hand - a mammoth undertaking even for that period of time. Motor lorries began to appear at Nelson cement works in the 1930's - they were used for the carriage and delivery of cement in sacks - and are referred to in detail further within this story. The Cock Brand symbol visible on the main chimney was also to be found on all the company's transport and was also adorned on the jute cloth cement sacks. Lots of women were employed at Nelson to clean and repair these bags - this was a very dusty and unhealthy job, and a levy was paid to all customers of Nelson who returned their empty sacks.

This is a fantastic picture of the Stockton cement works which for me as an historian is priceless. Look to the far right of the picture, and you can just make out some of the original bottle kilns used in the very early days of cement making.

Nelson cement works was dismantled shortly before the Second World War as it was considered as being too old to rebuild.

Early Assoc Company & RPC Operated Transport Lorries, the Thornycroft Connection and other types

Chas-Nelson continued with Thornycrofts, even after the RPC buyout, which were used alongside Leyland Cubs and Beavers. The Strenuous model shown here was to be fitted with pneumatic tyres and electric lighting – both very much looked forward to, even in 1926. The illuminated headboard would also be something of a novelty, even for the Nelson's drivers. This modern innovation must have seemed out of place in company with the bulb horn and strapped up starting handle. The double dropsides fitted on both sides would account for some physical effort each day on the part of the driver before manual unloading. The wooden driver's cab is of no frills construction, offering no more than basic protection from the weather.

All these Thornycroft models were in operation over a 10 year period between 1921 and 1931, but research has found that Nelson kept many of them in regular use almost up to the start of the Second World War.

A2 Thornycroft 4WH Dropside 1921. Solid Wheels. 2 ton operation

Thornycroft 'Strenuous' 4 wheel drop side 1926. Pnuematic tyres 4 ton operation

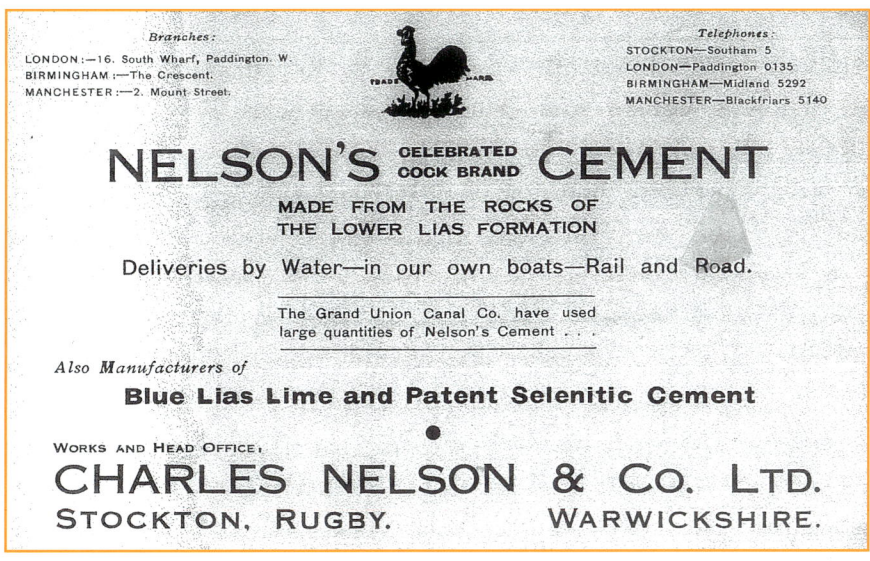

This advertisement for Nelson "Cock Brand" cement, draws attention to its origins with three variations in delivery transport."

The two Leyand Beaver 4 wheel platform lorries shown in the photograph above loading cement bags in a two-tier layout, were eventually to grow in number to six identical vehicles put into regular service from about 1937 onwards. This photograph came to me from the British Commercial Vehicle Museum at Leyland who now hold the copyright and who allowed me to include this scene of how things used to be long ago.

AWD 132 and 133 were what became known as "Oilers", but the actual model/type was classified as a TSC 8/9 already fully described in RPC Transport Part One. Period touches in this remarkable picture are numerous. For a start, the foreman talking to the driver in the right-hand lorry wears a long dust-coat and trilby hat; these along with the flat caps and general working clothes represent a period in industrial history now long gone. The restraining holding straps on the starting handles became commonplace, and the "no frills or extras" appearance of both of these lorries portrays a hard working environment, very different from this new century.

133 carries a normal loaded height of cement in sacks, possibly around 6 tons. The location for this superb photograph is Southam Works of Rugby Portland Cement.

The second superb photograph on the next page is also taken within Southam Cement Works. I can identify it by the double-fronted cottage in the middle of the yard, immediately in front of what was then the bag-loading shed. This assumption is further confirmed by the overhead covered roof extension which in later years under RPC control was extended to include all bulk/

bag-loading areas and operations well into the 1980s. The house was demolished in the 1970s and the Despatch/Transport, its primary use, relocated to a central position near the works canteen and other buildings. Identification of the type of lorry shown in this second picture, being loaded with a five ton 100 bags load in double rows, centres on a 1930s Armstrong Saurer 4-wheeler lorry. This is further corroborated by the shape and design of the fuel tank, the apparent lack of any rear fitted mudguards, and the spare wheel carried behind the cab. Points of interest also include simple platform-bodied construction which lacks the robust bodywork normally associated with bagged material loads of the period.

Below, you will again see the Thornycroft Taurus 4 wheeler dropside of Charlie Watson, because he was quite rightly one of Rugby's very first outside contractors for the carriage of bags. His lorry, being his own, did not carry a fleet number. Certainly during the last four to six years I have traced the Taurus's registration number and this is shown. I also learned from a variety of sources that this particular Thornycroft may still survive somewhere. Such a discovery within the old vehicle world might still be possible. During my research for this second book on RPC Transport I have traced Mr Watson's nephew who still lives on Rugby Road, Long Lawford. He remembers delivering cement to all parts in school holidays with his uncle. Whether the success of Charles Watson's Taurus Lorry had any bearing on RPC Transport's activities prior to the 2nd World War, based on its dependability, I don't know, but what is certain is that four identical lorries based on the Taurus model, each with its own 4wheel platform trailer, were put into fleet service.

Mr Watson's Thornycroft carried registration number WD 5868 as seen below. The driver's opening windscreen would be something of a revelation, even from 1931 onwards. This second photograph was made available to me from an unknown source after the release of my book on RPC Transport in 2002. The difference between this picture and the one on P21/Plate 35 of Book 1 is that I now have its registration number.

The Rugby Cement operated Taurus lorries and their trailers were, as far as I know from information received, in service before and after the Second World War, and because of the Wartime Regulations Permit held by the company, these lorries were required to back load urgent deliveries, mainly of foodstuffs, to both the American and English wartime airfields. The law then allowed for a second man for trailer operation, because full working days unloading bags of cement and reloading a multitude of transhipment goods, would test the stamina of the driver and his mate. The original Thornycroft Agent for the Midlands area pre-1930s and onwards, was in Digbeth, Birmingham. This was situated not very far away from the RPC Birmingham Depot in Sampson Road, Sparkbrook.

Ken Whyment started with RPC Transport in 1949. Prior to joining the company he was required to undergo a driving test with Stan Roberts the then very popular garage foreman. Stan drove the vehicle on the outward journey, then at a certain point, the candidate for employment took over. The consensus of opinion in these now far off days was that if Stan allowed you to drive the vehicle back into the confines of the Rugby Works yard, then you had passed muster! Ken's first thirteen weeks in RPC employment were to be spent doing a variety of jobs far removed from that of cement in bags deliveries. Both he and Ned Parkes, a former Mitchells & Butler driver, led a varied life during this time, collecting the sandwiches or fish and chips in Jock Henderson's little Ford 10 cwt pick-up. Often referred to as Jock's Ford Van, its registration number was PNX 91 / F/N 259 and is shown overleaf attending to two Thornycroft Sturdy 4 wheel flats in Rugby Yard.

The lorry alongside carried registration number JAC 386 and fleet number 193. Another Sturdy is visible under the bag shed roof.

Another name supplied to me in recent years is that of Eddie Matthews who lived at Clifton, and who was involved driving Bedford 4 wheeler covered box-tippers on some of the early bulk deliveries. From what I've been privileged to know from Freddie Hack, Eddie Matthews was something of a practical joker towards his RPC colleagues. Sadly I only met him in his pensionable years, and so did not really get to know him. In 1949, four years after the end of World War II, I am led to believe that the entire number of lorries based at Rugby Works totalled just fifteen Thornycroft Sturdy 4 wheel platforms which are shown photographed over a weekend, all with sheeted bodies.

Sheeting was, until the late 1960s, a daily necessity for drivers of flat lorries. The late Chairman and Managing Director of Rugby Cement issued a warning that the loading of bagged cement on to wet or damp bodies was not acceptable. This photo should be treasured by all the employees who worked for the cement company over very many years. It shows how the railway ran through the centre of the works. These empty wagons which had brought coal in for kiln burning are awaiting collection. The absence of other lorries, the oil stains in the almost deserted yard and the roof of the bag shed are now all distant memories for very many people. Ken Whyment's early service years would eventually see him and other RPC Transport drivers involved with newer Thornycrofts called Sturdy Stars. The new cab design was shared with Guy although the two firms were not connected. These new lorries are fondly remembered as "tin tops" but before I describe them in detail I must include some other photos of Sturdy models from the late 1940s which have come to light since my first book appeared.

EAC 485 Thornycroft Sturdy is shown with its mixed celebratory load. The white roofs of RPC lorries were a standard feature of company livery up until the 1960s.

Newer Sturdy Star models appeared from 1952 onwards. They were fitted with a direct injection diesel engine of 4.1 litres and they came to be known as TR6-/D1. A 16 foot 6 inch body capable of carrying 6 ton loads, became standard fitment.

More photos have surfaced over the past four years, and the adjacent photo shows one Rochester based Thornycroft Sturdy 4 wheel flat in typical every day use, but why there were two individuals in the lorry cab escapes me. FNX 762 is shown traversing flood water at the Rochester Works tunnel. Picture the driving conditions of almost 60 years ago with the very small driver's rear-view mirrors plus the need for hand signals, flashing indicators being a decade away. RPC Transport were themselves to account for perhaps 60 examples of these ZE 5 ton Sturdy lorries out of a possible 2,000 production models built between 1945 and 1950. It would appear also that the sister vehicle picture shown above was also Rochester based with its mixed load of cement sacks, together with a small diesel-powered mixer of the early years. The home-made self proclamatory sign appertaining to the shortage of housing for the nation, complemented by a flag on each of the rear platform corners and the V on the radiator, shows the vehicle taking part in some sort of victory parade.

Shown climbing the original A4091 Middleton to Tamworth Road, F/N 188 is a standard Thornycroft Sturdy 4-wheel platform lorry of Rugby Portland Cement Transport, carrying a smaller than usual load judging by the lumpy sheet. JAC 275 was, I understand, based at Rugby Works.

Of special interest is the road works sign warning of a man working down a hole surrounded by simple barriers. The Bedford lorry of Tamworth Egg Packers also dates from the 1950s and both lorries are roughly 1¾ miles North of the Belfry Golf centre. In later years the road number was changed to the A446. The absence of flashing indicators on both lorries shows a less stressful period in road transport when driver hand signals and less crowded roads were the norm.

Shown on the right is the interior thought to be the original Rochester works bag shed where a fair percentage of these "tin-tops" as they came to be known, were to be based.

The newer cab design was by Motor Panels, and Guy vehicles of the same period were similar apart from radiator grills and badges.

Fleet Number 235 is shown being loaded within the described gloom of a packing shed.

Fleet Number 235 carrying reg number LWD 898 is shown at the former coach builders Frederick Louch of Rugby

Shown in this fine photo is F/N 251, a later "tin-top" model carrying registration number NAC 5 and leading two earlier Sturdy Star models. The second lorry is KUE 873 which carried F/N 217. Photographs of this nature, with three company lorries in line, are extremely rare. I am informed that it was taken in the Medway area of Kent, possibly close to the RPC Rochester cement works. Perhaps this occasion was to illustrate the fleet use of Thornycroft lorries for readers of technical magazines, or transport periodicals of earlier years.

This photograph which was passed on to me by Phil Moth of PM Photography, deserves inclusion here because it shows the two Thornycroft 4 wheeler models favoured by RPC Transport. These were to see fleet service certainly between 1947 and 1957.

The Chinnor Cement and Lime Connection with RPC Transport before 1963

For as long as local people at Chinnor can remember, the cement works nestling in the shadow of the Chiltern Hills was a serious part of village life. Closed for just under ten years, certainly from the middle 1990s, Chinnor cement works finally succumbed to complete dismantling in the early part of 2008. Plans for some kind of massive redevelopment were submitted to Cherwell District Council, who in keeping with the natural beauty of the area, have apparently limited both numbers of housing or industrial projects. At the time of writing, housing has replaced the cement works.

Despatch Wharf, Chinnor Cement and Lime Co, August 1930

The photograph shown right dates from August 1930 and shows the Despatch Wharf, which much later became known universally as "Chinnor Bag Shed". A real variety of period transport is shown employed at that time for the delivery of cement in sacks. Later on, lime produced at these works became a by-word in construction circles. Shown left to right, the types of transport standing at the loading dock include two horses, the one on the left is munching from a feed bag fixed under its head, whilst the other is coupled to a single axle cart and is being comforted by its owner. A Leyland 4-tonner dating maybe from the 1920s is separated by the horse and cart. The next lorry in line is an even earlier produced Leyland with a cab design which, to the uninitiated, takes its origins back to the First World War. The first of two (shown) Chevrolet-Bedfords produced around 1934 and based on the popular 2 ton chassis, carried a Chinnor head-board and is registered UD 3708. The next lorry shown is unidentifiable, and the second Chevrolet Bedford completes this line up, being registered UD 4183. Of particular interest also are the railway box trucks awaiting loading alongside the wharf where even in these early times manual loading of cement bags in all weathers was only for the fittest people. This is a really fantastic photograph which epitomises times past as well as early forms of motor transport. As previously mentioned, in later years the bag shed would be extended with additional buildings added, along with storage silos when "Bulk Deliveries" came on stream.

The first-time visitor to Chinnor Cement works would be pleasantly surprised to travel down the work's drive, seeing first on the left hand side the Transport Office building from where all drivers in later years were given their instructions (both company drivers and contractors alike). Continuing on, the late Victorian, main office / reception also on the left-hand side, greeted you. There, the Works Manager and the Secretary, Rita Chapman, had separate offices, together with a room for Duty Supervisors working 24 hour shifts, and the all-important boardrooms.

The track railway lines visible under the excavated material were used by trucks to convey it to the cement works prior to the making of cement. It was not unusual for quarry equipment of tracked chassis to spend many years in use doing the same job before being removed from regular use. Working conditions in quarries and extraction pits in earlier years as well as in post-war times were really only for the fittest of individuals. Countless generations of local families spent their working lives at Chinnor Cement doing all manner of jobs in all weathers. I have seen for myself the extensive workings in Chinnor, the huge perimeters of which are shown overleaf in this superb aerial photograph taken some time in the 1950s or early 1960s. The nearness of both the houses and the adjoining farm land contrasts with the dust covered areas of Chinnor Cement works caused by fall-out from the works chimneys over decades. Different wind changes in every working day compete with the movement of quarry dumpers and equipment raising the dust off ground levels. Judge for yourselves the sheer size in acreage of the huge ground complex and imagine working there day after day.

Shown hard at work in Chinnor's vast quarry workings, is their Ruston Bucyrus 24-RB excavator.

Shown here are two types of 8-wheeler chassis which were popular in the Chinnor Cement Transport Fleet in the post war years.

Both types were operated around 22 tons gross. This AEC platform had both its cab and bodywork built by Duramin of London. Shown right on its initial delivery to Chinnor on trade plates, this Mammoth Major design originated from the early 1930s, but deliveries to Chinnor began in the 1950s. By then the basic chassis had improved. Later registered EUD 893 carrying F/N 34 it was the first of several platform bodied 8 wheelers which were to give many years of service to the Chinnor Fleet.

Other favoured 8-wheeler chassis in service about the same time as the AECs were the Albion HDs. Initially they were ordered to work as short-wheel based box-covered tippers used to move bulk cement powder.

Well documented in Part One of this story, these Albion chassis were altered in later years to carry bulk tanker bodies and discharge blower equipment.

As far as I know, these Albions performed their duties admirably before being replaced by Fodens. Shown here in some second hand disposal yard, what a wonderful project for lorry restoration this Albion might have made. GBW 828 carried F/N 38 during the whole of its working life with Chinnor Cement and Lime.

CHAPTER 2

More Post-war Reorganisation
New People in Charge
Eastwoods Cement Acquisition
Pressure Bulk Deliveries

The following information was published in the *World's Carriers* newspaper dated October 15th 1949, which I am extremely grateful to be able to use. Thirty eight lorry drivers in the service of Rugby Portland Cement Company were each ordered to pay 10 shillings "damages" on summonses brought by the company following a recent strike at the company's Southam Cement Works. The initial dispute was caused by the Southam-based packers/loaders who put forward a wage claim in June of that year (1949). Negotiations followed, but the packers/loaders withdrew their labour without notice and so, in effect, this action left the Southam-based lorry drivers with nothing to do.

Sadly, however, due to lack of action in the first instance from the Company to meet the drivers, those from both Southam and Rugby walked out on September 3rd 1949. Two hours later, after clocking on for work, the Company brought the proceedings in respect of the Rugby drivers alone, because the Southam drivers were already under notice. By a majority decision, the Bench found that there had been a breach of contract and therefore ordered each defendant to pay ten shillings damages. The same penalty was imposed upon all of the drivers concerned, with no order being made for costs.

Shortly after the Rugby Cement Book became available to members of the public, some of them proved to have had more than a passing interest or connection with Rugby Cement over the years. Several local newspapers had advertised my labours over the twenty or so years of preparation of the book. Numerous people ventured into Hunt's Bookshop in Rugby's High Street to find out more. Mrs Hazel Dale was then in her early 90s. She purchased a copy of my book, together with her son Roger, who lives at Tysoe near Stratford upon Avon. Nothing strange in that, you might think, until you, after spending almost a quarter of your life span researching information, are suddenly lifted back into the old century with a bang, so to speak.

During the early part of 2003, I was contacted by Roger Dale (on behalf of his mother) with a view to arranging to meet them both because, in their words, they had information regarding Rugby Cement, which referred to the pre-war year's operations which they thought I would want to know.

My first visit to 35 Rugby Road, Long Lawford, just less than three quarters of a mile from the cement works was, for me, a superb revelation when I met both mother and son because Hazel's late husband, Wilfred Frederick Dale, was the guiding light behind W F Dale & Son, the road transport company which had held A licences and had operated platform lorries on behalf of Rugby Cement before the Second World War.

I was destined to spend over two and a half hours in both Hazel and Roger Dale's company that day, obtaining new information but more to the point in question, I was able to learn that Wilfred's father, Hubert, had in fact begun the company.

Their base for a good number of years was a yard which had a low arched roof to traverse in and out. This being situated just off New Street in Rugby. Local people familiar with the area will remember it in later years as belonging to Deacon's Dairies. WF Dale & Son carried bagged cement certainly up until the start of hostilities in 1939. Further information was received from three surviving drivers, now all in retirement – Ken Whyment, Dick Smith and Neville Walker – both Ken and Dick worked for WF Dale as lorry drivers prior to joining Rugby Cement.

Dick Smith still remembers with absolute horror to this day, that one of two very elderly Foden d/g cabbed 8-wheelers had to be started daily on the handle. Both were platform-bodied and may have had the 112 bhp Gardner 5lw fitted. There was also a Thornycroft Sturdy 4-wheeler painted in Charles Nelson's colours. When work was slack on cement for Dales' employees, lorries were sent out on nationwide general haulage. To experienced lorry men, this became known as "tramping". WF Dale & Son did not restart operations after the war simply because Wilfred was called up for military service, added to which during hostilities a Government appointed contractor called Transport Services Ltd oversaw many urgent wartime deliveries, including cement in bags from both Rugby and Southam Works.

Wilfred Dale died some years ago. Roger, his son, is a computer businessman who lays claim to be a well-travelled individual. Hazel, his mother, was blessed with a tremendous memory for her 90 years. She could remember vividly seeing cement in bags, being delivered by horse and cart. Hazel was born in the shadow of the original cement works at Rugby. For the benefit of local people living near the current cement works, the remaining white farm house behind Parkfield Road council houses marks the spot. Hazel's current house, less than ¼ mile from the New Rugby Cement works, together with two immaculate gardens neatly laid out, bear testament to a lady well into her maturing years, who was still not content to let other people do things for her. On my last visit to her house, which carried the name of "Thornycroft" on her front door, her last words to me were "You've got to keep going haven't you?" Sadly, in late 2006, I was informed by Roger Dale that the gallant lady had passed away.

When the war ended, the Labour government implemented transport nationalisation. Firmly opposed to outright control of his own business activities, Halford Reddish, the then Managing Director of Rugby Cement, approached Transport Services with an offer to buy out the entire "C Licence" operation in view of the nationalisation looming on the horizon. Thankfully he was to be successful in his bid for full control.

Hauliers and own account operators took part in organised protests using their vehicles to carry the message of their opposition. Rugby's prominent local haulier of many years standing was well represented by all of his lorries opposing the Government's threat. Photographic evidence of the scale of the project of Goddards lorries on the Fletchamsted Highway in Coventry carrying prominent placards complaining loudly about government intervention are shown on the following page.

These two black and white photographs, kindly loaned to me by Jamie Goddard, show in No 1 photo, the entire WG Goddard fleet at that particular time, parked on the near side of the Fletchamsted Highway in Coventry. Firmly opposed to the

government's policy, Goddards were joined by other local road transport firms all protesting vigorously. Prominently placed placards adorn all usable vehicles. Goddards first lorry was the Bedford removal van shown heading this line up of similarly adorned lorries. The offside carriageway is also crowded with more protestors.

Shown in the second photo is a long forgotten design which came from Bedford, which although ahead of its time did not catch on. A Neville-bodied tilt-cab is shown on a 4-wheel tipper chassis, also a member of the Goddard fleet, with the body sides holding numerous placards in respect of total opposition to the Government of the day.

The larger photograph shown overleaf shows just how serious the threat of nationalisation appeared to be at that time. Operators took the protest on to the streets of London, past the Houses of Parliament. Shown alongside each other united in protest, even though opposite in business circles, (i.e. trade name difference but selling the same product), is the only recorded 'O Type Bedford of RPC Transport alongside a Blue Circle Cement Leyland Comet 4-wheeler platform-bodied. The location in this striking photo which has survived is Marble Arch W1, well known to Londoners and visitors alike. The seriousness of this, by then national protest, can perhaps be estimated by the reader in that the campaign was brought to the capital. JKE 582 was later sold to Goddards Transport, not long after this protest.

Two prominent British cement manufacturer's transport lorries side by side in the London protest against nationalisation.

Sir Halford Reddish – Chairman & Managing Director, Rugby Cement

When Halford Reddish took control of Rugby Portland Cement in 1933, the business end was at a very low ebb for the company. Consequently no one in these early years was to know that this gentleman would eventually, through his own energies, foresight and careful planning, completely turn around the fortunes of Rugby Cement. The years between 1933 and 1938 were to see the rebuilding of Rochester, Rugby and Southam cement works, during which time Mr Reddish also introduced full time working for all employees, thereby eliminating seasonal layoffs. He was also to bring about the commencement of RPC Transport which, in his own words, was started to provide a service to his customers. During the Second World War, all essential services came under Government control. This was to include the operating licence of RPC Transport, whose activities came under Transport Services. With reference to Rugby Cement's contributions during the war years, I am unsure apart from what has already been written. Although Halford Reddish had been appointed Chairman of Rugby Cement in 1938, a year before the war, he was to vigorously continue his energies after the war when he regained total control of RPC Transport. During the middle 1950s, both Eastwoods and Chinnor Cement, who would both later be bought out in the early 1960s by Rugby Cement had each, in their own ways, experimented with pressure bulk deliveries. Four years prior to these buyouts, Halford Reddish was knighted. His philosophy of business being a partnership between management and labour, was then extended to all employees, through the introduction of works committees (not trade unions), together with profit sharing (national ordinary shares) which were made available to every employee. Fiercely patriotic and extremely supportive of both Royalty and the Conservative Party, his own energies, certainly from the 1950s onwards, ensured record profit-making, which in turn meant continual growth within Rugby Cement. Sir Halford Reddish was, in my estimation, a unique individual with legendary business skills. He refused point blank to allow or accept union membership within his company, his view being that he was not prepared to be told how to run his company. The well being of all Rugby Cement employees, plus in later years after 1962, those of Associate Company personnel, was foremost in Mr Reddish's mind, his philosophy being that a happy employee was a good employee. Consequently, over very many years, certainly from 1933 onwards, he developed this practice through his managers and supervisors. RPC Transport, however, continued to be the "apple of his eye" and he would not have anything said against its operation. Long before productivity and cost effectiveness nonsense, together with ever changing working practices (Sir Halford himself often worked a 10 hour day or more), he did not differentiate between staff members or weekly paid employees who for reasons of their own were habitually late for work. Sir Halford frequently expressed his views to the people concerned when reprimanding them. Despite being born as long ago as `1898, just two years before the beginning of the last century, Sir Halford Reddish was destined to be far ahead of his time. His energies and eventual achievements, together with his concern and kindness towards his fellow men and women within Rugby Cement and elsewhere, put this individual into a class of his own.

Mr KJ Harvey - Transport Manager, Rugby Portland Cement Transport

Ken Harvey was born into a Kentish family, who themselves were involved in road transport in pre-war years. With the approaching conflicts, Ken Harvey enlisted in the RAF and trained as a Sergeant Pilot, flying 4-engined bombers such as Halifaxes and Stirlings. Shot down over Germany with his crew at some point in 1943, they were to spend the remainder of the war as prisoners. Along with many hundreds of their comrades, they were force-marched through Northern Germany into Russia, experiencing intense cold weather amidst deep snow drifts. Many of the prisoners were inadequately dressed for such conditions and died along the way. Fortunately, Ken Harvey and his crew survived into repatriation after 1945. From what I have learned about this man, his crew would have followed him wherever, because he too was blessed with the same consideration for his fellow man as was Sir Halford Reddish, whom he would later work alongside in his early years as Assistant Transport Manager at Rugby. There are some former RPC drivers, now in their pensionable years, who remember with mixed feelings and mild hatred when Ken Harvey became the Transport Manager. His views on doing the job for which he had trained, together with his years in the RAF during wartime, had produced an individual who believed in everything which was correct and proper. To this end, he rigidly obeyed the rules and expected all RPC drivers to follow suit. In his capacity as Transport Manager he therefore did his job with a high degree of professionalism.

Albert Southam - Assistant Transport Manager

Albert Southam joined Rugby Cement during the 1950s more or less straight from school. He was destined to spend his first few months of transition learning first-hand about transport operation under the watchful eyes of Fred Williams, Southam Cement Works' Distribution Manager. Under Fred's guidance, Albert would go on to learn all the basic techniques plus general aspects concerning movement of cement in bags. Box-tippers were still used for bulk loads then. Control of drivers and lorries, together with customer's requirements, were all part and parcel of an Assistant Transport Manager's role. Consequently, when Albert Southam relocated back into "Crown House" he was well versed in all aspects of the job he was required to manage.

Harold Garratt – Fleet Vehicle Controller

Harold Garratt also joined RPC Transport at some point in 1955. Both he and I would meet at evening classes at the former Rugby College of Technology where we studied book-keeping. However, thirteen years were to elapse before we would meet again, when I (author) joined the company in 1968, by which time Harold's main job was that of Traffic Controller for the Group. Other people who worked within "Crown House" then regarded Harold Garratt second only to Ken Harvey in being his right hand man! Harold was destined to spend a total of forty four years with RPC Transport before retirement in 1999.

He was largely responsible for vehicle taxation, insurance, MOT preparation, booking requirements, together with all on-line main servicing schedules of the fleet. He was also concerned with vehicle allocation within the Group, which involved new chassis entering fleet service, together with time-served vehicles and disposals. All of these jobs presented a mammoth challenge which he handled with aplomb.

Don Ward - Transport Clerk

Don Ward started work in September 1950 in the Transport Department at Crown House. His prime occupation at that time was responsiblity for cost estimations. His calculations were based on driver's daily timesheets which recorded the working day hours, together with loading and unloading, also journey times in the outward direction and returning to base.

According to Don, most RPC Transport drivers put in a full 11 hour day, added to which on many occasions telephone messages from drivers running out of time and requiring to be collected came almost daily from the "Beggar's Bush" Public House, New Oscott, Birmingham. RPC Transport operated completely within the law right from the start, and so any driver running out of driving time HAD to be fetched in. This necessitated sending two drivers out, one to bring the driver back, and the other to drive his lorry back to base. "Topper" Brown was the RPC Transport Manager when Don started with Rugby Cement. His Secretary was Marjorie Fletcher. Other names from Don's past include Ken Harvey, who was the Assistant Transport Manager, and Albert Southam. Topper Brown would confer with his Secretary as to which route – A or B – he was taking when travelling the RPC delivery routes to check up on his drivers. This at times led to confusion as to his own whereabouts. Don also reminisced about efficiency status practices asked for by Sir Halford Reddish. This involved checking teleprinter seven sheet delivery copies and log sheet examinations. Don remembers that Albert Southam produced a graph showing that there were only two transport companies at the particular time who were operating at 100% efficiency. They were the London Brick Company and Rugby Portland Cement Transport. Sir Halford refused point blank to accept 100% and would only rate a 99% rate, silly as it might sound. Other names from those far off days include Ron Birch, the Chief Buyer and Ray and Pearl Hayward. He also remembers when Harrold Garratt first joined the company. Because Sir Halford was completely teetotal, and as such would not allow the sale of beers, wines or spirits within the RPC Social Club which was then situated across the road in North Street above an Insurance Society Office, many Crown House employees opted not to use these facilities and so for more years than anyone could remember, the Social Club and all that it offered was to be made use of by the Rugby Welsh Society at the ridiculous rent of one penny per year's rent.

Other vivid memories of his time in Crown House include him being the only employee in the Transport Department on the day when the present Queen was being crowned at the coronation, Sir Halford demanding that those employees who were in the building remain at attention until the ceremony ended.

Don Ward left the employment of Rugby Cement in 1954. He later set up Ward's Travel Services in Railway Terrace, Rugby. David Holton, who himself later became Payroll Manager at Crown House remembers in later years booking train travel, etc. through Ward's for many years. Later on Don Ward formed his own export packing service, initially in Somers Road, Rugby, but in later years moving to larger premises in Albany Road off Torrington Avenue, Canley in Coventry. Finally retiring to a quiet and peaceful life, Don Ward lived in a delightful area known as Moreton Paddocks near Moreton Morrell in Warwickshire not far from Wellesbourne. Don, reminiscing about his four years' service working for RPC Transport refers to a period when, like most companies at that time, it was getting back into its stride after the Second World War.

Whilst significant at the time, the aftermath facing construction companies in general was enormous, and personal accounts such as Don Ward's help to tell the story more vividly and honestly as to how working conditions and experiences were at that particular time. I am grateful to Don for allowing me to use this record of his time with RPC Transport. Rather sadly for all concerned, Don Ward died in early 2010.

Brian Male - Driver / Fitter

Brian Male joined RPC Transport in the 1950s, shortly after completing military service in the army, being attached to the REME Royal Electrical and Mechanical Engineers. He was, I suppose, even then more familiar with lorries than even some of the bosses at RPC. Being young, and into motor bikes and beer, in that order, Brian needed the money paid to RPC drivers at that time. His recollection of the regimentation of rules within the cement company even after so many years of obeying orders did not, I suppose, come lightly.

Being part of a group of drivers on Saturday morning, who after deliveries of bagged cement in the Birmingham area had all congregated within the confines of the old A45 Meriden Café, he was just about to bite into an outsize bacon sandwich and a mug of tea when "Topper Brown", the RPC Transport Manager, burst into the room with an armful of drivers' log books. "Topper" said, in a gruff voice, sort these out and report to me at Crown House on Monday morning when your name is called.

Brian also remembers the trouble which erupted when trouble makers within the RPC fleet and Crown House Management wanted union membership. The upshot was that one week the Company made all drivers redundant, sorted out the trouble makers and other unwanted individuals, bad timekeepers etc., and re-instated the next week many of the original drivers who wanted to work for RPC Transport. By paying them a higher rate of pay, way beyond the best paid lorry driving jobs in the Rugby district at that time, they were able to keep their drivers happy.

Later on, Brian Male was put on "JANKERS" for ten days after an incident with his Thornycroft Trusty 8-wheeler tanker. Their handbrakes were notorious for sticking on and the difficulty in releasing from their position just inside the driver's door (then). Brian was walking past his lorry one morning, so he thought "I'll just drop the handbrake from this angle". Unfortunately for him, after his folly he slipped on a patch of oil in the yard, by which time the Trusty had run away down the yard and smashed into another lorry, causing considerable damage.

Called to the "House of Crowns", Ken Harvey put Brian on a week of nights, starting at 6pm. His main job then was to bring drivers out of driving time back from Southam Works. He also had to go with one other to fetch drivers stuck in Birmingham and elsewhere when their time was up. Before he left the company, Brian was relocated into the RPC Transport Garage. Brian also has vivid memories of the Servis Time Recorders fitted to all RPC lorries – the 1950s idea of the Tachograph, which in itself was not too bad an idea if you kept your nose clean.

I am unsure exactly as to how many "S" type Bedford 7-ton box tippers came to carry the RPC Transport livery, but judging from researched information there were identical types based on the Big Bedford, as it was known - N/C (normal control) and F/C (forward control). The 5-ton were N/C whilst the 7-ton were F/C. The photograph shown below is another angle to the same picture in Part 1, but this shows the tipper F/N 285 with its box body tipped with the rest in the normal position on the chassis. Taken within the confines of Rugby Cement Works, this Weld Alloy advertisement captures these Bedfords exactly as they will no doubt be remembered by surviving drivers. The four main bulk silos still present a landmark on Rugby's skyline, as they have done for many years although in recent years much rebuilding on the site has taken place, so that the old packing-shed roof has all but disappeared. The roof-top catwalks still survive, but additional buildings have been added. The Bedfords were fitted with the manufacturer's own diesel engine together with these Weld Alloy bodies, which featured a one-piece constructed unit well suited to bulk powder transport because it was both sealed and built to prevent leakage. The strength of these box-tipper bodies is best appreciated in the main view of VAC 386, to which greedy boards are fitted.

The levelling rails were positioned to facilitate the statutory dust sheets which covered the entire load. Two identical lorries complete this unique picture of almost fifty years ago. TAC 699 F/N 299 and LWD 129 F/N 234. Shown overleaf loading bulk cement powder under the then dust protective covering is an identical lorry, TAC 698 F/N 280, the location being the old bulk shed at Rugby Works. Les Smith, better known to all of Rugby's drivers as "Chunky", with another title, which cannot be referred to, drove both O and S type Bedford tippers. He told me in one of his lighter moments that he helped in the construction of the M1 Motorway driving these box-tippers.

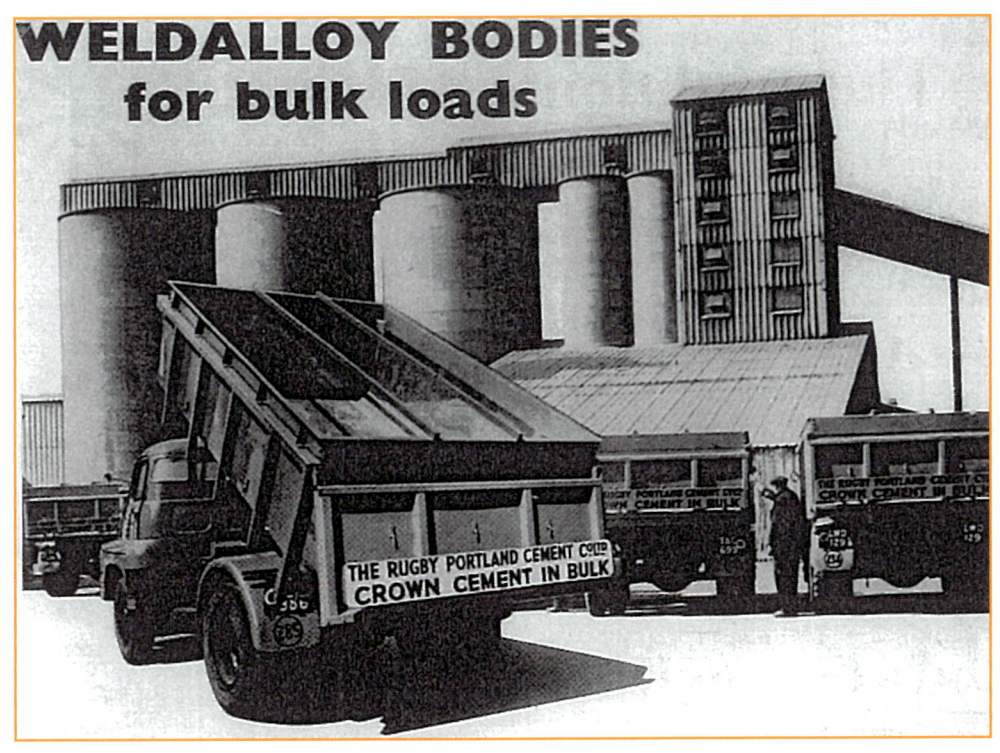

Drakelow Power Station near Burton-on-Trent was another "bulk customer" for deliveries in those years. Shown right in its daily environment is fleet number 280. The basic loading techniques of those times were that after the vehicle was positioned beneath a loading point under the sheet, bulk cement was loaded to a visual height just beneath the greedy board extensions.

In June 1956, after doing National Service, Peter Bunyard, like his father Albert before him, joined RPC Transport. His brother Alan was then also employed by the company. According to information supplied by Peter to me, not everyone was in agreement when Peter took over his father's earlier Bedford LWD 129. This arrangement had previously been decided by Jock Henderson, the RPC Fleet Engineer, as Albert was about to receive a newer Bedford tipper SNX 807 F/N 265. George Foots complained bitterly about the new arrival, but his cries were ignored by all concerned, mainly because he was not employed at that time on the Bedford tippers. Peter remembers from long ago, Neville Walker and Harry Gherry with split-screen Commers. He also cast his mind back to meeting Cliff Masters and Eddie Matthews who drove a vintage Foden 8-wheeler platform F/N 528, probably an ex-Eastwoods Cement Lorry. Other names from a dim and distant past include Dennis Saukins and Aubrey Tomlinson. These box-tippers were really only the tip of the iceberg in the infancy of proper bulk cement deliveries, which as the years went by, brought pressure tanker lorries.

However, in these early days, customers were slow to provide sufficient storage for between 5-7 ton loads. The original premises belonging to the Mix concrete Company at their Duston / Northampton plant are shown to good effect here. Bulk cement powder was delivered under a sheet by these Bedford tippers, and simply tipped into the "Hole". UAC 386 with a

Here's an example of the customer providing his own unloading arrangements. Mix-concrete of Northampton have supplied an unloading pit from which the cement is conveyed by elevators to the hoppers in which it is stored prior to being mixed with aggregate. Thanks to this arrangement, The Rugby Portland Cement Co. are free to use simple bulk carriers, in this case a Weldalloy tipper.

possible F/N of 285 is shown reversing up to the unloading dock prior to the sheet being loosened and the body tipped. The two vertical elevators shown would then transfer aggregate, sand and gravel along with the cement powder. Metered amounts then went on conveyors to the batching plant machines.

Box-tippers paved the way for bulk pressure deliveries later on. Ford ET6 Perkins powered diesel lorries were followed by Ford Traders which came later. Judging from remarks from retired Rugby Works-based cement drivers, the ET6 Ford, based on the standard SWB 4-wheel drive chassis were not universally popular, but numerous versions were bodied as covered bulk tippers working between a 30-40 mile radius from Rugby Works. The same basic chassis was to be used for the early pressure tanks and at least twelve such Ford 4-wheeler PV (pressure vehicles) fitted with bulk tank bodies started the RPC bulk service to customers.

One of their number is shown top right.

Ken Offord, one of Rugby Cement's early drivers on the ET6s, is seen in this family group in front of Ken's regular lorry at that time. The young girl in the centre of the group is Avril (Ken's daughter), now Mrs A Johnson. A similarly bodied PV/Ford ET6 VNX 232 carrying F/N 295 is shown below in the early days of bulk storage at Birmingham Depot. This ET6/PV was discharging into the overhead silo via the heavy rubber pipe shown at the rear of the lorry. In later years aluminium sheets would be fixed to the initial uprights. Later still, motive power would be used to load bulk vehicles. Today's stringent health and safety inspectors would cringe at the sight of upright ladders used to assist both maintenance and bulk loading. The building shown behind this ET6 catered for cement bag storage.

Another photograph supplied to me by Avril Johnson was one of her dad's next semi-permanent bulk cement tanker.

Based on a 1957 introduction of the Ford Thames Trader 7152 AC carried fleet number 322. This is a fine working photograph, because it shows an RPC Trader discharging into bulk storage. Again, the heavy flexible rubber pipe is being used. These lorries were fitted with a 6-cylinder diesel engine and a 4-speed synchromesh gear box. Almost all of the Rugby and Southam based Trader P/V lorries assisted in the building of the M1 motorway before it opened in 1959.

Ken Offord was based at Southam Works. His involvement with both the Ford ETC and these Traders happened long before I joined the company, consequently I never got to know him at all. My own beginning with the RPC Transport Company, known and locally referred to as "The Portland" was destined eventually, after the compulsory bulk training sessions with a seasoned driver, to bring me into contact with very many different types of drivers and individuals. George Foots had been with RPC for quite some years prior to his joining

The two photographs relating to Ken Offord were passed to me by his daughter Avril Johnson in 2006.

the newly-formed Night Shift Drivers. Here he was destined to work alongside George Anderson, Freddie Hack, Ken Whyment and Bill Gardner. From my own memory, George "stuck nights" for perhaps six or seven years, before finally opting for retirement in the late 1970s. His time as a driver with Portland began during the days of the Thames Traders.

Shown standing beside his own Ford Trader 4 wheel bulk tanker registration number 7779 NX which carried F/N 348, George is pictured in his younger years. I personally was not to be made aware of George's reactions when things did not go according to the way he thought they should go. It was really because of this that I think he initially opted to go on nights.

In later years, during his retirement, he forged a friendship with Sylvia, whose surname escapes me, who for a time ran the RPC works canteen. Later on they married and set up house together in Long Lawford, but ill health and numerous hospital visits gradually wore George down. I, will be indebted to both George and Sylvia for snippets of his life as a Portland driver, when both he and his Trader, along with other cement characters helped build the M1 Motorway before 1959.

As with all authors, when your attempts at eventual publication of your masterpiece or whatever comes to fruition, people in general begin to remember that hidden away in some pocket, drawer or even in the loft in some boxes are Rugby Cement photos. On numerous occasions since 2005, letters or phone calls have alerted me to relevant material.

Below is a copy of a photo made available to me by persons unknown, and shows Thames Trader bulk-tanker 4297 AC F/N 311, next to a similar vehicle and the Commer maxiload 2 stroke lorries, that started to replace the Traders certainly from about the early 1960s onwards. F/N 311 was given to Billie Jenner, who was to stay with RPC Transport for many years up to 1988. He eventually became one of the first owner-drivers. After the RMC buyout of Rugby, Billie eventually retired and now spends his retirement with his wife, staying both in Rugby and in Ireland where they also have property.

These two photographs, passed to me as late as March 2010, show a new weighbridge, which by 1958/59 replaced an earlier structure at Southam works.

Construction of the new facility is well on the way. The buildings behind, including the white looking shed, were demolished.

The new weighbridge is shown bottom right together with a Ford Trader bulk tanker, on the bridge, which carries registration number 4297 AC with F/N 311. In the distance on the left, a Thornycroft Swiftsure platform lorry is parked behind the workshop.

Both photos were supplied by Dave Allsop of Southam who deserves my sincere thanks.

Trinidad Cement Ltd was in effect another associate company of RPC and had been for many years. The following photos, which directly relate to TCL activities (before and after their independence) did not come into the author's possession until after 2002, but it is felt that they should be included at this point in the story.

This mobile drilling unit is based on what is reckoned to be an ex-W/D Thornycroft Nubian 4-wheel drive chassis. Bearing in mind that this photo was taken in 1953, health and safety requirements as we know them today in this new century, did not really apply to this two-man gang. This, I think, is a seismic drilling outfit to try and determine clay-bearing deposits prior to excavation from variable depths in the earth's crust. The absence of any protective gear, or indeed equipment, even in 1953, beggars belief, but the urgency at that time to search for usable materials so necessary in the manufacture of cement more than justified using just the basic available equipment at that time.

Shown below is a Bedford A-Type 4-wheel platform, the design of which was introduced in 1953. Carrying what is reckoned to be around a 5 ton load of bags - 100 separate sacks, two centre rows of 4 bags high, complemented by inverted bags along the sides, complete the load. It was registered TC859 with fleet number 8. Possibly because of the hot climate in Trinidad, the rear of the load could be secured by ropes, eliminating the need for sheeting. Over the years, from information since received from former RPC engineers and friends within Transport, I have been privileged to learn that several parts of the early kilns used at South Ferriby cement works were in later years dismantled, to be replaced by modern equipment. The early ex S/F material was later shipped over to Trinidad and rebuilt in the TCL works. All this work was in the early days supervised by South Ferriby engineers. Like so many of their United Kingdom fellow associate members, Trinidad Cement Limited delivered cement in bags for many years, but the middle-1950s brought the introduction of bulk cement deliveries. The birth of the lorry-mounted concrete mixer completely revolutionised major and minor building projects. Gone were the days of hand-mixing cement for large jobs. Bags, however, continued to be wanted by most builders' merchants, but for most of the UK's major cement manufacturers, the writing from then on was on the wall. Consequently, the introduction of more and more pressure built road tankers became the order of the day. Trinidad, in their infinite wisdom, introduced higher operating weights, mainly for 6-wheel chassis, and although RPC Transport had used the same basic A type Bedford chassis in a shortened 4-wheel chassis form for bulk operation, shown discharging "On Site" during the 1960s at the construction of the St Albans by-pass, PUE 893 is apparently well down on the rear axles.

Early types of concrete mixer equipment are visible above this Bedford tanker. The absence of flashers, plus the small round driving mirrors, reflect past operation. I am indebted to Peter J Davies, the lorry historian, who very kindly passed this photograph on to me. These Bedfords were operated at the 13-ton gross limit in the United Kingdom. A worrying aspect for the RPC engineers was the fact that when the bulk tank was tipped, the front end of the lorry lifted off the ground. It was therefore decided to send these Bedfords over to Trinidad Cement Limited, then part of Rugby Portland Cement, where upon arrival there, an additional axle would be fitted to each of these lorries (as TLC operating weights were much higher).

The unique photograph above shows all three ex-RPC Bedfords about to depart for London Docks on the first stage of their journey. PUE 893, PAC 597 and PUE 200 on the right are all accordingly painted and lettered in TLC livery.

Since this photograph was taken Rugby Cement has seen two complete rebuilds of these works under two separate owners. The backdrop of building in this view shows the original cement works kiln house, chimney, conveyor belt, plus empty railway coal trucks waiting to be collected.

For local people who've lived within sight of these cement works over many years, and former RPC employees, drivers and other individuals who've worked nearby – this is how these works will be remembered.

Billed as the first twelve-wheeled bulk cement tanker, opposite, to carry a 15-ton load of bulk cement powder, nine Thornycroft Trusty lorries joined RPC Transport some time in 1957. From enquiries since made, I have found out that three were based at Rugby, with a further batch at nearby Southam Works, whilst the remaining three were based at Rochester Cement Works in Kent.

The lorry shown in this Mike Jeffries painting is part of a 2008 calendar of his work featuring old commercial vehicles at work. F/N 365 was based at nearby Southam works and its regular driver for most of its service was Jack Reynolds, one of Southam's characters. The sequence shown here involves the tank being raised by two rams as it is slowly emptied of its load by tapping the rear of the tank as discharging continued. An experienced RPC bulk driver would then elevate the tank higher to assist discharge, eventually raising it to its full height of 3 rams high. To facilitate full discharge of any cement powder remaining within the tank in this position, the cement door was closed and pressurisation of the tank up to 10lbs began. When this safe pressure was built up, the cement door was opened and technically any remaining cement powder particles shot up the pipe. As to the location of this painting, I have yet to find out. All the characteristics of these venerable machines are portrayed in this working shot. It is, however, worth noting now that prior to these Trustys entering RPC Transport, the Basingstoke Factory of Thornycroft Lorries was on strike, and so the cabs for all nine Trusty chassis were constructed by Bostock/Barsby, the Barwell Leicestershire coachbuilders, under the supervision of Thornycroft engineers. Having myself driven one of these Trustys during my early years with RPC Transport, I can fully confirm the strength of construction built into these chassis, which is equally portrayed by two photos taken by me at the 2006 Classic Commercial Motor Show at Gaydon.

Shown to the right is a colour photo which dates back certainly to perhaps the late 1950's - 60's, taken from the top of the original Rugby kiln house roof. This photo shows empty coal wagons waiting to be collected, along with a bulk rail wagon alongside. The bulk cement conveyor belt from the mill into the packing shed and old bulk storage is shown in the centre of the photo. Top right is the old Parkfield Road garage, with a selection of lorries and cars outside. The biggest chassis appear to be two Thornycroft Trusty 8-wheel bulk tankers, whilst parked on the left of the yard is a Foden short wheel based 8-wheel bulk tipper, with the original ERF twin steer recovery unit alongside. The railway line to Leamington Spa, Marton and Southam is just visible at the top right and steam from the works chimney occupies all of the top left hand area of this unique but well remembered area of the cement works.

Dragged out of Rush Green scrapyard, Hertfordshire, where it had lain for just over thirty years, 1146 UE F/N 364, was purchased by father and son, Jon and Fred Lawton from Etwall near Derby, who intend to rebuild it back fully. They've certainly got their hands full here. Willi Flowmer, a locally well-known preservationist contemplates the perhaps enormous job of rebuild. Unseen to onlookers, the cab is propped up by various lengths of wood to prevent the roof falling down. For the Thornycroft front grille to remain for fifty years since being built is impressive. Even the massive steering wheel remains.

The second photograph shows the remains of this Trusty from the rear. It is worth noting that the rear axles are still fitted to the chassis. These will include the double-drive arrangement (fitted from new), but speaking again from my own experience, the traction in rough areas of quarries and ready-mixed premises did not entail the use of the D/D bogie. These Trustys did their job efficiently and without fuss. They were regarded by the drivers who drove them regularly at that time as being the best. Two of them were still in regular service eleven years later when I joined the company in 1968. F/N 364 and 374 were kept for the more inaccessible bulk jobs where access was difficult. I was to drive both of them separately during summer holiday relief before I had any sort of permanent lorry.

My own memories of these by then "elderly lorries" will live with me for many years simply because of their utter reliability, not to mention their often at times unexpected and troublesome characteristics to the unwary drivers put on them for a day's work.

The photo shows the ravages of many years' standing in open fields. The interest shown at the Gaydon event in that "old wreck" more than justified bringing the RPC Thornycroft for everyone to see. Many ordinary people, including myself, thought quite rightly, "someone has got an almighty job on their hands" to even begin to remedy almost thirty years of neglect, but at least the remains have now been saved. I'd personally like to think that in later years we might see a reincarnated RPC Thornycroft Trusty 8-wheeler bulk tanker – who knows?

Having tried to obtain early pictures of Eastwood Cement activities, certainly since 1982, I was recently surprised to be sent, via email, two photographs, which I think date from the 1950s, perhaps later.

The photo above shows Eastwoods Lewes based drivers. I am not able to recognise any of these gentlemen, so can only add the list of names with which I have been supplied.

Shown left to right – John Bellard, Fred Goldsmith, Bill Wickham, Dick Tucknot, Charlie Ward, Charlie Mewitt, Ray Gravell, Don Beach, Gill Haylar, Aubrey Taylor, Cliff Deacon, Frank Woolmer, Dick Hyde, Jack Hood, Brian Mockford, Jam Simmons, Jordy Lewis and Arthur Redmill.

Bearing in mind that almost fifty years have passed since the Eastwoods Cement Company was absorbed into Rugby Portland Cement, getting these pictures from Geoff Isted has been a real eye-opener.

The second offering from the Sussex-based factory of Lewes Works, is a long-wheel based Dodge Kew 4-wheel drive dropside shown opposite. This particular lorry fits in exactly with the following article which captures the Eastwoods Cement approach to post-war years' operation exactly. I'm informed by Mr Isted that this lorry in question, MXU 619, had Fred Goldsmith as the regular driver. Observers of this post-war building site with a very basic scaffolding tower, cannot fail to also notice the standard load pattern of Eastwoods cement bags waiting to be manually unloaded.

Unlike other swop body chassis, MXU 619 has fixed dropside bodywork and all loads would be sheeted. Like so many of her sister lorries of their time, a Perkins diesel engine was standard fitment. The old Lewes three digit telephone number of 500 and the small rear view mirrors on long stalks are of a bygone age. All of these Eastwoods cement works had their own preferred way and practice of loading bags, as can be seen on this Kew Dodge.

Brian Peeps began his career as a driver with Eastwoods Cement based at South Ferriby cement works on the 17th April 1961. These details are on his former contract of employment. His first lorry was a bonneted Dodge 4-wheeler platform lorry, fitted with tipping rams and blower discharge equipment. Demountable bulk tank or tipper bodies could be held on the platform by spring retention bolts and hooks. This system was admirable as the photo overleaf shows.

NYE 225 carries F/N 605 and dates from around 1954. Perkins R6 engines were fitted; these Dodges came to be known universally as Parrot Nosed.

This photograph is superb, in that it shows the reader how the operator utilised the chassis for three separate bodies, whereby powdered or bagged cement could be delivered to the customer in exactly which form he or she wanted it.

F/N 605 is shown blowing out an 8 ton bulk load at the former RMC Red Lion Works at Alford, which was situated between Mablethorpe and Skegness.

Brian Peeps later transferred to later styled LAD-cabbed Dodge 4-wheelers fitted out as LWB (long wheel based) dropside lorries. All loads were sheeted. The cab structure termed LAD was similar on the Leyland and Albion, as well as the Dodges of that period, the only visible differences being the front grilles and manufacturers names. Brian's new regular lorry was 2005 ML, again fitted with a 6354 Perkins diesel.

Other SWB LAD/ Dodges had the same engine and carried swop-body tanks on box tipper bodies or flats. Normal load weight was 8-ton of bags or bulk on outward journeys to customers. Inbound trips back to South Ferriby involved loads of coke from Barnsley, Yorkshire Pits, or from Leeds gas works at Tursley. Additionally, if we were in the Doncaster areas, return loads of kiln fuels would be singles (small coal) from both Monk Bretton or Thorne Collieries. All loads in and out were sheeted down. The basic LAD cab designs were introduced from about the middle 1950s, and offered better visibility for drivers. More powerful engines offered better payloads, but, as Brian Peeps said, comfort for driver's basic needs was extremely low, even with a new chassis, because for a start they had no heaters or windscreen washers when it rained.

On Saturday mornings drivers were to be occupied servicing their lorries. Bodies were tipped up for greasing and wheel nuts were checked all round. Mansion polish for the mats and other bits, plus car polish for the cab, were used.

Shown below is Raymond Ward, leaning on the front of his regular lorry 1074 MM, whilst his friend Brian Peeps, in similar pose, holds up his lorry 2005 ML. This photograph refers back to a period in road transport when lorry driving was a way of life. The roads were far quieter than they are now. Eastwoods Cement drivers were issued with overalls and uniform caps etc with the company name embossed on to metal badges on their caps. I remember going with Chalky White delivering bulk cement in two SWB Dodges to the RM Douglas cement/ready mix plant in Perry Barr, Birmingham. We each had a box-tipper with fixed bodies in RPC ownership. I seem to remember now from almost forty plus years ago that their F/Ns were 112/113 and they were scrapped shortly afterwards. This was my first experience of driving a tipper lorry, with not much physical effort needed, apart from driving the lorry and following Chalky through the Birmingham Streets. No M1 Motorway in those days! When we got there, the bodies were raised, and the tail boards were opened. Both 8 ton bulk loads went down on to an underground conveyor which took the cement powder up to the automatic plant.

Shown right, Raymond Ward stands in front of his regular steed, whilst the gentleman on the right is Harold Blanchard. The stark, basic design of these LAD/Dodges is shown to good effect and the smallness of those small driving mirrors on long stalks, where the driver, had to be like "Quasimodo" just to look behind into that small area of glass.

These Brian Peeps photographs, taken almost sixty years ago, portray to you, the reader, the stark, almost basic conditions of being an Eastwoods Cement driver; preventative maintenance spoke for itself much later on when heavy vehicle design improved. Much reference by myself in Part 1 of this story concerned Foden and Bedford lorries, but as you will see, within these pages, using one chassis with three separate bodies appealed greatly to Eastwoods Cement. It also made for better customer relations because deliveries were made using the exact body suited to each particular customer.

Shown right is a bold statement from Homalloy, circa 1954, who built a lot of bodies for Eastwoods Cement, but not them all. Dodge LAD designs followed in the middle 1950s, but Austin Morris/

WITH "UNIVERSITY" BUILT

Homalloy
LIGHT ALLOY

Commercial, and some Albion medium chassis also carried the Eastwoods name.

Thirty four lorries, out of a total of 80 overall, were Dodge LAD rigids/artics. Together with new Bedford KMAs (fitted with TK cab designs) in both rigid and artic form, all of these had the Perkins diesel of the day. According to a *Commercial Motor* report, the artics pulling 12-ton loads were averaging between 9-10mpg, whilst rigid lorries carrying 8-ton loads returned 17mpg. The Perkins 112 brake horsepower unit would in effect produce adequate power / acceleration for its day, bearing in mind that the Barrington based lorries were averaging 800 miles each per week, on fairly long journeys through East Anglia, and all of this was long before the advent of rebuilt major roads and motorways.

Peter Dimes, a Barrington based driver throughout both his Eastwoods and Rugby Cement days followed his father into transport. He remembers taking over the driving of 749 BLA, a Bedford KMA / TK styled artic fitted with the 4-in-line platform trailer after the original driver (who was Rodney Witt) experienced a rather frightening experience involving a roll-over whilst on a delivery of bagged cement to an Ipswich Suffolk customer. From what I have since learned from Peter, the previous individual was too cautious of the braking system, and after this episode he never drove bag lorries again.

Peter Dimes himself stayed with BLA until it was replaced, and in later years, after 1968, I remember meeting and talking with him at Rugby or Barrington when on stock deliveries of bags. Certainly over the past five to seven years we have again met and shared nostalgic times, mainly at the Barrington Open Day events.

The Dodge LAD chassis design started life in the late 1950s when road speeds were lower than those of today, and also the number of road users was limited. These two aspects generally made lorry drivers' jobs more enjoyable.

The combined harsh use of clutches, gearboxes and suspension, all of basic design, and not as sophisticated as today's modern equivalents, coupled with building site work, normal operations on metalled roads and on builder's suppliers' premises took its toll. A mixed bag of coats, hats and working footwear to cope with harsh working conditions and ever changing weather is shown in the opposite photograph. Drivers ready for the off at going home time are also pictured here in typical pose.

Working clothes of the period include flat caps. Ordinary jackets and dinner bags cover RPC overalls then. Two of the well remembered LAD Dodge short-wheel-based covered tippers provide the backdrop to this very cheery scene. L-R are drivers Les Brown, Harry Maddock, Ron Storer and Fred Kirk. They took bulk cement to Leeds, Sheffield and Mansfield almost daily on regular runs. The man visible in the background of this photo is Bob Goodsen.

Byron Bennett was a driver based at South Ferriby for very many years. He gave both Eastwoods and Rugby Cement more than forty one years service. Two of his following colleagues – John Todd and Brian Peeps kindly supplied the photgraphs and the accompanying detail.

South Ferriby cement works was rated an A depot. The transport manager there was to be responsible for a total of 44 lorries of mixed types, operating a delivery radius of 70 miles from the works on the banks of the Humber.

Shown resting on the front bumper below is a young looking Byron Bennett as he surveys the then South Ferriby works atmosphere.

Byron's regular lorry was registered 4261 MF and carried F/N 90. All semi trailer chassis in use with Eastwoods Cement at that particular time were based on the 4-in-line configuration, manufactured by BTC (British Trailer Company).

Demand from customers fluctuated from day to day, and whilst drivers were kept to their particular units, bulk orders being the priority meant that flat trailers used for the carriage of cement in bags could be standing. Single front spot lamps, certainly up until the middle 1970s, were a feature of all RPC-operated lorries. Shown alongside Byron is the

rear of 192 BXV, a flat artic 4-in-line trailer, whilst to the immediate right hand side, is an almost new ERF L/V bulk tanker.

When Byron felt he'd done enough lorry driving, he then transferred into the very busy Transport Office at South Ferriby, where he was to be kept fairly active in the company of Bernard Johnston on the left.
Byron is shown centre, with an exceedingly young looking Mervyn Smith, who was in charge of the Despatch Office. Mervyn started his career with RPC Transport in the 1950s, based at Southam works, working alongside his oldish cronies like Neville Walker and Clive Mumford, now sadly gone. When it was going home time Mervyn would hide inside the bulk tank, purely to get more paid time. Reg Coles, now long since dead, and Fred Saunders (alias Reg Harris), also deceased, were ex-colleagues of Mervyn Smith. A "reborn pensioner" since his triple bypass, Neville Walker remembers a humiliating result of a race between the packers / loaders and the drivers from Southam bag shed to the works main gate. Mervyn beat Neville and by quite a few yards into the bargain.

The backdrop of these three Despatch staff shows the destinations and drivers' names, together with the fleet numbers and start times, all in chalk on a blackboard. This was a far cry from today's computerised logistics. These three gentlemen looked after daily requirements of despatching loads/drivers to customers. Later on, development of a night despatch staff/driver came on stream at South Ferriby as it did elsewhere within RPC Transport, certainly during the late 1960s and early 1970s. When Mervyn Smith retired from Ferriby Despatch Office, the Company lost an exceptional individual who continued to retain a superb sense of humour as well as respect from everyone. I personally met him and his wife for the first time in later years at Rugby School Close, when the RPC cricket team displayed their skills.

Mervyn has been away from Ferriby for a number of years, and lives in retirement at Winteringham, just up the coast road from the cement works.

Long before the RPC Safe Driving Award Dinners and Medal Presentations, the South Ferriby drivers and the garage staff organised a Drivers Dinner at the Angel Hotel in Brigg, Lincolnshire. Thanks to Brian Peeps' excellent memory for faces, he knew them all. I as Author did not, but would ask you, the reader to find you and your partner below.

On the front table, shown left to right, are as follows:
Harold Blanchard and wife, Ray Lawtey and wife, Brian Peeps and wife, and Mrs Swin, wife of George who worked in the garage stores. Even with all the names supplied to me by Brian Peeps, it would be difficult to sort it out. If you were there, find yourself and your partner amongst this happy collection of faces!

The Eastwoods story is vast in itself, purely and simply because long before the takeover in 1963 by Rugby Cement, they were the nation's builders merchants in England and Scotland. There was not much that they did not deliver in the building and construction industry. I attempted in Part 1 to refer to and write about their vast fleet of road delivery lorries, but I could only really write about the photographs, which at that time (1980s) were passed on to me from both former Eastwoods plants at Barrington and South Ferriby. Maintenance schedules were rigorously laid down in the early days for drivers, plus later on the inclusion of base workshops where trained staff coped with a variety of tried and tested chassis over many years of daily and nightly use.

Above is a 6-wheeler Foden lorry which is shown close to delivering its last load.

Its visible and mechanical condition are both 100% after probably a fifteen year life of carrying bagged cement on its back. KGJ 625 carried F/N 525 and dates from about 1955, maybe earlier. Perkins engines were standard fitment for 4-wheeler chassis, but the larger lorries were Foden, powered by numerous Gardner variants such as are shown here. Of particular note on this Foden are the fore-runners of flashing indicators, the lazy arm trafficator, shown on the outside quarter light panel. Shielded in its vertical shaped box, one was fitted on either side of the cab.

Lewes Cement Works (Originally Eastwoods Cement) RPC take-over 1960s.

The origins of the cement works at Lewes in Sussex, date back as far as 1902 when the Lewes Portland Cement Company started operations in the Snowdrop and Southerham chalk pits during that year. Both the clay and chalk excavated material was eventually moved to the kiln by a succession of small locos until after the RPC take-over in the early 1960s. Diesel-powered replacement locos made their appearance for a short period of years, before the closure of these works. The kiln on this site had been working non-stop since around 1928, and cement from it was used to form, the rather awkward looking, but functional, Mulberry floating harbour of the D Day Landing.

A fact possibly unknown to local inhabitants and the cement works employees other than those engineers who looked after it was that the power required for that early kiln was reputed to come from a World War One German submarine Maybach diesel engine. Shown above is a joined up photograph taken some years back under RPC ownership which should give the reader a good indication of the age of the Cement Works. A local publication stated in 1981 that Lewes cement works would be closed in July of that year with the loss of 55 jobs. Ownership by RPC had lasted a mere 19 years, but cement had been made at these works for 79 years. The reason given for the impending closure was that Lewes being very old in terms of buildings and equipment meant that the works overall were becoming uneconomical.

Before we can come forward a few more years, this other interior view of Lewes cement works gives an even closer picture of the old style buildings within these works. Eastwoods Lewes Cement prominent lettering is displayed on top of the storage silos conveyor shed. This, along with the two lorries of the period, portrays the past of the cement industry in this part of the Sussex countryside which contributed so much to the construction industry.

There is very little information known about the Foden S20 short-wheel-based 4-wheel quarry dumper shown amidst the confines of Lewes works. Possibly limited access for tipping, whether into a building or directly on to an underground conveyor belt, may have accounted for the short length. Of prominent interest to readers is the front bumper, together with its protective radiator grille. The Dodge kew 4-wheel bulk tanker in the background is typical of early road bulk pressurised delivery chassis. These yellow painted lorries, with their boldly black painted Eastwoods letters, hark back to earlier times when road speeds were lower and the pace of everyday life was acceptable.

The decision was taken in the middle 1950s to plan and build Britain's first motorway, linking London initially up to Crick in Northamptonshire, but it was to be 1959 before this was completed. Massive reconstruction after five and a half years of World War 2 was really only in its infancy, but some principal towns and cities were gearing up gradually for what is now remembered as the building boom of the 60s/70s. The demand coupled with ordinary day requirements from builders' merchants and the general public, meant that more cement, particularly in bulk form, was often to be asked for at short notice. The 4-wheeler pressure chassis were really only the tip of the iceberg, and so Eastwoods' engineers, in conjunction with their Transport Department, designed a triple pepper-pot pressure delivery chassis to fit their maximum 8-wheeler chassis in use at that time. The construction of these new pressure chassis has been described in Part 1, however the two photographs now available to me of these well remembered lorries, each show the immense pipework involved in the design, which must have appeared something of a gamble even to those involved in such a bold effort. However, these "Klingers" as they were known, paved the way for bigger loads.

Each tank had a capacity of five tons, and only one tank could be discharged at a time.

Some idea of the piping and bulk tank and catwalk aluminium construction can perhaps be appreciated from the photograph. All the manufacture of the tank bodywork was built by YEWCO (Yorkshire Electric Welding Company). Power for discharging came via a Volkswagen engine, driving through a blower. This was positioned on the outside rear of the chassis. A centre-mounted full length delivery pipe, linking the base outlets of all three tanks, exited at the rear of the chassis which, when coupled to bulk/delivery canvas hoses, allowed deliveries to be made. The above photograph features a Barrington-based Foden FG/6 8 wheeler chassis which originally had been supplied in flat platform guise. They were operated at the 24GVW rate, allowing a straight 15 ton load of cement in bulk to be carried. Although this chassis, and perhaps one or two other similarly re-bodied Klingers featured the YEWCO-built bodywork, after the switch to aluminium-built equipment, Reynolds T1 Aluminium were to be responsible for future new chassis pipework. Various adaptations to catwalk access ladder positions on the early designs and the overall final concept of this new bulk powder design, changed constantly over the first few years of their appearance in the Eastwoods fleet. Gardner 5LW engine variants which, along with the then Foden-designed gearbox, really sorted the men out from boys amongst the drivers. I can only remember my own physical, often exhausting energies, trying to keep a slow moving heavily-laden lorry on the move, whilst struggling at times with the gearbox as one had to remember to wait for the "revs" of the Gardner.

With experience came ease, but it took time and lots of patience. Once mastered, driving these Fodens was something you never forgot.

In the above photo NLP 568, a sister lorry, is shown loading bulk cement at the South Ferriby Eastwoods cement works. The loader with his hand on the tap, so to speak, is watching the flow of bulk cement powder into the rear bulk tank. All three tanks would be visibly loaded to just under the lids. This is a superb photo taken of a working lorry. The complete off-side of the lorry is shown to good effect, and the old Winterton three digit phone number contributes to this picture. Having, over the years since I began my research into RPC Transport and its Associate Companies, been fortunate enough to meet and converse with surviving drivers who worked for both Eastwoods, and ultimately Rugby, I have listened to the various comments regarding jobs of the day where these Foden Klingers more than proved their design in support of customers far and wide. Many of today's hi tech bulk pressure tank designs owe their origins to these Klinger lorries.

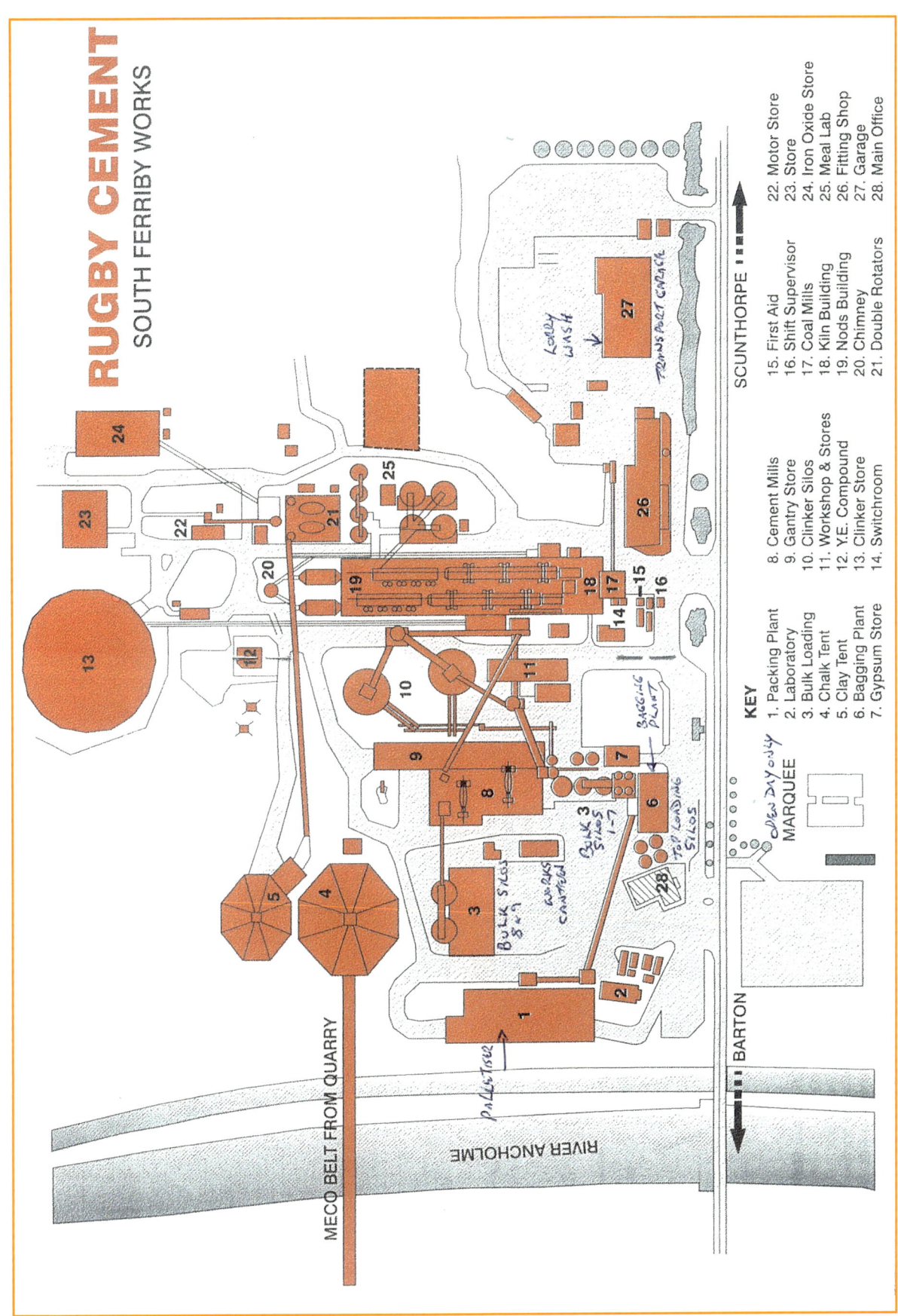

The interpretation of South Ferriby Works Interior given to "Open Day" visitors below shows the plant process in numbered form.

Shown below is another daily scene, this time taken within the Barrington Cement works near Cambridge, also then still operated by Eastwoods Cement. Bulk cement powder is being blown into the rear pot of a triple Klinger pot lorry. When fully loaded these Fodens would weigh nearly 24 ton, each pot tank held 5 tons, 3 x 5 = 15 tons, but only one pot could be emptied at any one time. These Fodens helped build the M1 motorway before 1959, and some driver individuals who are still alive today, will tell you about being up to your necks in mud just trying to connect your discharge pipes. Barrington based Klingers delivered to most of the bridges and culvert junctions in Hertfordshire and Bedfordshire. The driver is watching the level of cement powder filling the pot tank and he is in a position to stop the flow of powder when he gauges a full load. The lorry shown is a Foden S18 8-wheeler chassis dating from around 1954. Fitted with Gardner oil engine and Fordens own gear box, these lorries demanded the fittest of drivers which along with an in-built design strength saw most of Eastwoods lorries still in use 12 or 13 years later

CHAPTER 3

Raw Material Extraction & Equipment, Barrington Light Railway & Works Characters, Rail Bulk Deliveries Eastwoods Cement

It was a special hardy type of employee who worked in the quarry industry of post war years. Shown right in this Southerham - Lewes Sussex quarry, with little or no emphasis on health and safety, are two workers using powered pneumatic drills to break up large clay bearing lumps. Manageable sections plus a good bucket load would then be loaded by the RB24 Ruston Bucyrus excavator into the waiting Foden Scow bodied 4-wheeler. The excavated clay would then be transported to the wash mill and screening conveyors prior to cement making, which because it was and still is a constant manufacturing process operated 24 hours a day.

Most of the former Rugby Cement owned/operated cement works were located alongside quarries where clay and chalk were excavated. Various methods of extraction were to involve many different kinds of machines. In the following selection of photographs, some idea of the harsh working conditions for both man and machines can be understood. The demand for cement became never ending, certainly after the 2nd World War.

Shown overleaf in the former Rochester Works quarry, in Kent, is a 22-RB excavator. "Ruston Bucyrus" was a household name, and their excavators survived in similar conditions for many years. The clay would be extracted from the sides and banks by another similar machine fitted with a rammer, which broke up the shelved clay. When excavated, the clay was then loaded into Foden dumper lorries and transported to the wash mill and screening plants, prior to cement manufacture.

In another series of Tony Higgins photographs, taken within the confines of Southam Works in Warwickshire, the nature of quarry machines can be appreciated. The spartan cab design of almost all such equipment used in the vast quarry workings at Southam, certainly from 1955 as I remember, will no doubt illustrate to the reader just how daily working conditions appeared. Generations of families worked in the quarries. Several layers of clothing plus, in later years, the advent of compulsory safety equipment, such as viz-vests, hard hats, overalls, gloves etc., were indeed a far cry from earlier years, where the ever-changing British weather conditions were to account for a job which appealed only to the hardiest of individuals. Yet, as in most of the areas of cement making, the same groups of men did the same job for countless years.

Resident in Southam quarry for more years than even I can remember, this offside view of the 54-RB might give some idea of the harsh every day conditions described. The skimmer bucket is similar to the Rochester machine. My mechanical knowledge of such machines and equipment is limited, but I know that this was diesel-powered. When this photo was taken the RB had endured countless years' service.

The "Dumper Shop" takes almost centre stage in this view from behind the former arm of the canal where barges loaded bag cement in earlier years. Shown awaiting attention in one form or another is the 6-wheeled Foden ½ cabbed scow bodied dumper and the Aveling Barford 4-wheeler in similar guise. The rear end of another unidentifiable tipper is visible in between a cluster of bits and pieces. In the background, just

visible, are RPC bulk lorries and the main conveyor belt from the kilns, which transported powdered cement down to storage and for use in the bag packer.

Shown above is an Aveling Barford 50-ton 4-wheeler quarry dump-truck parked in front of the "Dumper Shop". Its closed driver's cabin, offered the driver some degree of daily comfort. The immense construction is very apparent to the reader, and its appearance makes it ideal for the job for which it was designed. These tiny cab/driving mirrors appear inadequate in lieu of the size of this machine, but then this dumper was only used within the cement works. Fitted with both a horn and an audible siren to warn employees of its presence, it too worked a lifetime in Southam Quarry.

Parked and probably abandoned on the edge of the Southam Quarry, and operated on hire from Abelson Plant, this Caterpillar bull-dozer was, in its heyday, used to clear excavated spoil from the main working areas. It was also used for loading dumper trucks. Its main task in later years was concerned with levelling off redundant working areas, using loads of kiln dust etc brought over from Rugby Works in covered box-tippers.

Clinker is an intermediate product produced in the manufacture of cement, large stocks being produced in the continuous 24 hour production process.

Shown on the right is the new clinker storage facility which was completed at Southam Works in the early 1980s. Prior to this building coming on stream great heaps of 'brought-in' clinker delivered by outside haulage contractors were a prominent feature of the landscape at most of the Rugby Cement Works. Clinker is fed directly to the mills and large quantities were moved on inter-works journeys by hordes of tipper lorries before these new storage facilities were available.

Much later on, with the advent of more up-to-date quarry equipment and the inevitable safe working practices, these BM Volvo Moxy articulated 6 wheel dumper trucks were to make their appearance, certainly in both the Southam and ultimately in Barrington near Cambridge quarries. These later machines had the drivers' well-being catered for.

In the photo shown to the right, the backdrop of buildings to this works locomotive and its five loaded coal wagons is the original Rugby Cement works. The works chimney is prominent at the rear of the kiln house and attendant buildings, as each loaded coal wagon was detached by the railway worker and raised via the coal tippler (arrowed). It was then loaded back onto the railway line and shunted backwards allowing the next loaded wagon to be put in place. When all the wagons were unloaded and coupled in-line they were then shunted by the works Manning Wardle loco to join up with other empty wagons shown centre. They would then be shunted onto the branch line to await collection by a British Railways locomotive; from memory two loaded coal trains of perhaps ten or a dozen wagons were delivered into Rugby Cement works every week.

Seen slowly and very definitely rusting away into oblivion this former Rochester Cement works steam powered Sentinel loco and ten open bodied 16-ton coal wagons await their fate. The building to the immediate left of this train is the former packing shed for loading platform lorries with cement in sacks. The building with its covered roof alongside, catered for the loading of both bulk rail wagons and in earlier years the loading of bags into covered box trucks. A side elevation shows 'out of use' regular buildings within Rochester Cement works, the redundant steam shunter and the already described empty wagons awaiting their ultimate fate which in some probability would be the scrap man. Originally delivered new into the Totternhoe Lime Works near Dunstable, Bedfordshire, this was one of a half dozen similar steam Sentinel locomotives.

Barrington Light Railway. Eastwoods Cement (Ultimately RPC)

Almost ninety five years after it began in support of the cement works in Cambridgeshire, the Barrington Light Railway ended its days transporting chalk and clay based materials from the adjacent quarry around Barrington cement works. This original narrow gauge railway, which began in 1910 powered solely by steam-powered saddle-tank locos, was to be changed entirely to diesel operation in 1963.

The photo below shows "Vulcan", an Andrew Barclay loco Number 1145/09 taken on site at Barrington Works in September 1960; also of interest is the exposed kiln.

The photo overleaf taken within the cement quarry, shows a diesel powered Ruston Hornsby loco waiting for its four 16-ton open wagons to be loaded by the electrically-operated dragline excavators.

As each new terrace of levelled clay was cleared, new areas prepared allowed for excavators to be moved nearer to load material into these quarry trains. The starkness of each level of clay etc can clearly be seen. I have been privileged through my friendship with Barrington Works Raw Materials Coordinator John Drayton to be taken on a tour of these seemingly vast quarry workings, where 4-wheel drive vehicles do find difficulty traversing the slopes of the quarry. However, the view from the top of these workings far outweighs any concern for the future operation. Anyone working as a Quarryman in ever-changing weather conditions had to be a hardy individual.

An article written from the *Old Glory* magazine is included at the end of this article, and shows aspects of this much loved operation and their successors in transport.

Shown above is Dora, an Avonside loco which I do believe has survived into preservation.

Avonside 0-4-0 ST Dora, suitably adorned with a wreath, brings another four empties into the quarry. The wreath signifies the closure of the quarry railway operation.

Dora arrives at the loading excavator with her empty wagons.

Redundant and unwanted, these two electrically-powered excavator / face-shovels stand forlornly on the quarry floor, waiting perhaps for a sympathetic owner to buy them. Having served the cement quarry at Barrington, possibly through two owners, at the time of a visit some years back their future was uncertain. Perhaps the scrap man put them out of their misery. Sadly, another part of our industrial heritage lost forever.

Shown on the right is one of four Volvo BM Moxy diesel powered rear ended tippers which replaced the Barrington Light Railway operation. These remained in service until the end of Barrington Cement works, which closed around 2005/6.

Sending bulk cement by rail

The rebuilding of both Rugby and Rochester Cement Works in Kent which has already been described in Part 1 of this story, enabled both cement works to contribute hugely to the building booms of the 1960/70s and into the early 1980s. The introduction of both the concrete mixers and ready mixed concrete oversaw rapid growth of pressure delivery chassis, mainly 8-wheeler based lorries, for all of the United Kingdom major cement-producing companies. The eventual ability of experienced RPC bulk drivers, together with the three way-valve fitted to most of their lorries did, when required, completely revolutionise bulk deliveries to customers who, by the nature of the location of their sites, created the need for rail bulk deliveries to the nearest sidings.

Shown above is a good indication of the rail bulk/bags loading area at Southam Cement Works in Warwickshire. The main line is the two tracks on the right, whilst of the two centre lines, left goes into the former bags loading in railway box trucks, whilst the right hand line is concerned with top loading for bulk rail wagons. Some degree of protection for the loading staff is provided by the roof covered areas. The lines shown far left give access into Southam works areas including the railway servicing/shunting areas. Sending cement bags out in railway box trucks ended some years back. These silos, together with their attendant buildings, and the now redundant 130ft works chimney have been local landmarks for well over three quarters of a century, perhaps more. The piles of kiln bricks are reminiscent of hurried emergencies of years back. These will probably lie there undisturbed for some time.

Taken from behind the production area of Southam Cement Works, the superb photograph opposite shows the diesel shunter locomotive to good effect. Not knowing too much about railway engines I would suggest that this is based on a Ruston Hornsby.

The brick-built building on the far right was the fitting shop for quarry dumpers and plant. Various other buildings shown accommodated the electrician's shop, kiln house, personnel and others. Various sets of railway lines are shown. These ran around the back of the works and into the quarry areas. From what I have been able to research on the rail bulk services operated by the company, loaded bulk wagons were sent to Norwich (Thorpe Sidings) from Rochester Cement Works in Kent. They also, from time to time, were sent to the Southampton Rugby Cement depot, and Greenford depot in Middlesex as well as to a depot at Bow in Central London. Both Barrington and Rochester works would contribute in the early days of bulk rail deliveries via main line services to Greenford and Bow. Chinnor Cement Works sent out both cement and lime in sacks via railway box trucks, but I am unsure in the knowledge regarding bulk. Rugby Works was involved for a time sending bulk SR cement to Chinnor when work began on the building of the M4. Equally, Rugby was involved sending bulk OP (ordinary Portland) cement up to Banoldswick in Lancashire.

Rail bulk activities at Lewes, in Sussex, were marginally referred to in Part One, but more in depth information follows later on. Barrington's activities, mentioned earlier, had several of these Ruston Hornsby locos doing sterling work within the works.

Provision for an entirely new rail bulk-loading facility was to be included in the Rochester Cement Works rebuild mentioned further on within

this story and shown below in the early stages of construction. The reader can perhaps imagine and maybe shudder at both the immense size and storage capacities of these two towers. In this superb photograph, dating from September 1979, are two Rolls-Royce powered Sentinel diesel shunters, shown within the skeletal construction of the new rail bulk loading building. This would eventually protect both the rail and cement works personnel from adverse weather conditions. Cement powder, by its very nature, requires dry storage after manufacture, and also whilst it is being loaded, whether into bulk tanker lorries or rail storage wagons. The structure of these storage silos allowed for the passage of these diesel shunters to drive through their base, thereby allowing safe and dry loading practices for all concerned. Barrington's contribution regarding quarried material into the former cement works, together with manufactured cement, both in bags and later in bulk on both lorries and the railways, has already been told, but the photograph shown below did not become available to me until late in 2009. Shown with a full load of Procor bulk cement

wagons, one of Barrington Works' Ruston Hornsby diesels shunters makes its way up the branch line to the main railway junction. These new-style storage wagons carried in excess of 40 tons and were, like their predecessor, discharged by air pressure on arrival.

More Memories of Southerham (Lewes) Cement Works - Sussex

Two letters received in the early part of the year, from Maggie Collyer, who lives in Chatham, Kent, provided additional information for Part Two of this story, whilst also enquiring on the availability of Part One. Using her own words, relating mainly to her second letter to me, it transpires that her late father was the driver for the Lewes Cement Mills Atlas No 17 Steam Loco. More information came to her via her brother who provided the facts that it was a saddle-tank 0-4-0 with inside Stephensons valve gears. When this came to the end of its useful life, it was replaced by a diesel whose story follows this article.

Maggie's father decided then, as he was approaching retirement, that perhaps a younger man should look after the diesel, and so this is what he did. Maggie also informed me that she got to ride on the footplate of the old Atlas from time to time. More of her memories as a young child of the Southerham Works, as it was known locally, concern the Works chalk lorries, which were Seddon tippers. She also remembers the twice daily times of blasting, the sounds of which would be heard all over the town and other forgotten things like the engine's whistle as it crossed the main road pulling clay wagons into the cement works. The crossing itself was on a hair-pin bend where upon hearing the whistle a simple bar was swung out, blocking the main road, so that the loaded trucks could be shunted into the works. Health and Safety regulations of today's environment were light years away from these perhaps long-forgotten and best remembered days. Local people living in Lewes who have a copy of my book, Part One, may be interested to know that if they look closely at Plate 16 at the bottom of page 12, they will see the redundant Atlas Loco standing on the line, centre right of the photograph. Maggie's late father's name was Fred Horstcraft, a name which according to her was local to Sussex. I am informed her husband's family came from Battersea, London.

Eastwoods Cement – Southerham Cement Mill Lewes, owned by Rugby Cement from 1962 onwards

The origin of Lewes Cement Mill, together with the buyout by RPC after 1962, and subsequent change of Lewes into a depot in the late 1970s, has already been written, but as is the norm with all extensive research, additional material from unexpected sources has become available. Shown on the next page is a photograph of a diesel locomotive which, supplied new in 1959, served both Eastwoods and Rugby Cement until the Lewes Works was dismantled. Based on a four-wheel-drive arrangement, this loco was powered by a Gardner 613, 6-cylinder diesel engine with electric start. It weighed 22 tons and was built by the Drewry Car company, its works number was 2591. Used regularly to shunt wagons between the works and the trans-shipment buildings, it worked steadily for more than twenty six years. After the cement works were dismantled, the loco was stored at Lavender Line, Isfield, which in turn, as far as I am led to believe, is connected to the Spa Valley Railway Society.

Since 1997 extensive restoration/remedial work has been carried out on 'Southerham', including the fitting of air brakes. Following fire damage, work to rewire it began in 2006. Since then, the lighter shunting duties and smaller works train have enabled the Society to ensure that its second life is less stressful, but still in keeping with its original occupation as a diesel shunter.

For their combined kindnesses in supplying detailed information regarding renovation/remedial work done on the fomer 'Southerham' diesel-shunter, I should like to thank both Paul McKinnell and Trevor Harrison who are both heavily involved in the Spa Valley Railway Society where the loco now lives.

The following two photos show new buildings which replaced Lewes Works owned by Rugby Cement before it finally closed towards the late 1980s. Photo One shows the front entrance, now fenced off (i.e. no entry), and currently used in conjunction with a Scania dealership. The backdrop of the former use as a cement works is bounded by rocks and surviving undergrowth. Photo two, the loading / unloading areas for countless former Rochester-based RPC drivers on "bags" (i.e. unloading stock or otherwise) should bring the memories flooding back.

I am indebted to Steve Hastings, of Gillingham, for supplying me with these photos and for Dave French of Uckfield a fellow Foden Society friend for initially organising information on the former 'Southerham' ex-Lewes Works diesel shunter. To him I offer my sincere thanks.

John Drayton was part of the daily scene at Barrington Cement Works near Cambridge for more than 30 years. So much so during that time, that if he was to suddenly have left for whatever reason, it would quite simply, in my opinion, have meant sheer disaster for everyone concerned. I say this quite often, and honestly, in total respect for this man during the first twenty years I have had the pleasure of knowing him.

During my research into the history and post-war operational activities of Eastwoods Cement, John Drayton, and the former works secretary, the late Margaret Green, were instrumental in providing enormous assistance to me whilst writing Part One of the Rugby story. Any members of the public, retired, or indeed current employees of Rugby Cement / Cemex, who over the years have been privileged to attend Open Day events held at these works in Cambridgeshire, organised from start to finish by John Drayton, could not fail to see the respect and trust in which he was held. John's exact knowledge in a personal sense of the many and varied characters who have worked at the cement works are listed accordingly:

New Year honour for quarry man

Matthew Gooding
matthew.gooding@archant.co.uk

A LONG-serving quarry manager has been made an MBE in the New Year's Honours list.

John Drayton, 59, who manages the Cemex plant in Barrington, receieved the award for services to the quarry industry, and geology.

Mr Drayton has been working at the Barrington plant since 1970, and was recognised for helping to make geology accessible to the public.

He said the honour came as a "complete shock".

"You get told you've been nominated but don't find out whether or not you've got the award until New Year's Eve itself, so it was a really nice surprise," said Mr Drayton.

"I'm waiting to hear when I'll actually go and pick it up, but it'll be some time in the next six months."

Having joined the cement works as a carpenter, Mr Drayton has progressed through the ranks at the firm, holding the positions of yard foreman and general site foreman before being appointed quarry manager.

He said: "I've been interested in geology and archaeology for about 20 years.

"We used to have a Dr Peter Sheldon, who was a professor at the Open University, visit the site twice a year, and I got talking to him and it's grown from there into a full time hobby."

With the Barrington site having been made a Site of Specialist Scientific Interest, Mr Drayton regularly takes groups of school children and university students on tours of the quarry.

He also gives talks to clubs and societies.

Over the years, the quarry manager has made a number of important historical discoveries at the site, including a host of Roman artefacts, and a shark's tooth, which was unearthed last year.

In 2005 he uncovered the remains of an ichthyosaur while conducting a routine geological search at the quarry.

The bones and teeth are now on display at the Natural History Museum in London.

"That's probably one of the best memories I have, but there have been so many good times," he said.

"Another proud moment was having a railway engine named after me. I donated it to the Rutland Railway museum and they named it Mr D.

"It used to take me to and from work every day along the works line so that was a special moment."

While the future looks bleak for Barrington Cement Works itself, with the site set to cease operation in the next couple of months, Mr Drayton will remain at the quarry in the role of caretaker.

"I'm really grateful to have the job, and it will allow me to continue to do the tours and give talks," he said.

JOHN DRAYTON: "There have been so many good times."

Award 'complete shock' to plant manager

Tubby Wisely managed fifty years' service at Barrington. He originally started with Eastwoods Cement straight from school, and ended his days both as a general handyman, plus driving a van for the works. More nostalgic memories of happier times during Eastwood's ownership came from the life of Peter Dimes when I met him and his wife at the 2003 Open Day at Barrington. He remembers his father having MXU 322, the only 2-stroke-powered Foden FG/6 8-wheeler platform amongst hundreds of Gardner variants. Gerald Strange, another driver from years back, had one of the Canadian ex-army 4-wheel Dodges which were fitted with ½" wheel studs when in use with the army. Because of the all up weight in covered box-tipper bodies nearing 13 tons (load weight between 8 – 10 ton) these nuts sheared off on a fairly regular basis, causing total wheel loss. The "Nut Cracker Operation" referred to in Part One concerned a converted Foden S21 / 8-wheeler platform. These were used for bulk pressurised deliveries to American Air Force base construction work at Tiverton (Devon), Molesworth (Northants) and Alconbury (Cambs) in and around 1955.

TLO 103 carried F/N 491 and dated from around the late 1940s and bodied as an 8 wheel platform it was allocated to Ernie Saunders. He drove this for an unspecified time until he received a similar lorry TJJ 733 which again, as mentioned in Part One, was later converted as one of the first "Klinger" three pot bulkers.

Humorous happenings were the order of every day at Barrington works. Unofficial pranks played by Eastwoods drivers on their colleagues were very high on the list. One of the best remembered characters in Peter Dimes' experience centred on the former Eastwoods Weybridge Depot in Surrey. The Manager there was Bill Murphy. He had a really fantastic sense of fun and laughter. The original dead badger episode in Part One, in the cab of a Dodge 4-wheeler was passed around Lionel Pegham, but Bill Arnold was the instigator of such an act of folly! Another name from times past was Ralph Coot who drove another 8-wheeler Foden S21 platform. Doug Cobb was the bulk / bag loading shed foreman whom I became extremely friendly with during my early 8-wheeler platform days at RPC Transport whilst taking 15-ton loads of sulphate resisting cement in bags to Barrington, and returning to Rugby with an equal load of masonry in bags. With a regular 5.30am start from Rugby works on Saturday mornings, plus a three to three and a half hour journey to Barrington, which was 70 miles, each way, from Rugby, Doug's words to me still ring in my ears after almost forty years have passed: "Why can't you buggers from Rugby get here earlier. Normal arrival time at Barrington with me and my old faithful Foden S21 / 8 wheeler varied between 9.00 and 9.30am, just as the packing shed loaders went to tea break. Once I got to know Doug Cobb we became good friends and he often helped put the last few bags on to my Foden to speed my exit from Barrington.

Two 'Gold' pints

Congratulations to Tom Cook and Vic Allum who, on the 4th November 1992, each donated their 50th pint of blood. Tom and Vic both work in the Garage at Barrington Works, live in the same street and have been donating blood for more than 25 years.

Well done!

The photograph shows Vic (on the left) and Tom (on the right) being presented with their gold badges by Janet Weedon the Team Leader of the Blood Transfusion Service based in Cambridge.

The caption to this picture is self-explanatory. Both of these gentlemen worked in the garage at Barrington's Cement Works for quite a few years. Whilst I personally did not know Vic, I do remember one particular trip to this part of the country and an early morning visit to Barrington when the rear brakes on my old Foden were sticking on! Tom Cook on the right-hand side of this picture was the gentleman who was given the task of sorting out my problem at that time. Many years have passed since that incident, and so I wonder where and how these two gentlemen have fared since these wonderful days of RPC Transport.

Again, on these now far off, but well-remembered trips, friendships were made both with the late Cliff Crawley, a former bulk tanker driver, and my good friend / fellow platform driver, Keith Collett. Their combined feelings and remarks on the policies and instructions on a daily basis from Crown House would have a parson doubled up with laughter. Sadly, again for all the wrong reasons, Cliff passed away too soon. But for me, his passion for fun and laughter at someone else's expense is never forgotten. His kindness to me in my early days of building some of my RPC model tankers was made possible by his expertise, owning a Myford Lathe which turned out cylindrical shapes based on my measurements. More memories came flooding back when half a dozen Rugby drivers took six brand new lorries (bulk tankers) to the Flying Horse Café / Garage (Mobil) just outside Northampton, on the A428 at Yardley Hastings one Saturday morning. By prior arrangement, organised via Crown House and the Transport Department, six Barrington drivers converged at the same spot bringing half a dozen time expired chassis, a few of which were barely roadworthy.

Peter Lander was an Eastwoods driver for a limited period of service at the cement works. He came as a visitor to the 2003 Open Day, accompanied by his charming wife. The man remains a natural born comedian, whose exploits in his early days would have you literally in tears of laughter. It wasn't long before he started reminiscing about his long forgotten days with the cement company. Whilst undergoing driver training instruction with Brian Peters, Peter Lander had a nasty habit of falling asleep, so much so, that first thing every morning Brian took to locking the passenger door meaning that from then on Peter became responsible for the driving. Sometime later on, well after Peter Lander passed his instruction and became a fully-fledged Eastwoods driver, a rather more serious situation occurred as he and three un-named drivers were involved in an unfortunate and unforgettable incident at Great Yarmouth. Despatched to an oil and gas pipeline contract near the railway station on the edge of town, Peter and his three colleagues were informed on arrival at the site by the foreman that the ground storage area was not yet ready for the cement delivery. On hearing this, the four drivers left their vehicles parked up and went for a walk down the sea front. A couple of hours were spent this way when they were suddenly confronted by a police car with a loudspeaker asking the four drivers to return to their cement lorries immediately. Upon arrival back at the site, it was found that the Eastwoods drivers had parked their cement lorries over the main railway line at Vauxhall Station, thereby preventing the trains from Norwich entering the station.

After unloading, the four drivers returned to Barrington works, whereupon they were put on immediate suspension with a distinct possibility of being sacked. However, when the workforce at the cement works heard what had happened, they all downed tools and came out in sympathy for the drivers concerned. This action forced a re-think from the Barrington management. Later on, however, Peter Lander left the cement works in pursuit of another career.

CHAPTER 4

Chalk or Cement and There's a Foden Lorry for the Job

ADDITION TO THE ROLL OF FODEN DUMPER OPERATORS —
THE RUGBY PORTLAND CEMENT CO. LTD.

THE Rugby Portland Cement Company Ltd. has recently added two large production units to its Rochester Works, raising the productive capacity to some 400,000 tons of portland cement per annum.

Large quantities of chalk are needed to keep this continuous-process plant in production and, to ensure the supply, six 9-cubic yard Foden Diesel Engined Dumpers have been purchased. Large electric excavators dig the chalk in the nearby quarry and load it into the Foden dumpers which convey it to the materials store. The whole of the chalk supplies are now moved in this way.

This type of dumper was originally developed by Fodens to fulfil the requirements of the Steel Company of Wales Ltd. at their Cornelly limestone quarry, following an investigation of the latest American practice.

The bodies had to be built to withstand exceptionally rough usage at loading point and also the severe abrasive action at tipping and involved consideration both of design and the choice of steel used in construction.

When the prototype was tested it was found that a slope of 20˚ was too severe, causing the load to slide off suddenly and the front of the truck to lift. A decrease of slope of 10˚ corrected this. Further tests indicated the provision of the protective plating to cover radiator, headlamps and to protect the fuel tanks.

Next, a high speed tipping pump was developed for quicker discharging of the maximum load—in 15 seconds. Other refinements have been incorporated since the Dumper was first described in the *Foden News* (July 1949) and this special job which, to "recap" was aimed to excel anything available in Detroit, seems destined to be the Dumper that will end dumper discussions for some years to come.

The article opposite was written to coincide with the order from Rugby Portland Cement to Foden Limited in 1964 for six of the new diesel-engined quarry dumpers, used primarily to convey excavated chalk to the works. Working conditions in both dry and wet weather offered little or no health and safety precautions or any kind of protection to quarry employees. With a constant 24 hour process of cement production at the Rochester Works in Kent, these dump trucks were to be worked extremely hard.

In the lower photograph these conditions can perhaps be better envisaged, with a good load being put on to the dumper by a diesel-engined Ruston-Bucyrus excavator. As one area of the quarry was excavated the next face of chalk was prepared to repeat the process all over again. The top chalk from the massive area was mixed with underwater chalk, dredged from the blue lagoon using a submerged multi-bucket excavator which discharged onto a conveyor system.

Whilst this Foden is obviously shown on demonstration, this was to be the daily arduous life of these Dumptruck chassis for many years. In fact, some of them were to be in service for well over twenty years. The immense cab protection and

strengthened tipper body sides indicate the enormous strength built into these Fodens. Safer, single-tyred rear bogies coped admirably in relation to traction

problems encountered on the extremely rough areas on the quarry roads. Some idea of the daily punishment inflicted on these dumper bodies can be imagined as bucket loads were deposited in the tipper's body. In the lower photograph the tipper looks to be well worn, but still able to do a hard day's work. Nine cubic yards equates to around 20-tons of crushed chalk, and these Fodens coped admirably over many years.

Neville Walker started as a driver with RPC Transport in 1950. He was destined to give the company a total of 39 unbroken years of service, until his redundancy in 1989. Like so many of his colleagues, Neville was to drive Thornycroft Sturdy 4 wheeler bag lorries to begin with. F/N 226 was his first semi-permanent lorry. This carried registration number LUE 118.

Some characters recalled from these far off days include Dabber Worrall (who was based at Southam Cement Works), Happy Alder and Johnny Weston.

Over the next sixteen years, and beyond 1966, Neville was set to be involved with quite a number of bag lorries. He graduated on to Commer 2 stroke flats, the type fitted with a two piece screen. F/N 298 carried registration number WUE 593.

Neville's final four years "on bags" is remembered, with mixed feelings, on a former Eastwoods Cement Foden S18 8 wheeler, renumbered by RPC Transport to carry F/N 489 shown opposite. It had the 2-stroke Foden diesel engine. A very young Neville Walker is about to climb aboard. His

memories of this lorry include many days spent in the garage due to frequent breakdowns relating to the engine. In an effort to deaden the in-cab engine noise Neville covered it with a blanket. This eventually resulted in the blanket catching fire! Neville transferred on to bulk cement tankers after 1966 and eventually, like the remaining few company-employed drivers, in 1988 took and passed his Class 1 Artic licence. As mentioned above, he left the company in 1989, and enjoys retirement with his wife, Joan, in Rugby. Fortunately for me, as his friend and the author of this second book, he still retains his superb sense of humour and proportion, whilst still having a foreboding mistrust of Scottish generosity, regarding my spending of money.

Photographs of working lorries with their drivers convey the true meaning of lorry driving many years back. Prior to the RPC takeover in 1962, this Foden 8-wheeler, fitted with the S18 cab design carried dark blue livery all over, with Eastwood's Humber Cement in bold white lettering on its tipper body sides. These SWB short wheel based covered box tippers delivered bulk cement on outward journeys from South Ferriby Cement Works to customers with underground storage capacity. However, returning loads of kiln coal back to the cement works would occupy later hours. Shown here in charge of NUE 853 is driver Jack Johnston Rees in typical pose.

The world of lorry preservation was light years away when these Foden lorries were helping to rebuild Britain after five and a half years of war. LYM 753 started life with Eastwood's Cement at Barrington Cement Works near Cambridge in 1951. It was sold off ten years later into a life within the fairgrounds, to Tom Smith & Sons of Leighton Buzzard (Showmen), Bedfordshire. They removed the 2nd steer axle for one reason or another.

LYM stayed in Smith's ownership until an auction of the family's transport in 1992. By then, however, LYM 753 was hidden in the undergrowth. It was purchased in "as found" condition by Sandy Turner who lived near Bradford, Yorkshire. Sandy was later to restore the lorry back to 100% originality by refitting the 2steer axle with much of all work being done in his back garden. Sold within the past 4-5 years, LYM 753 now belongs to Keith French, a pig farmer who lives in the Basingstoke, Hampshire area. Keith and his family are owners of other preserved lorries, as well as LYM 753 which is kept in Sandy's livery for the moment. This is my photo taken at the 2007 Macs Café Gathering in typical surroundings.

A Gardner 120 horsepower engine coupled to the Foden gearbox of its time, presents an unequalled combination.

The middle 1950s was to see the launch of the Foden S20 cab design. This is probably better known as the Greenhouse Cab on account of a lot of glass used in its build up.

Registered in its early days with Eastwood's Cement, XLE 676 carried F/N 486. This was later re-numbered F/N 51 in RPC ownership, and driven for a while by Stan Vingoe who, when the regular Night Shift began in the late 1960s at Rugby Cement works, teamed up with Alf Measey. Their attitude and appoach with everyone changed with the weather. Later on, Alf Measey supported Bill Appleby in the despatch office, before he eventually retired.

I drove XLE 676 during my early days in 1968 with RPC Transport, delivering cement in bags, all "Handball unloaded". This lorry was taken off me in December 1968 as I received a better Foden in the shape of 4274 MF, a 1960s S21 bodied 8-wheeler platform.

XLE 677 represents fairground transport of years back.

Prior to the buyout of Eastwoods Cement in 1962, together with the acquisition, a year later of Chinnor Cement & Lime, it is evident now, after much research by myself, that both these companies had absolute faith in the many Foden lorries which they'd operated for years in varying wheelbases and uses. The strength built into each Foden chassis, coupled with the reliability of design in every sense of the word, appealed to many operators. More evidence on this statement is to be found when you read of the development of quarry dumper chassis manufactured by Foden Ltd. Mentioned early on, photographs and relevant texts bear evidence of this true opinion.

Shown above on "Internal Use" within Rochester cement works in Kent, XLE 676 has suffered visibly due to harsh use. The N/S front windscreen is missing and the front bumper is broken on each corner. The lorry was to be used during the last few years of the total rebuild of the cement works at Rochester. XLE 676 was later to be sold for scrap. Two of her sister lorries survived into 2nd ownership within the fairgrounds, one of which, XLE 677, is shown to the right.
Photographed by Rod Spooner at the Hull Fair in October 1978, and owned by Marshall Waddington, a prominent Yorkshire-based showman, 677 carries Luton bodywork, plus a generator power pack positioned at the rear of the lorry. Painted in a sort of crimson-red/white livery, plus a replacement driver's door,

Many years after the advent of the Commer vans or, in later years, Ford Transits which originated from 1965 onwards, RPC opted for diesel-powered variants, certainly when Central Garage opened in 1970. As with all car-derived vans, and the Transits, their tasks were as varied as the weather. In the early days the Commer vans / minibuses were used for ferrying drivers between Rugby and Southam works. At other works pick-ups and vans were used by the various garage fitters. All lorries and smaller vehicles, cars etc., used by both RPC Transport and the parent company Rugby Cement, were to be registered in Warwickshire.

Development of the Land Rover originally began as long ago as 1949. Shown is an early registered variant 4845 WD outside the Rochester offices. This particular RPC version was a general runabout for the works. We had a similar model kept within Rugby Works, which I drove on two occasions, picking up engineering spares in the Birmingham and Black Country areas on behalf of the works stores. Almost sixty years have elapsed since Land Rover shot to fame! Go down into the depths of Barrington's Cement Works quarry with John Drayton (the Quarry Supervisor), up to your knees in clinging clay, bouncing around in his ageing 6-wheeler, and you will be instantly amazed at the performance in terrible conditions, likely to test any chassis to the absolute limit. You will see why this "anywhere" chassis remains popular with every branch of industry.

Another totally unexpected photograph, shown opposite, was part of well over 2,000 separate photos thrown in to the skip after the closure of Rochester works. Based on the Austin Somerset, very few of these picks ups found their way into regular use on the UK mainland as very many of them went for export. MOA 941 is Birmingham registered, and although I personally have no knowledge of this particular pick up, I can only presume that this particular photo was taken of the RPC Austin at some carnival or other.

I've yet to find out exactly where the location is (Upper Halling?). Both the other vehicles in this picture date from the 1930s. The car on the right is, I think, a Morris, but I am unsure about the lorry in front of "Crown Portland Cement".

On the subject of former Eastwoods Cement Foden 8-wheeler platform lorries, many soldiered on under RPC Transport colours until the early 1970s. The already described 1001 MH, a sister lorry which would eventually carry a re-issued F/N of 108 was earmarked by Central Garage foreman Arthur Alcock to be their own fleet recovery vehicle. He outlined his plans to his fitters and the transport engineers. He then went on holiday. Arthur wanted four axles to carry heavy recovery equipment, plus other necessary spares because Rugby had used 4-axle bulk lorries since 1957 and had had total reliability and success from day one. The evidence was there every day for people to see. The folly of a completed recovery unit on three axles was not lost on Arthur when he returned from holiday, and he voiced his fears to the engineers.

Shown at the rear of the "Central" F/N 108 is shown in a perhaps good setting amongst time served redundant ERF bulk lorries.

The folly of the three axles was to be proved time after time when the Company started operating 30 tonne 4-axle chassis for bulk deliveries. A broken down 30 tonne chassis fully loaded tanker caused extreme embarrassment to RPC Transport when the wrecker lifted off the ground at the front when coupled to its charge. After this, the front cradle was fitted to hold balance weights to alleviate the problem. F/N 108's conversion for general recovery was not a success at all. However because of the short-wheel-based chassis, long haul distance towing was well within what capabilities remained.

Shown below is another former Eastwood's / Rugby Cement Foden S21, ex platform chassis bodied 8-wheeler getting ready to exit the former cattle market ground in Rugby. Tommy Connells artistry has really transformed this S21 Foden cab design, with a combination of red and crimson, plus gold lettering interspersed on the panelling, giving a new image in presentation. Fitted with an early version of a curtainsider body for easier access, 8912 MK is almost ready to leave for pastures new after the October Fair in 1976. Shown in company are a 1960s AEC Mercury and an Ergomatic cabbed Leyland behind.

Ken Harris (Assistant Transport Manager)

Starting life on the "shop floor", so to speak, Ken Harris began his working life with Rugby Cement in the packing shed at Rochester Cement Works in Kent. He rose in stature to the dizzy heights of foreman in charge. A change of direction and job description came about in 1966 when he was offered a chance to join RPC Transport at Crown House in Rugby. According to Ken's daughter, who was then about 10 years of age, this appointment was to be the vocation for her father who, after the family re-located up to Rugby, was rarely home before 7pm. Looking back many years now, I can see why Ken Harris was chosen for this job. His years at Rochester, working closely alongside people at the sharp end, had produced an individual fortunately blessed with an ability and a polite approach to anyone. Ken was therefore able to converse with drivers and senior staff alike. My own involvement saw me getting caught one morning by him returning from a Leicester

builder's merchant delivery, when urgency forced me to stop for a "call of nature" on the A426 Lutterworth-Rugby Road and also, in later years, when my KM Bedford HUE 738L was stolen from Rugby Works by a couple of late night revellers who missed the last train home. This would be around 1974. I remember going to Foleshill, in Coventry, to collect my lorry, travelling in Ken Harris' car, along with Roy Eddings, who would later replace "Jock" Henderson as the RPC Transport Fleet engineer when Jock retired some months later on. Other than these two instances described, I did not come into direct contact with Ken Harris for the remainder of my company service.

The extensive growth of RPC Transport has already been described in Part One of this story. What has not, is the enormous responsibility of Ken Harvey, together with the daily activities of Harold Garratt, and, both Albert Southam and Ken Harris in their joint roles as Assistant Transport Managers. All four were directly in charge of what would turn out to be, later on, one of the largest privately owned road transport fleets of its time. Well over 500 separate lorries, vans, pick-ups, fleet recovery and works vehicles, came under the auspices of the RPC Transport licence held at Crown House. Some 480 drivers were spread across the Group, many of them, certainly by the late 1960s, had twenty or more years' service under their belts – perhaps more.

Visits by both Albert Southam and Ken Harris across the RPC Group were to form a large part of their duties in connection with the licence. Drivers who had the misfortune to attend court appearances would, like me be both afraid and concerned. We were supported and put completely at ease by both of these Assistant Transport Managers. Such situations and experiences have since been described to me by drivers / colleagues from across Rugby Cement. Equally, drivers involved in accidents through no fault of their own, who in some cases because of serious injuries were to spend long periods of time off work, either in hospital or at home, were in turn never forgotten. Nor were their respective families. Individual requests made to Ken Harris from drivers at Leeds Depot, together with those at South Ferriby Cement Works, on a number of subjects concerned with the job, always received the same answer: "I'll look into it". To this end in particular, the Leeds drivers, as opposed to others within the group at that time, nicknamed Ken Harris as "The Mirror Man". Ken Harris's overall contribution to both the cement industry and Rugby Cement Transport over very many years was to be both recognised, and rewarded, in the 1980s with an MBE. For a man who, like many others, began his career on the bottom rung, this was a deserved honour. Going down to Buckingham Palace, accompanied by his wife and daughter to share that "once in a lifetime experience", is still vividly remembered by his daughter Diane.

After the 1962 buyout of Chinnor Cement, all of their lorries which were considered mechanically and visibly perfect were in time to be resprayed, apart from two of the later mentioned S34s, one tipper and one platform. The remaining four were disposed of fairly quickly. Several S21s further assisted RPC Transport for a while.

Chinnor Cement and Lime operated a mixed fleet of transport lorries out of their cement mills at Chinnor near Oxford for very many years. Visual and mechanical presentation of the whole fleet was of paramount importance to a succession of managers over the whole period. Purchased outright by Rugby Cement in 1962, a small percentage of mainly time-served BMC swop-body chassis were to be disposed of although I can remember seeing one bulk tanker version still parked undercover at Chinnor in the early 1970s.

The remainder of the fleet were repainted in Rugby colours as and when convenient.

Shown left is a rare lorry indeed, one of Chinnor's best remembered Foden 8-wheel bulkers. Registered XUD 77 and carrying F/N 872, this picture shows a Buckinghamshire registered lorry in Rugby's ownership, and was taken by a passing driver on the other side of the road. It is absolutely unique, and very much a part of this second book on Rugby.

This 8 wheeler platform lorry started life with Eastwoods Cement at Barrington Cement Works around 1958, carrying F/N 775 and registration number 1001 MH. I am unsure as to how many years passed before it was converted to its secondary role of fleet recovery, but I do remember the work was carried out within the Barrington Garage workshop.

One of several Foden lorries which, over many years, have served Rugby Cement and its Associated companies, carrying Chinnor Cement livery, and based on a middle 1960s design which was universally known as the S34 Plastics Cab. It is shown here with a spare wheel mounted off side centre. This practice ended because retaining bolts sheared off during empty running. The Chinnor livery is prominent even in this picture,

one of six versions of the Foden S34 cabbed 8-wheeler chassis operated by Chinnor Cement. All were powered by the Foden 2-stroke engine, namely the 126 horse power unit. These lorries were bodied as a covered box tipper EUD 97C and EUD 99C (explained above) in the form of a bulk tanker, along with two platform-bodied 8-wheelers. All were fitted with a 7-speed Foden gearbox and a non-tilt cab.

Painted in Rugby colours is an ex Chinnor Cement covered box-tipper. This is possibly ex F/N 82. What a wonderful restoration project this would have been had it been saved. Instead it went for SCRAP!!

Note the angle of shot of this photo taken deep within the bowels of the Kensworth chalk quarry near Dunstable in Bedfordshire. The huge NCK/Rapier excavator itself should give some idea of the daily scene which quarry workers saw every day of their working lives. Even the man walking towards the excavator appears small. The former RPC Transport ERF 8-wheeler dates from around 1963-74 and is almost certainly ex-Barrington Works. Shown in its new role as a workshop / servicing unit, it carries the original bodywork taken off its predecessor lorry. Chalk quarried at Kensworth is mixed with water to produce slurry, the chief ingredient in the manufacture of cement. Pumped underground via a 57 mile pipeline which, in some places, lies parallel with the M1 Motorway, this engineering project was started in the 1950s and was viewed, by many in the then construction circles, as being suspect, in that it would not be a success. However, this process has more than proved itself for more years than anyone can remember. This much needed product is continuously pumped directly into the Rugby cement works.

This machine shown below replaced the NCK Rapier excavator in recent years and is fitted with a rammer ended bucket which loosens the ridges of chalk before loading the excavated material into a 50 ton dumper ready for transport to the next stage.

Prior to the closure of Southam Cement Works, a secondary pipeline for slurry movement followed the former branch railway line between the two works. The location of this pipeline was to be brought to the fore some years ago when a leak was discovered near the railway bridge area south of Bilton, Rugby, on the A4071. This bridge / road area was swamped with chalk slurry, resulting in a road closure for several days in both directions. The main 57 mile pipeline direct from Kensworth Chalk Quarry was completely renewed between 2004 and 2007 following a review of such practices by Cemex, the current owners of Rugby Cement Works.

CHAPTER 5

RPC Transport 1950s & 1960s Commer / ERFs

In the intervening years, immediately after the end of the 2nd World War, the immense task facing this country of rebuilding the country's industry, together with housing on a massive scale, necessitated switching drivers on a regular daily basis between Rugby and Southam works. Clive Mumford started as a fitter in the 1960s. Although he lived in Southam, his shifts involved the old Parkfield Road garage at Rugby Works driving the already mentioned Thornycroft Sturdy and Sturdy Star Platform bag lorries. Clive's duties included draining off all the radiators each night and refilling them each day before operations re-started. Going out to breakdowns was all part of a normal shift. Sometime later on, Clive was to be appointed garage foreman at Southam Works.

Harry Gherry was one of many long-serving drivers spending almost the whole of his career with RPC Transport. He began his employment driving Nelsons blue painted Commer 2-stroke flats. The photograph shown to the right is just such a lorry - 3034 UE carrying fleet number 377. This particular lorry was driven by Doug Proudhoe before he, along with several other drivers, switched to become garage fitters. Several of these Nelson Commers were still in use in 1968 when I joined the company in June of that year. Harry Gherry switched on to new 2-piece-screened Commer flats when Rugby purchased new chassis. When I'd finished bulk training, I was aware that Harry, along with other famous characters, like Cliff Masters and my late great friend Titch Partington, were all employed doing other jobs within the garage. Whilst Harry dealt with fuel returns and ordering new fuel deliveries, of both diesel and petrol, he also took care of all routine servicing paperwork for the fleet. You could never turn your back with Cliff Masters as his capacity for fun and laughter, often at the individual's expense, was often fully supported too by the late Dick Kendrick who was second-in-command of the vehicle stores. Dick always had an eye for the fair sex.

A cricket team formed in or around the 1950's-60's is shown below with some of the faces I knew.

Back row, L – R
Unknown, Unknown, Unknown, Bill Appleby, Fred Adams
Front Row, L – R
Jack Parton, John McDonnald, Dick Smith, Unknown, Unknown.

The frontal view of a Nelsons Cement Commer shown right has since come to light, and is included to show off these well remembered frontal shapes. The ruggedness of the cab design can perhaps be judged. The small cab mirror on a double bracket are just two basic frills of years ago.

The smaller photo opposite, taken some years back, shows two Commers, one a bulk tanker closely followed by a bag lorry and one of the Southam quarry 4 wheeler dump trucks, I think, based on an early Aveling Barford. The scene is near the main office block in Southam cement works. Of particular notice is the early compressor unit being used to break up concrete prior to a replacement covering. From memory, the make of the compressor is either

Blaw Knox or Ingersoll Rand.

Also shown opposite is an accident scene many years back on the main A426 Rugby to Coventry Road and concerned a former driver whose vehicle sank into the ditch whilst returning to the cement works. Although very little damage is visible, the result of the ground giving way under the Commer tanker meant that vehicle recovery in some form was required to extricate the RPC vehicle from this position.

The evidence of the hurricane lamp means it was used as a warning to other road users during the hours of darkness. All these incidents took place long before the use of road cones and other modern day traffic hazard warnings.

From memory of my early years on Commer Tankers, the driver of 381 5297 UE was the

late Cliff Masters. Whether he himself was responsible for the alarming situation, I do not know. Cliff Masters is sadly no longer with us, but those of us who worked with him over many years can relax in the fact that his ability to always have you looking over your shoulder when he was around went to the grave with him.

One of the most imposing structures within the main part of Rochester Cement Works was this former bulk cement covered loading area, with ongoing supplies of bulk cement pumped directly into storage from the main works alongside. This well advanced facility served RPC Transport from perhaps the 1950s onwards until the new plant came on stream in the 1970s. A brand new ERF K/V 8 wheeler bulk tanker is shown entering the facility, 383 GAC F/N471.

The shine on all of the bodywork is all too evident, as this lorry has just entered fleet service. 6975 UE, a Commer 2 stroke tanker is alongside and carried F/N 399. A sister lorry is shown parked on the left. I am readily informed by Jim Hastings, a former Rochester based driver, that four separate bulk tankers could be loaded together. All bulk lorries were loaded directly on weighbridges, thereby eliminating overloading. This new kind of loading system was only at Rochester works, but all future RPC Transport Depots would, in effect, utilise a similar practice. Safety for both bulk loaders and drivers, plus a quicker turnaround and less time-wasting, made this structure a prominent feature of the cement works well into the late 1970s.

"On The Move" (opposite) is a RPC Leeds based ERF K/V bulk tanker registered 239 HAC, F/N 479. This kind of photograph is unique because it shows the lorry "in action". The ravages of wear and tear on the wheels and tyres are consistent with visiting the ready mix plants. The tank bodywork on F/N 479 is reminiscent of one of the early Metalair designs. Notice the air pressure pipe hanging down in the centre of the tank. Front mounted access catwalk ladders and these pressure pipes would be incorporated in later designs of bulk pressure tanks together with side mounted access ladders. I am indebted to Peter Seaward of the H/S Photo Collection, Leeds, a friend of many years standing, for allowing me to use this photograph. Absolutely superb!

Thirty one identical ERF K/V 8 wheeler bulk chassis (as opposed to forty five), mentioned in part one of this story earlier, were to see out the whole of their working lives with RPC Transport certainly from 1954 onwards. Introduced to the road transport world two years earlier in 1952, the ERF K/V Kleer Vue was involved for two more years before Rugby Cement received their ERFs.

Shown below in this Tony Higgins photograph is F/N 463 carrying registration number 373 GAC. As far as I have been able to research, this particular K/V was kept at Rochester Cement Works for much of its fleet service.

A one lorry/one driver system was to be responsible for RPC lorries achieving colossal mileages. This system alongside the procedures for fleet servicing laid down many years previously, contributed to the exceptional mechanical condition of RPC Transport Lorries. Platform lorries used for cement in sacks also came into this category, although bulk deliveries, certainly from 1970 onwards, took preference over bags (contractors could be used for bags), and platform drivers were often required for bulk deliveries at a moment's notice.

Bulk tankers were inspected every 12 months by insurance inspectors, and any which developed leaks or cracks were scrapped immediately with all useful parts removed from time expired chassis including remaining road fund licences. When applications for new licences were completed and the money drawn from the cash department the individual tasked with obtaining the new licences, collected them from the former North Street post office in Rugby. Replacement bulk chassis were then sent out into the groups operating areas, fully equipped and licensed for 24 ton bulk operations. However, when RPC Transport introduced 30 ton bulk operation, useable bulk structures were stretched with additional sections welded within. These were then fitted to pre-30 ton A Series and B Series ERF Chassis.

Shown parked next to 463 is John Gilbert's Commer Maxi 4-wheel box covered tipper. When he relocated on to permanent nights, this lorry was removed from permanent use.

The photos overleaf show more presentations to company

employees for one reason or another. Sadly for me, knowing all of the boiler suited drivers, and for reasons concerning old age, many of the faces in these photos are no longer with us. This makes it more pertinent for me to describe their well known characteristics.

Shown top right on the far left is one of the best known drivers who worked for most of his life for RPC Transport, Nobby Lines. Prior to his retirement he worked as a retained driver for Central Garage. Next to him is John Cant, another long server, who sadly did not live very long after retirement. Next to him is Neville Walker, who everyone knew as Noddy. The two gentlemen behind Noddy, I didn't know. John Gee is the dark suited gentleman making the presentations. Next to him is a youngish looking Roy Bates, better known as Woofer. Next is another unknown and Mr Baker, Southam Works' Manager, plus another unknown face from the works.

Shown in the central photo is Jack Brain who was in charge of the Despatch Office when I started. He was a giant of a man, an ex Guardsman, and rumour had it he got that job because he could not get up in the mornings. He is pictured 2nd left, I think on his retirement presentation day.

Maurice Jenkins is far left with Ken Harvey second right.

Shown in the bottom photo, are some of the more character based men! Billy Boyle is the first person from the left, he was a tipper driver for many years before transferring into the Despatch Office, who, when called for, his sense of humour was a delight to watch. Next to him is Wilf Childs, who lived at Braunston. "Always on Earlies" was his nickname! The next man is unknown to me. Mr Baker is next who by this time had transferred to Rugby (as Works Manager). Next to him is Charlie Harris, a retained driver who worked in the Tyre Stores. He came out to me once when I had a double puncture on a building site at Matlock in the summer of 1974. Maurice Jenkins is centre stage next to Charlie. Captain Dick Goode stands behind him. Dick's humour in everything he did ranks him as one of the nicest drivers I ever worked alongside. "Happy Alder" is next. When this photo was taken, he was off lorry driving, but drove the mail car during office hours. Next to him is Harry Gherry and then Paddy Donahue who was a charge hand packer in the Bag Shed.

The idea of rewarding most long serving employees at occasions of this nature featured very heavily in the thoughts of our former Chairman / Managing Director, Sir Halford-Reddish. Equally, after 1968, when I joined, and at the end of record profit making years, employees were presented with additional shares, or commemorative sets of spoons or coins etc. There were more than a fair share of long serving individuals amongst the Rugby Works based drivers of the late 1960s period.

John Todd
South Ferriby Transport
Sept 1967 – Feb 2009

In September 1967 I was heading home from a 6 – 2 shift as a fitter on the blast furnaces at Appleby Frodingham Steel works as a young lad of 23 years old, fed up with working shifts and married with one son. My route home took me past the cement works at South Ferriby where I'd heard, through the grapevine, that Rugby Cement were taking on drivers. So I stopped on chance to ask if there were any jobs going. Mervyn Smith, the Transport Manager, arranged a test drive there and then with a British School of Motoring Examiner in a Foden S20 8 wheeler loaded with bagged cement. After a little tuition on the gearbox, I passed, and was offered a job. On the following Monday I was put in the capable hands of Tom Maw for training on bulk pressure lorries. Tom became both my mentor and good friend who, in these early days, kept me from getting into too much bother. My first week was spent learning how to blow his ERF tanker where my first delivery was to the Deniff plant at Immingham. On completion of my training, I was put in charge of 4274 MF, a Foden S21 8 wheel Klinger – 3 pot tanks bulker carrying F/N 495, fitted with a 1600cc petrol Volkswagen engine to power the blower – fondly named Humphrey on account of the 3 humps (pots). I lost many a piece of skin on the index finger of my left hand when trying to engage low first or a low reverse.

I (Author) know that feeling extremely well, having had that same experience in both Foden S20 and S21s. I lost this lorry when the power weight ratio came in, as the engine was too small for it to carry 15 tonnes, along with the weight of the pots and the lorry. After this I drove every type of lorry Rugby had, except the artics which followed later on. I quickly began to prefer driving ERFs as opposed to the Fodens I had driven earlier. This statement is honestly given in relation to all ERFs allocated to me between 1967 – 2000. In

1989 Rugby Cement decided to introduce the ICH owner/driver scheme. It was sign up or look for another job. I signed up for the only ex-fleet lorry available for me at that time. A739 JAC was an S108 Foden Haulmaster 8-wheel bulk lorry – ex Rochester Works. Whilst discharging at Tarmac's Topmix Selby Plant the near side 4 foot of the chassis broke off causing £50,000 worth of damage. This was caused by someone in earlier Company owned years who had drilled the manganese bronze chassis lorries (against instructions from Foden, the manufacturers). The lorry was later rebuilt completely, and is now on fairground work with John Armitage, a local man from Barton on Humber. The fleet then went to artics and I bought a new ERF E11, powered by a Perkins 375 engine, the best tool a man could have had. It served all of its eight year contract. I then followed this with another ERF/E11 6 wheeler artic fitted with a Cummins 440 engine, but kept this only for thirteen months because the ICH scheme was disbanded when RMC Group purchased all of Rugby Cement and took transport back in house. They later appointed TNT to look after the daily / nightly running of the transport operation. I was appointed Driving Assessor, and in-between deliveries I also spent a lot of time in and around the transport office, right up to the Cemex take-over, and up to my eventual retirement in February 2009.

On the whole, looking back at forty one and a half years spent at South Ferriby, which initially started out as a six months trial, I thoroughly enjoyed my job. I made a lot of friends, and a lot of enemies.

Shown on the page opposite is John Todd's three pot Klinger Foden 8 wheeler, just having loaded (or about to load). The driver is seen on the access step ladder. Before and after loading the pot lids were required to be opened and closed. This scene at the South Ferriby Cement Works dates from the late 1960s when new bulk loading weighbridges, plus ancillary equipment, were being constructed in front of Silos 1-7. Two 6 wheel Denniff transite mixers are shown on site. This particular kind of building project would require enormous amounts of ready mix concrete. Of particular interest is the box compressor and the complete lack of viz vests and safety helmets such as we are accustomed to in this new century. Bulk cement deliveries were not new, but the loading system for these Klinger lorries is shown by the raised catwalk joining the silo and pressure loading point, itself the best there was at that time. How times change!

The connection between myself and John Todd's initial service at South Ferriby Cement Works was only made known to me in late 2009. John joined RPC Transport in September 1967 and my own service began in June 1968, nine months after him. When he lost 4274 MF and graduated onto ERF bulkers, I was given F/N 495 in October 1968 after it had been rebodied as an 8 wheeler bag lorry as I'd expressed an interest to go on to bags. I kept this grand old Foden until August 1971, when I received a brand new L/V square fronted ERF 8 wheeler platform. Due to an increase in bag tonnages out of Southam Works, F/N 711 was transferred there, and I reverted back on to 4 wheeler platforms (see Part One RPC Transport). 4274 MF remains in the ownership of WJ Warwick who is based up at Selston Winter Quarters in Nottinghamshire. This is visible on the left hand side of the M1 Motorway, just before J28 (A38). I spoke to Billy Warwick less than three years back who said it was the intention of both him and his son (also William), to restore MF back into regular use of the fair. For any lorry chassis to survive almost fifty years and more is an

exception to the rule. Perhaps we shall see this veteran Foden take to the roads in the future.

More details remembered regarding KV/ERF 8-wheeler bulk lorries come from the memories of Mick Lowe, a South Ferriby night driver, whose own story is related further on. He says we had F/N 462 and 464 at Ferriby. 464 was fitted with a super singles on the drive axles and reckoned to be a "flyer". She would do 44mph!! One bad aspect of those KVs concerned the curved front windscreens. If it was raining heavily, and a large lorry went past you at speed, the wind rush caught, and flicked, the wipers back over the windscreen, so that you the driver, ended up with a wet arm as you tried desperately to reach the offending wiper to pull it back down. Happy days are here again, or words to that effect!! My own memories concerning these KVs refer to the back of the tanks as no two were the same and unless the regular drivers painted "O" for Open or "S" for Shut on the cement door, horrendous accidents could and did happen to the unwary driver. I vaguely remember this happening to me at Birmingham Truckmix at the Minworth Birmingham Plant one afternoon in 1970 when air pressure / cement powder blew me halfway across the yard!

Between 1964 and 1969, a total rebuild of the cement works at Rugby took place. Buildings and plant which had seen constant use, probably since the 1930s and perhaps earlier, were demolished.

A brand new kiln, together with all the ancillary and supporting equipment, would eventually replace work worn machinery. The small chimney which had dominated the Rugby skyline for decades was replaced by an even taller structure, believed to be 300 feet high, and surrounded by state of the art dust precipator plant.

This photo taken from ground level shows parts of both the old and new cement works buildings, together with a real variety of Company lorries, plus a fascinating view of staff cars parked in available spaces within the works yards areas. Prominent in centre stage is F/N 232, an ERF L/V 8-wheeler bulk tanker carrying registration number MAC 498E. It was at that time the daily responsibility of Ernest "POP" Lineham, a driver of many years' service. Shown are two Commer Maxiload 4-wheeler lorries - F/N 223, a platform version which carried 8 ton loads, as did the tankers behind. The K/V ERF 8-wheeler tanker shown on the right hand side is F/N 448 registration number 195 DAC. Its regular driver for some time from new was Eddie Leonard. Morris and Austin cars of the late 1960s period, plus a lone Ford Cortina next to the railway line fence, hark back to a "daily scene" for Rugby Cement employees and drivers which, for all the wrong reasons, has now gone forever.

The stark difference in reversed height of the two chimneys at Rugby's Cement Works rebuild can be judged in this height variation picture. On-going new building work means that the old kiln must continue working until such times as the new one is started. The absence of private cars in this photo suggests that the area behind the works on Parkfield Road, earmarked for employee's car parking, had come into regular use. The building immediately on the left, screened partially by the tree, is the clocking in and out area adjacent to the Time Office. Out of sight, but immediately behind, was the Despatch and Transport Office. The corrugated iron roof of the Central Laboratory building is just visible. This was separated from the Despatch Office by a through roadway linking both sections of the new Rugby Works Transport yards. Following on from these, in this rather dull picture taken in 1966, the main works and Manager's Offices fronted the base of the new works chimney, which itself was to dominate the Rugby skyline until the early years of this century, before its ultimate demolition. Half a dozen RPC Transport bulk tankers occupy centre stage in the main yard. There are three ERF lorries in front with three smaller 16 ton

Commer 4-wheelers behind. Parked against the railway fence is one ERF K/V 8 wheeler bulk tanker and a Commer tanker and a flat. The roof of the packing shed is on the far right with the old cement works main kiln house/conveyors linking the bag shed. The main works gate / entrance fronts the A426 Rugby to Coventry road. This offered daily and nightly access for all RPC Transport lorries coming and going on deliveries. The small shed shown was the then main Weighbridge office. Sid Edwards was the man in charge. At that time he was a seemingly motivated individual, whose working days revolved around sending you, the driver, out with exact bulk and bag tonnages. Some people thought he was a bit miserable, but after I'd been at RPC Transport a while I found his sense of proportion and humour, although a little dry at times, more than made up for the general attitudes of most employees at Rugby. When the new kiln came on stream, early in 1969, Sid Edwards transferred on to the new 4 bay bulk loading weighbridge covered area. This was situated immediately behind these already described buildings within a completely new screened off area of the new works complex. In recent years, since both RMC Rugby and the Cemex takeover in the early 2000s, these two large bulk silos and the weighbridges have been out of regular use. In time, demolition I think may well result. Sid Edwards was a "Cockney" by birth, not often giving much away, but like many of us driver loaders / packers all slung together each working day, now and again a supreme sense of fun and laughter would prevail where the true qualities of each individual would come to the fore. In recent years, with takeovers/buyouts, humour is often sadly lacking.

Anyone who is anyone and who worked for Rugby Portland Cement at Southam Works, certainly from the late 1950s period onwards, must remember Jack Saunder's venerable fleet of Atkinson lorries. Some of them were to be converted to artic units from rigid 8 wheelers. Suspect braking and stopping performance regularly brought daily problems. Saunders's workshop and yard parking still stands on the A423 on the left hand side of the village as you head out towards Marton etc. The building next door for many years was officially known as the Rhine Hill Café, but to countless hundreds of RPC Transport drivers it was probably better known as "Auntie's Café".

Shown in close proximity to each other, two RPC bulk lorries are shown below. The front vehicle is a Commer 2 stroke 4 wheeler, whilst at the rear stands an ERF K/V 8 wheeler. During the daylight hours between 6am and

6pm, RPC drivers would, and could, dally here between trips. This picture dates from possibly the early 1970s, judging by the Ford Zephyr car. Sadly, since these idyllic care free days of motoring, "Auntie's" has been sold. It is now a Chinese Water Garden Diner with a select clientele.

Aubrey Tomlinson, already mentioned, later transferred off driving into the packing shed. Much later on, he became foreman in charge of all packers and loaders. He reported directly to Chris Shepherd who was the supervisor of all Packing and Loading, including the new bulk loading area, which was destined to come on stream in the early 1970s. Chris's main job entailed checking all loading tickets for both bags and bulk, together with delivery tickets (copies). He was also concerned with weighbridge loading receipts (as attended to by Sid Edwards when he was in the main yard weighbridge office). Aubrey looked after day to day operation of the bag shed and bulk rail loading.

Many characters come to mind from these days after I transferred permanently on to Bags. They include "Abdul", better known to his friends as Phil Saunders, whose passion was Rugby Football. Phil worked the Fluxo packers with Tommy Donahue, a loveable Irishman who took every opportunity to have a snooze in the top packer's rest area. The fitter who was responsible for all of the machinery within the bag shed was called Ralph Berry.

These three men were the best of friends, and could always be found in the rest area already mentioned at break times and when work was slack. Albert Goode was a bag packer/ loader when I started at RPC Transport. He was very heavily built and, like many other RPC employees / drivers he used to cycle to work from his house in Hillside off Dunchurch Road. Albert too was seriously into Rugby Football, and he, Aubrey and, at times, Abdul, were often deep in conversation about local team failures and successes. Sadly, however, Albert collapsed and died some time later. Bob Barnacle was Senior Bulk Loader, he'd worked for RPC for many years – his passion was steam locomotives.

In the photograph shown below the entire range and scope of packed Crown cement products are shown to good effect. To bag drivers such as myself, and hundreds of customers in builders yards, and on sites alike, who would become familiar with such items, it is perhaps prudent for me as an author to describe each bag and its contents, together with the purpose of each product. Starting at the top, and going down, we have six main types. The first two bags are OPC, Ordinary Portland Cement, used for a variety of brickwork and general building requirements. The yellow edged bag is Masonry cement, used to complement rural and countryside buildings.

Rapid Hardening I'm not sure about, but can only presume that it, and the next bag down, Sulphate Resisting were used where large damp water filled areas predominated such as sewer and water distillation plants. Chiltern Lime was a byword in agriculture terms, and had been for almost a decade. Crown White, the bottom bag, was a prepared cement for fireplaces and bathroom work, together with larger jobs such as Sport's Centres, where tiling works predominated and was another byword in building and construction circles for more years than anyone could remember. OPC, Masonry and Sulphate Resisting were on most loads whilst the remainder were kept or prepared for special jobs when ordered by customers.

Shown opposite this BTC (British Trailer Company) in-line platform semi-trailer is coupled to a TK Bedford Tractor unit. The versatility of unit and trailer together is shown admirably.

Registered 192 BXV, this is a Perkins powered lorry. Reflectors on either rear corner of the trailer come from years ago.

The bottom photo shows the 4 in line twin pepper-pot bulk trailer shown in convoy with its ERF L/V 8-wheeler bulk lorry companion. This particular chassis was the first of eight similarly registered ANX lorries ordered purely for the carriage of cement in bulk. They were destined to be shared out within the Rugby Portland Cement transport fleet at both Chinnor and South Ferriby Cement Works. The bulk tank bodywork featured a nearside front mounted catwalk access ladder plus side pipe carriers. Known as ALC tanks, they were made by Amalgamated Limestone Corporation, and carried 15 ton of cement powder. This particular one was given F/N 130 and was driven by Ray Lawtey. This was the first L/V cab design from ERF which featured the front panel lift up for daily checks. Some of the ERFs would eventually clock upward of a million miles whilst in RPC ownership. Photos of lorries with their respective drivers are rare indeed, and this double combination of Bedford TK and ERF L/V lorries shown in convoy is unique.

Many original photos are known to have existed, particularly of the people who made up the bulk of the RPC Transport story, and whose daily/nightly efforts were never really appreciated. Here I refer to garage staff, many of whom I have never met. In the case of South Ferriby, my initial enquiries were made to John Todd, who was in charge of the transport office there, then under Cemex. John, in turn, very kindly steered me to Brian Peeps, whose photographs are here for you to enjoy. I shall be eternally grateful to both these gentlemen for their kindness.

South Ferriby RPC Transport night garage staff
Back row left to right: Foreman Ken Belt, Unknown, Arthur Green, Alan Gardner
Front row left to right: Don Tyson, Tony Clipson, Jack Broughton, Brian Johnson.

Such photos are rare indeed. All of them so much a part of happier times of long ago.

Way back in 1961, ERF Limited brought their L/V Long Vue cab design to replace this by then well received KV, or round front model. For me, in any personal sense, purely from both my driving experience with RPC and from my study of this model over the following thirteen years up to 1974, prior to the arrival of ERFs (first tilt cab design the B Series), I thought the L/V design was the most attractive shape to emerge from this Sandbach lorry builder.

One of the first 8-wheeler chassis supplied to South Ferriby works for bulk operation is shown opposite, with the very happy driver. ANX 474B was supplied to RPC Transport in June 1964. It carried an ALC (Amalgamated Limestone Corporation) tank body which featured a front mounted catwalk and was the forerunner of pressure tanks of various designs, all of which were popular. This ERF Chassis number 12198 worked solidly for around fourteen years before being disposed of. The driver

shown close up was again Ray Lawtey. Over the following years of the L/Vs popularity, the front panel of these models would undergo many changes.

Although I never got to know any garage personnel at South Ferriby, which in later years would have been a bonus for me, the idea of using front wheel caps did not feature at either Rugby or Southam works during the whole of my service with the company, so perhaps the garage foreman there was a bit more lenient in his approach to the drivers, the idea being that all non-essential weight (eg wheel discs, spare wheels etc.) were removed to save on weight. Most of these ERF bulk tanks tared around the 8 ton 11cwt mark, allowing for a straight 15 ton load weight. A sister lorry is shown overleaf in one of the many advertisements where Rugby Cement lorries were to be featured. ANX 478B carried F/N 134 and the ERF 2LV cab, similar to its sister lorry F/N 130. This view has already been described in Part One, but the benefits of using ERF chassis are well documented in this advert.

From 1964 medium numbers of these new L/V cabbed ERF sub 8-wheelers would swell the RPC fleet over the following six years. Based on the 68GX2 model, which to the historian is a 6 cylinder 8-wheeler Gardner, well over a hundred such lorries would be fitted with bulk tank bodies and blowers etc., and all relevant chassis equipment before being sent for painting and lettering. When this was complete, these lorries were sent out within the Rugby Group to replace time served chassis.

Two identical ERF tanks, or so it would appear, stand side by side within Rochester Works. Not so!!

F/N 172 has the 2LV cab whilst F/N 208 supplied new in March 1967 carries a revised front grill where thicker, more prominent squared off panels are shown. Other than this change, both cab fronts appear identical. However, F/N 208 carries one of the then newly introduced Knutzen of Malvern bulk tank bodies, which carries a centre mounted catwalk. The large cylinder to the left of F/N 208 is one of five new kiln sections delivered into Rochester Works during a ten year rebuild of the works between 1969 and 1979. Some idea of the immense size of these sections coming into Rochester Cement Works on a Sunday with police motorcycles on escort duty can be imagined - not very heavy in weight, but oversize in shape. Robert Wynn & Sons, the experts in moving items of this nature, appear to make the job just that bit easier with their Scammel Contractor three-axle tractors. All this happened just over 40 years ago.

Towards the late 1970s, cement manufacturing processes were constantly being monitored and evaluated with regard to additives being introduced to the

continuous process. A former Chinnor Cement half backed 8 wheeler bulk tipper, LUD 680E was used for a time between Southam Cement Works and Rugby, transporting liquid sand. Because of the nature of the load carried, it was used for a time with its original rear end design (i.e. half backed open tipper).

Later on it was converted to the design shown overleaf. It was loaded through the top hatch from an overhead pipe via weighbridge checking. Unloading via gravity discharge was merely by tipping the tank body, although, from my memory, this was only a short term project before the process was changed at Rugby to facilitate "On site" constant supplies of liquid sand for an indefinite period. This tanker averaged 3-4 loads per day, plus 2-3 loads during the hours of darkness before this system was ended.

Having basically described, in Part One, the RPC Transport story, what prompted all of the British Cement producers to introduce bulk cement chassis deliveries, and why? It is now possible, in this second publication, to concentrate on some of these very early, but basic standard 24 ton 8-wheeler chassis favoured by RPC Transport, which in later years were to be the mainstay of the Rugby fleet for many years.

Shown right is, I think, an early former ALC bodied bulk tanker which has just left the Rochester cement works, heading up the A228 road. These bulk tank bodies were manufactured by the Amalgamated Limestone Corporation. They carried front mounted nearside access catwalk ladders, and a few of these early versions carried the air release pressure pipe, shown on the off side of the tank body. This photo dates possibly from the mid 1960s, and shows F/N 172 registered in 1966 on JNX 316D. According to the RPC Fleet lists, and less than thirteen days later, F/N 173 carrying JNX 317D shown on the next page, entered fleet service carrying one of the first (if not the first) Knutsen of Malvern Worcs, built flat backed bulk tanks. The differences between the two bulk structures were many. For a start, the catwalk ladder incorporated the pressure relief valve for emptying the tanks of undue pressure after discharge and all canvas delivery pipes, and clips etc. were stored in a box. Also, on the nearside, vehicle markings are shown in the vertical position which, because of tipping bulk tanks and delivery pipes in use when discharging etc., would often not be seen and may have restricted access.

Fleet Number 173 was in effect the twenty ninth L/V cabbed chassis to be introduced into RPC Transport over almost a two year period, 1964 – 1966. This photograph shows the lorry ready for fleet use, but it is not taxed. This particular ERF was one of an unknown quantity of identical chassis for bulk use destined to spend almost their entire working life based at Rochester cement works in Kent. The regular driver of F/N 173 for an equal number of years, was Mickey West. Whilst both described tanker vehicles were taxed for 24-ton operation – load weight 15-ton – the Knutsen bodied version would in time equip almost all of Rugby bulk chassis right up until the introduction of B/C Series ERF rigids, and an ultimately articulated version. Certainly during the mid 1970s, all the flat backed bulk tanks were changed to coned ends. This came about mainly because of problems caused by blocked pipes and customer silos, which were not checked as often as they should have been. Discharging procedures dictated by RPC Transport Department Managers meant that the driver should remain at the rear of the tank (ALWAYS) to keep his eyes on the air pressure. Flat back tank designs required less haste when tipping. Because of the flat rear design sudden weight pressure on the pads incorporated into the rear pipework of these early designs caused blocking. This, in turn, could, and did, block the delivery pipe right into the customer's pipe and so on. With the introduction of cone backed designs, cement powder found its way via the delivery outlets in a more gradual movement. However, from my own early P/V (pressurised vehicle) tuition, I can still remember Jock Anderson saying that too much air pressure causes dust. Too little and you might block up. There has to be a happy medium where you learnt to get it 100% correct.

It was always my intention as author of my first book on RPC Transport to try to include photographs which showed former Rugby based colleagues, but it is only within the past twelve years since 2002 that these particular photos have been made available.

This occasion I think concerns the presentation of 25 years' service certificates. Shown left to right:

Peter Bunyard, unknown, unknown, Bill Alder in 4th from the left. His miserable outlook on life, resulted in his nickname "Happy Alder". Next to him is Harry Gherry who, in later years, would transfer into Parkfield Road garage doing fuel return MOT requirements etc., He later transferred, with all garage staff, into Central Garage, when it opened during the early 1970s. His son, Paul, followed him as a driver with RPC transport, but left for pastures new after only a short time. The next face, the man in the grey suit and back tie, is Ron Sheasby the forehead of Ken Whyment behind him is just visible, and Roy Bates is the man on the immediate right. The gentleman making the presentation is unknown.

Shown against the starkness of the kiln house and old adjacent style buildings within Southam Cement Works is a Commer Maxiload TNX 770G which carried F/N 529, bearing signs of a hard life, and on full right lock.

These Commers are remembered with mixed emotions by the Author. Concentration in "wet weather" wavered slightly as they were prone to skidding if you were not 100% careful. The multi-coloured material sheets are remembered with mixed feelings. This was an attempt by the company to cut down on costs regarding canvas which had served its purpose admirably for years prior.

With a view to not keeping all their eggs in one basket, RPC Transport also operated the smaller engine variety of the Maxiload. Designed around the 13-ton gross vehicle weight range, shown overleaf are two identical platform lorries, one sheeted, whilst the other one loads up under the vast roof extension at Barrington Cement Works in Cambridgeshire.

These lighter chassis carried an 8-ton load of bags, and the gross weight worked out at 13 tons. OAC 595 and 597F were supplied new in 1968. Several were to be seen within the RPC Group from then on elsewhere. We had F/Ns 188 and 222 at Rugby works, driven by Chris Moon and Frank Goodyear respectively.

Len "Buff" House spent very many years with Chinnor Cement, long before Rugby bought them out. His experiences gained with the company earmarked him many times for training new drivers, one of whom was to be Alan Holland. Alan's own story comes later on in this second volume.

Shown right is Ron's regular 4 wheeler Commer Maxiload bulk cement tanker "in situ" discharging its load into RMCs Caversham-Reading storage silo. The twin ram stability is shown to good effect in that the tank is at full elevation and almost empty of its load. A good bulk driver on these four wheelers could empty out in under 20 minutes, depending of course on customer's care of their storage facilities. The well remembered Chinnor livery of slate grey and black wheels chassis/wings plus the orange front grilles is a distant memory. A full length off side photograph of this same lorry is shown in the second photograph

being parked up at Christmas Common.

LBW 791E dates from 1967, and like all Chinnor vehicles, was immaculately presented. A two shift system (i.e. two drivers to each lorry) ensured that all lorries were tidy. The Chinnor grey became a byword in the Mason's paint catalogue section in later years. This superb livery was to be discontinued after the 1962 buyout of Chinnor Cement and Lime by Rugby Cement. From what I've since learned, many of Chinnor's regular customer base refused to accept cement unless it was delivered by Chinnor Transport. Consequently, in order to respect both the former Chinnor customer base, together with the workforce, repainting of most of the usable fleet transport was delayed as long as possible. This act of change was to gain acceptance in time by all concerned - both the Chinnor despatch staff and their former customers alike, purely and simply because over many years before RPC Transport came along customer relationships with the management and the drivers had forged friendships based on keeping the customers happy. This, in turn, would eventually blend in with the aims and forthright decisions made by Halford Reddish regarding customer satisfaction.

A colour print out cutting from the much missed "Truck Magazine" shows the rear end of a Peter Gudgin's Commer Maxiload bulk tanker F/N 572 waiting to unload into an On Site PIG bulk structure.

Shown side by side, two such storage vessels were used during the construction of the M45 motorway linking the A45 at Thurlaston with the M1 just south of Watford Gap. Shown alongside are several other RPC bulk tankers discharging their loads into these large storage units. This idea was developed by the major cement producers of the period for large construction jobs where a constant pour of bulk concrete was required, to ensure ample supplies of bulk cement powder were readily available to the batcher. With ample discharge points fitted to these PIGS, loaded cement tankers could unload at any time of the day.

These structures often stayed on site longer than perhaps they should have done, simply because a long load "movement order" was required from the police before any ballasted unit could be used to move the PIG to another site! The structure is seen to good effect here over the pit inside the Barrington garage / workshop.

Shown right is a daily scene in Central Garage, whereby the extensive servicing and repair facilities ensured that RPC Transport received the best possible attention. There was not much, if anything, that could not be attended to both during daylight or darkness hours.

Pete Collins is seen on the left of these two individuals engaged on replacing new brake shoes plus checking for adjustment on one of two Commer Maxi half open ended bulk tipper tanks. These were mainly used for bulk deliveries to Hilton Concrete near Derby (2 loads a day over 5 days). F/N 182 JNX 552D and F/N 183 JNX 553D were supplied new in 1966, and were rarely parked up out of use. Other customers included Redland Tiles at Clifton, near Rugby, where cement powder slid out of the rear end when the tank was tipped.

Other customers where these two Commer Tippers went were Alexandra Stone at Kirkby Muxloe, Leicestershire, and their larger facility at Malvern in Worcestershire. Bearing in mind that it is now well over forty three years since the majority of Commer Maxiload chassis were supplied to RPC Transport, they came as short wheel based and medium wheel based tankers, box tippers and platform lorries. Like so many of my colleagues, I too was obliged to cover for holiday relief not long after I joined RPC Transport in June 1968. Fitted with the 2-stroke engine, I personally did not care much for them, but they served RPC well enough over a 7-8 year period. Consequently, I am never surprised to know, or be contacted and told, that former RPC Maxiload chassis are still in use, working in other jobs under second ownership, several later registered, mainly tanker chassis on both medium and short wheelbases. VNX 972H, came to RPC Transport in 1970. Given F/N 911, spending all its working life on bulk operations at Chinnor Cement Works in Oxfordshire and sold out of service some 14 years later, I now know it is currently under restoration by David Trant and his son at their farm in Oakhampton, Devon. In June 2012 I met both of them at the Gaydon old lorry event, and have since supplied them with full details of VNX 972H's life at RPC. Graham Munday a chargehand fitter at Chinnor garage looked after F/N 911 and he supplied all the details to me regarding this lorry for which I am indebted to him for supplying this information on this Commer shown overleaf.

This photograph shows a medium wheel based chassis, now in use as an internal farm lorry. Traces of RPC orange are visible under the black paint, and the lorry appears in remarkable mechanical condition. The conversion to box tipper use would be simple enough in lieu of the existing EDBRO tipper rams fitted, sold with the Commer chassis.

The lorry in this Central Garage scene shown below is F/N 182 flanked on either side by ERF lorries, both bulk chassis. The B series 8-wheel lorries had been delivered direct from the manufacturers. Being one of the later chassis recognised by the twin air filter pipes it would be fitted with automatic lubrication piping and discharge blower equipment. Later on a bulk tank body would be fitted. F/N 822, on the left hand side, was driven by Dennis Garlick, better known as 'Choo Choo' because of his interest in the Severn Valley Railway. This scene was at the South West end of Central Garage, where three well lit pits are immediately visible. Roller shutter doors allowed for easy access. There was to be a succession of bulk drivers who were to spend nearly the whole of their working lives with Rugby Cement, starting with the early pressurised vehicles (PV). Over the coming years, as and when newer lorries were introduced, these drivers, in order of Company service, would get a newer vehicle. Two such characters deserve special mention here, not only because of both their adventures with Commer Maxi bulkers, but also the sheer hilarity of these individuals, namely "Captain" Dick Goode and Peter "Branch" Gudgin. Captain Goode was reckoned to be a former member of the Indian Army. As to the truth of this statement, I have no reason to think it's not true. Dick's rendition of a situation in which he was to find himself several years back, would have any normal person helpless with laughter. Returning to Rugby Works, after a bulk delivery in the Hereford/Worcestershire

area, Dick pulled into the layby at Inkberrow, some 8 miles from Worcester on the A422 towards Alcester. Here he was to spend his official half hour break, required by law. Suddenly, a car with a young, seemingly oblivious courting couple, pulled in directly in front of him, and got down to some serious business! When these two lover's antics reached fever pitch, the *Daily Telegraph* was forgotten, and Dick's tea and sandwiches went everywhere. Needless to say, after cleaning himself and the cab up, time was not on his side, he resumed his journey back to Rugby. Listening later to Dick recollecting his moments of embarrassment to his colleagues, puts this man clearly in a class of his own.

Peter Gudgin's experiences did not prevent him from an equally agonising and embarrassing moment one bright summer's afternoon, when he too was on his way back to Rugby Works. Having delivered bulk cement to the Spun Concrete Works at Branston, near Burton on Trent, he was driving along the back road between Elford and Tamworth, the A513, when his folly of filling up on chips and gravy at the Spun works canteen before he left, suddenly and very definitely forced him to park up rather quickly! He scrambled out of the cab, jumped over what he thought was a hedge, and dropped his overalls and trousers in one go. Oblivious, in his earlier haste to complete an urgent toilet and re-dressing himself, Peter Gudgin slipped and fell into an overgrown patch of waist high nettles, with his trousers and overalls etc. around his ankles. He was very painfully stung all over his private parts! He was in absolute agony! Finally struggling up the bank, in a half dressed state, he was suddenly confronted by a line of bare bottoms facing him. In his absence, a coach load of ladies had pulled on to the same patch of ground as him. And with the same urgency as himself! One of the ladies suddenly saw Gudgin in his sorry state, and shouted to her friends "Ladies, we have a peeper", only to watch in horror as he collapsed in front of her.

Two of the ladies were nurses and treated Peter as best they could. Rugby Cement were contacted (no mobile phones in those days), and two drivers arrived; one to drive Peter's tanker back to Rugby, the other to take Peter, in the car, to the nearest hospital. Peter Gudgin returned to work some days later, somewhat subdued, but was soon back to his old self. How do I know all of this? I was the driver who brought Peter's Commer bulker back to Rugby Works.

Peter Gudgin was a born comedian. During his many years as an RPC driver he would always help the individual. I personally have many memories of working alongside him, and I remember the happier times. When he was made redundant on a week's notice, along with Sid Cave in 1984, Peter Gudgin was broken hearted. Sid was no different, never having been out of work in his life. Both him and Peter worked as retained drivers in Central garage, always eager to help or assist you in any way they could. Sid's mechanical knowledge was supreme in every sense of the word, and if ever you experienced problems with your own cars, he would help you out, often refusing payment. The word "redundancy" is now sadly part of this new Century, which for reasons beyond the control of ordinary employees and employers alike, is part and parcel of modern times. Indeed, many firms, large or small, have shut their doors for the last time. However, in the middle 1980s, ordinary employees, many of them with years of loyal service to RPC Transport, whether they worked the day or night shift, were suddenly confronted with losing their jobs.

Shown below is a scene which could be seen at any hour of the day or night at any Rugby Cement Works, or indeed at the depots. F/N 254, I've since learned, was based at South Ferriby, and this night shot leads me to think that the ERF bulk lorry was collecting a load of sulphate-resisting cement powder at Rugby Works. Supplied new in January 1968, and carrying registration number ONX 343F, the pipe shown on the left above the hazard board, brought induction air from the blower into the tank body. The centre coupling was both the original loading and cement delivery pipe controlled by an unseen valve. In later years, safer working practices for bulk loaders were introduced via consultation with management and the bulk loading staff. This resulted in small raised platforms to enable loaders to complete their tasks at a safer height. Later, air pressure (dust) methods were also introduced and much later on top loading through roof mounted tank hatches became the norm.

In this photo, the loader is tightening the spring loaded clips on the supply pipe from the storage silo, after which, 15 tonne of cement powder will be blown into the tank bodywork. All RPC bulk chassis involved weighbridge loading. This totally eliminated overloading, and quicker turnarounds were achieved. A good proportion of careful company drivers resulted in a very low accident rate, considering the enormity of the RPC Transport Fleet. The type of driver individual considered for employment with the Company did itself contribute itself to this statement, but the prime reason for safety lay in the fact that a fully laden RPC bulk tanker 8 wheeler could barely manage 30mph. This, alongside the fact that certainly forty years or more ago there was not the volume of traffic that there is now.

When Company lorries were

involved in accidents however, the overall damage was rather extensive, as shown in the photo, right. Long before the advent of the M180 motorway, at a place called Roxby Bends, driver Tom Beacock's ERF was involved in a really frightening collision, as the damage shows. This is the remains of F/N 254 (already described on the previous page), taken from the nearside front end after this collision. Tom Beacock was extremely lucky to walk away from this accident, although I've since learned that the shock of the impact affected him for a few days afterwards. His side of the cab appears to be complete apart from the missing cab roof. Tom may have been on his way to the RPC Depot at Leeds, with a stock load, or indeed to any customer in the Doncaster or Sheffield areas.

Fleet number 287 was given new to Lew Dickson in May 1968 at Rugby Works. Over the next fourteen years or so, and almost quarter of a million miles later, 533F found itself sold to the Stanworth Showland family from Stoke on Trent. They fitted box body work and painted it in crimson/grey.

In third ownership with the Pearson family of show people who wintered at Swannington

in Leicestershire, they removed the Luton bodywork completely, and then fitted a box storage body of their own. It was then repainted all over in white, with a pleasing light blue on the lower chassis and wheels. A square front panel from a new ERF was fitted after 1974. I photographed this unique survivor from the RPC fleet in 2002 at the Clarendon Park Fair, Hinckley, Leicestershire. By then, this grand lorry was 34 years old, and still on the original Gardner 150. It was

finally taken off the road around 2006, mainly because she was too slow for today's traffic.

The strength built into this chassis by ERF, plus Gardner reliability, are two reasons for the longevity of this lorry. F/N 288, a sister lorry new also in 1968, was given to another well remembered Rugby Works character, Alan Astley, whose prime passion was the bookies, and betting on the horses. Like so many of these long servers within RPC Transport, Alan could take you the quickest way to most of Rugby's bulk customers at that time, but he always found the best café which had fruit machines and other, so called, money making attractions. Something of a dilemma faced him one day when he was sent down to London when he got lost near Billingsgate old Fish Market. He never lived that one down for a long time afterwards.

F/N 288, registration number PNX 534F is shown opposite in one of the many advertisements used by the various tyre or component manufacturers who RPC Transport relied upon from time to time. When I started with the Company, it was using Avon Tyres. This caption photo shows the versatility of the strength in the Edro tipping rams and the wheels are now shod with Goodyear Tyres. The photo shows Alan Astley's regular daily steed, based at Rugby Works for a good few years.

Sadly, Alan Astley did not live long after retiring some time in the 1970s from the company. His sense of humour to his former colleagues was much missed after he left. His best pal was Lew Dickson and these two appeared to go everywhere together.

There are no two showmen whose ideas, and overall presentation of rides and transport equipment which although apparently similar, are not. For me, as the historian of former RPC Transport Lorries, this continues thankfully to be both a revelation and a bonus!

Many families within the ranks of the show people themselves, are now very good friends of mine, and I am constantly reminded when talking to them that most of the RPC Transport lorries bought by them initially, served them faithfully over many years.

Delivering cement in bulk to concrete mixing plants and 'on site' building projects, calls for a prompt and dependable delivery service if the highly intensified programme of motorway construction and re-development schemes are to be maintained.

To help meet this challenge, Rugby Portland Cement fit Goodyear Extra Tread 'S' tyres to their very large fleet of vehicles and experience has proved their choice to be a wise one.

Extra tread 'S' tyres are doing a great job for Rugby Portland Cement – they could do the same for you!

For specialist advice on truck tyres contact the Commercial Tyre Sales & Service Dept., Goodyear Tyre & Rubber Co. (Gt. Britain) Ltd., Wolverhampton.

GOODYEAR
Tyremanship – get it on your side

Shown right is a converted former Rugby ERF which, not only looks the part, but shows the skill of its owner twofold. YWD 282J was exactly eighteen years old when Rod Jesson photographed this grand old ex RPC ERF pulling its possible 30ft drawbar living trailer. By removing the 2nd steer axle and fitting composite box bodywork, this in effect would increase the turning manoeuvres so necessary for the showmen where access is, and can be, very difficult. The pleasing combination of pale green / light green is reversed between lorry and living trailer. This, and the roof mounted air horn and upright exhaust, together with the obligatory orange flashing light, presents overall excellence. 282J was photographed at the August Fair 1988 at Babbacombe in Devon. The wheel discs fitted to all three axles on the lorry add to the presentation of showmen's transport for which the owner, Chris Smith, has to be both congratulated for his efforts and hard work to achieve such a fantastic result. This photograph was taken some twenty five years or more ago, but I have no doubt that this grand old ERF, if and when it was removed from use, would be kept by the family concerned. I have no idea at all where YWD 282J was based in her role as an 8 wheeler bulk tanker during her Rugby Cement days. Her fleet number was 688, and was supplied new to the RPC Transport Company on the 1st August 1970. The chassis number was 19967.

Shown right is a scene which can never be repeated. It shows both an ERF and its two smaller brothers, Commer Maxiload lorries. This particular scene was commonplace at any of Rugby Cement's manufacturing plants, which, in their heyday of operation, spanned seven separate locations right across the lower part of England from the river Humber downwards. Shown taking centre stage is PUE 311F, and ERF standard bulk tanker carrying F/N 291, the 4-wheel bulk tanker which grossed out at 16 ton with 10 ton bulk loads as standard weight. The platform version shown on the right carried 10 ton of bags, and also worked out at the 16 ton GVW. The scene is at Southam Cement Works on a rather dull summer evening. 311F dates from 1968, and to any observer presents an unrivalled picture of mechanical excellence being perhaps more than ten years old, or more, when this photograph was taken.

The middle to late period of 1969 saw the beginning of the permanent night shift of drivers at Rugby Works. I can remember seeing my former training mentor, George "Jock" Anderson, teaming up with Ken Whyment. Mick Lowe, who joined the night shift gang at Ferriby later on, around 1973, often wound George up by asking him about his broad Glaswegian accent by saying that he sounded like a Cockney! George Anderson was one of fifteen children growing up in Glasgow. Life was extremely hard for all of them. He remembers his father, who ruled the family with his fist, sending George and his two sisters for his weekly bottle of whisky. Very early on in his childhood, George developed a taste for Scotch Whisky when he and his sisters helped themselves to "sippers" from their father's bottle. Before they gave their father the bottle they refilled it with cold tea!

Freddie Hack's name involves laughter wherever he goes. He was determined to spend a large part of his Company service on nights. One night, way back in the early 1970s, perhaps earlier, he remembers a frightening journey of almost eight hours partnering Ken Whyment when they took a brand new Foden 6-wheel quarry dumper down to Rochester works. The reader must be aware that this particular

lorry was basic in every sense of the word. It was built for off road use with a top speed of perhaps 30mph. Heaters were non-existent, and this journey was done long before the advent of the M25 and the Queen Elizabeth bridge over the River Thames. Fred remembers Big Taffy of the old Parkfield Road garage night shift fitters/greasers loaning him and Ken a thick leather coat. In view of the really intense cold driving this slow moving lorry, the coat turned out to be a real Godsend! Although I'm not exactly sure, I have a distinct feeling that this redoubtable pair returned to Rugby Works by train, mainly because, as Freddy put it later, by the time they eventually reached Rochester, both of them were literally frozen to the bone!

Other characters included Bill Gardner, on nights for a long time, later reverting back on to day shift (bulk). John Gilbert (alias The Duke of Wellington) always wore wellington boots everywhere. Maybe even in bed? He was very much a loyal company man, who always stuck to his guns.

Roy Cheatle joined the company a year after me in 1969. Apart from his training period, he opted for the night shift, and stayed on it right through to artics, until redundancy in the 1980s. Both he and his wife, Cynthia, are very good friends with me and my wife Diane. John Garrat swapped from days to nights and was very much a loner type of individual who did his job with little or no fuss. His own style of Irish humour occasionally came to the surface, but I, and many others, had very little to do with him.

Rugby drivers delivered two loaded bulk tankers into the yard, had a quick cup of tea, or whatever, and then jumped into two empty tankers for return to Rugby.

Once the Gloucester depot night shift started John O'Connor and Norman "Brummy" Marshall joined the night drivers gang. This pair were up to all sorts of tricks, mainly because Norman had a pair of greyhounds running three times a week at Gloucester dog track. From what I've been able to research since, they wasted so much time at the dog track, their return speeds 36-38mph at best, were to be observed very often by traffic police in both Evesham and Stratford. So much so, that eventually they were summoned in front of Bill Appleby, who was the night shift transport supervisor. I don't know the outcome, but things went back to normal running before they were soon back to the dogs.

George Anderson and Ken Whyment ran together almost until the day George retired from RPC Transport. By far the most memorable, but absolutely scandalous act of behaviour, by a dog owner in Evesham town centre, really infuriated Jock Anderson. During double Gloucesters (running twice to RPC Gloucester Depot from Rugby Works) with bulk tankers some time in the early 1970s, Ken and George saw this woman blatantly allow her two dachsund sausage dogs to complete their toilet in shop doorways. Having had a strict disciplinarian upbringing in Glasgow, this disgusting performance by a member of the public so infuriated George that he was determined to teach her a lesson she would never forget. Running possibly three nights out of five to Gloucester, during two of these nights they regularly saw this woman let her dogs foul the main street doorways of Evesham town centre. George said to Ken before they left Rugby on the Friday, for the second time around "When you see that woman and those two dogs, flash your off side rear winker" (Ken always led on the outward run, and George followed). Later on as they entered the edge of Evesham on the old A46 during the early hours around 1.30am, George suddenly saw the desired signal. Quick as a flash, he pulled the dead man handle ON/OFF. The sudden squeal in the dead of night, as air was blown into the tanks, caused both dogs to literally bolt like greyhounds out of the trap. The woman was pulled to the ground and dragged along until her head hit a doorway. In the short time of passing by, both Ken and George reflected on their joint actions and planned handiwork as the two dogs finally scarpered away in fright, dragging their leads to parts unknown.

Sad to say, however, George Anderson finally retired from RPC Transport in the very early 70s, but he was not fortunate enough to be allowed to enjoy a well deserved rest because he died not long afterwards. To me, personally, this was a very sad loss because he was one of my best friends.

Sometime well into the existence of night drivers at RPC Transport, at both Rugby and Southam, it was found that Nora Ryder, wife of Gloucester Depot Driver Harry, made celebration cakes. Christenings, birthdays, weddings etc. plus other celebratory occasions were all catered for. RPC Transport night shift drivers brought back, on request, from Gloucester, beautifully decorated cakes of all sizes and colours, packed in strong insulated boxes in lieu of bounce. This voluntary task did not come under the job description as such, but it fulfilled a lot of happiness for many people. Freddy Hack often ran in company, in later years, with both Ken Whyment, until he retired, and thereafter with Roy Cheatle. The seemingly plentiful supply of mixed vegetables on roadside stalls within the Evesham area was quite a distraction for Fred, until such times as he could stand it no longer. Now in his pensionable years, he readily admits to helping himself on more than one occasion. Many other well known companies from years past shared the A46 on night trunking duties with the RPC drivers. Friendships were begun with people from Grimsby Fish who ran from Grimsby down to Bristol and elsewhere. Freddy engineered an agreement from the regular fish delivery drivers, both from Grimsby and Hull, whereby fish being sent back as not delivered found its way onto whatever cab Fred was driving on a regular basis. Regular day shift bulk drivers finding their cabs stinking of fish, refused point blank to take their lorries out until they were fumigated properly.

Other names concerned with the driver's night shift at Rugby works, included jovial Bob Crisp, whose name still evokes fun and laughter. His passion for both double breakfasts and free beer, particularly if someone else was paying, earned him a serious resemblance to Billy Bunter. Barrie Bunyard was the third member of his family to work for RPC Transport. He too spent some time on nights before leaving to start his own business. Alan Bloxham was another night driver who always found something not to his liking, moaning about anything and everything.

Something of a motley crew of night shift fitters in Central Garage are pictured in a thoughtful, and perhaps, an intelligent pose. Mick Hennesey, the redoubtable 2nd night foreman, holding his cap, was held "in-fright" by visiting night drivers for the jokes which he constantly played on them, although they too occasionally managed to get their own back.

Shown above, left to right are Paul Grubb, Pete Brown (sitting), Pete Collins immediately behind, Kindu, an Indian fitter standing next to Mr Hennesey.

CHAPTER 6

ERF & Fodens
Drivers and Garage Fitters' Memories

A new breed of ERF 8 wheelers were to make their presence felt from about 1970 onwards, mainly on J reg plates. Shown right is one such lorry, again of 8 wheeler chassis form, but bodied as a covered box tipper, and registered ANX 484J carrying F/N 693.

This was one of the last 1970 registrations to come to RPC Transport. Bought initially to replace an ageing Foden S20 8 wheel tipper, 693's daily runs were made to the Alexander Stone Malvern-Worcester plant twice a day. The regular drivers, from memory, were Ted Shoebridge and occasionally John Ginger Gilbert of "wellington boot" fame. Whilst Ted was in charge of 693, he was another individual who made good use of both the front and rear towing eyes by extricating car and van drivers from ditches and culverts on the very bad road between Alcester and Worcester. This road was full of blind bends - treacherous for unwary drivers. Consequently, those whose right foot was forever pressed hard down on the accelerator played right into Shoebridge's hands when their vehicles ended upside-down, embedded in the hedges or ditches. This was where his weekly pay at RPC took on a completely new meaning when his lorry was used to pull them out of the various predicaments – resulting in cash changing hands – then again, nothing lasts forever! 693 did not have a very long operational life because pressurised bulk deliveries were gathering momentum, and so the covered box tipper use was at an end. Now and again, this 8 wheeler would occasionally divert to the Alexander Stone's second facility at Kirkby Maxloe near Leicester, and also when required to the RMC block plant within the huge quarry complex at ECC / RMC Croft near Leicester.

Shown overleaf in front of the original bulk and bag loading shed within Rochester Cement Works, two differently front panelled ERF 8-wheeler platform lorries are visible amongst smaller lorries of the 4 wheeler Dodge varieties.

Several other designed L/V cabbed ERFs came into the RPC Fleet, both for bulk and bag use. F/N 694, 5, 6 and 7 were fitted with the standard 150 Gardner. Later variants again of L/V but of square fronted panel design would be powered by the Gardner 180, whilst both versions remained at an operational 26 tons on taxed rating. This statement can perhaps be better appreciated by the photo shown immediately right.

F/N 713 carried registration number DNX 713K. This is the square fronted version. The lorry behind is F/N 694 with AUE 130J as its registration number. This has the original and best remembered design of the L/V (long vue) structure. F/N 694 was, I'm led to believe by Steve Hastings, written off in an horrendous accident on the A2 Swanscombe cutting (London bound direction) when a foreign driver hit it up the back end. However, contrary to what people might think, this lovely old ERF lived to fight another day, thanks to the skill and resourcefulness of the showman, as the following photograph shows. The remains were bought by Denzel Danter, whose family travel around the Wales / Hereford areas. This grand old ERF was then rebuilt with a full Luton framed body, which then carried Waltzer cars and equipment. Photographed by Rod Jesson at the 1984 Hereford Fair, this proves beyond all shadow of a doubt that old ERFs never die, they just fade away. 8 wheeler platforms taxed for 26 Ton use were to see fleet service from 1971 onwards. One of these was AUE 131J carrying F/N 695. This was given to Rugby Works' longest serving driver, Fred Saunders.

On an "official break", 695 was photographed by Peter J Davies, shown opposite, presumably on a motorway services area. Diff locks were fitted to this 8-wheeler platform and these came in handy whilst involved with on-site deliveries to the Cassington Reservoir construction job in North Derbyshire, where Fred was the only platform driver able to leave the site under his own power. All others had to be towed out behind crawler tractors or bulldozers. It was sold out of service in the middle 1980s to Clark Transport (a former RPC driver turned private operator) for £500 with two lorry sheets thrown in.

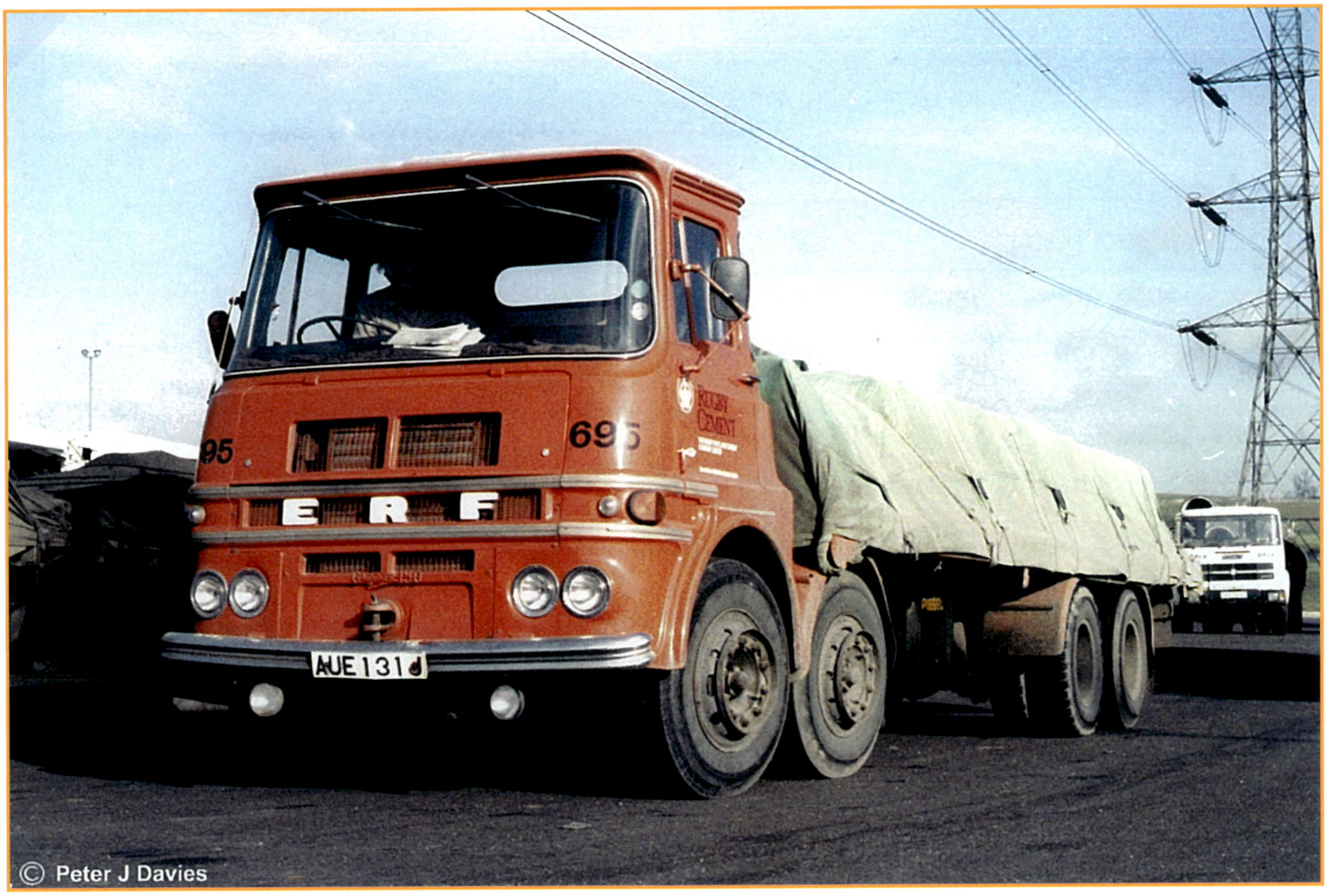

© Peter J Davies

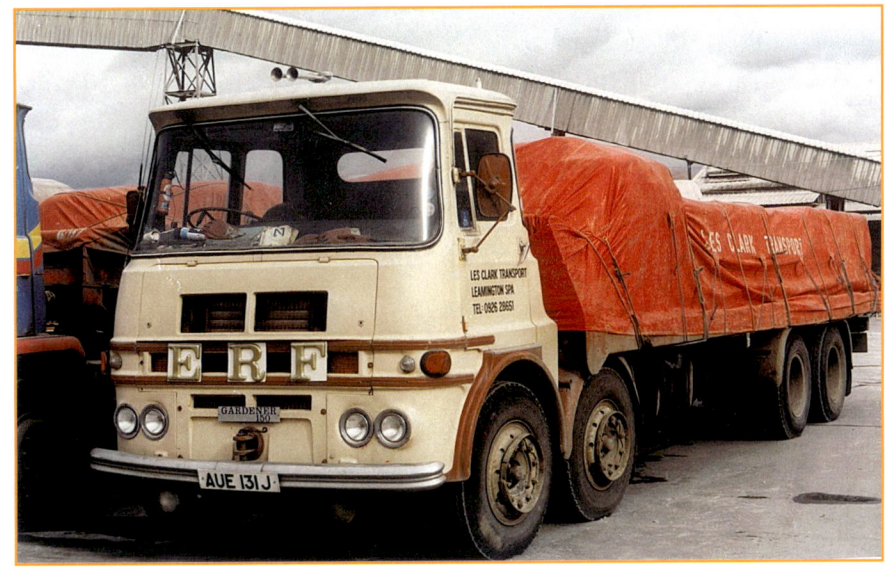

Had he concentrated on running this beautiful 8 legger sufficiently long enough he would have managed to replace it. Instead Les Clarke bought several other ex RPC lorries - both tanks and platforms all of which feature in this story. His misspelt Gardener name, plus his liberal use of Southam Works Yard for servicing purposes, all signalled his short term duration as an RPC contractor. AUE 131J was purchased for preservation in the late 1980s. Its third owner has never been found.

Gardner engines, of one sort or another, were to be a part of RPC Transport certainly in depth from the 1960s onwards. Several early variants were to be used prior to the period. Even earlier, compression ignition 5 cylinder versions of this legendary engine were in use during WW11. They were also used to good effect by the lorries belonging to Transport Services whose contract lorries were employed within Rugby's Cement Works during the war and immediately afterwards.

Receiving attention to the pump, is a standard Gardner 150 6LX power unit which was the mainstay favoured by RPC Transport until the advent of 180 powered Gardner ERF chassis around 1972 onwards and used to move heavier bulk / bag loads at 26 and 30 ton GVW. In 1974 the B Series ERFs came on the scene, but RPC did not receive theirs until at least a year later. By then 180 Gardner's had become the standard power outfit for 30 ton. The fitter shown adjusting the engine above is Mick McDonald who spent very many years in the RPC garage. His passion for football often saw him dashing around on Saturday morning shifts, hurrying away in time for the game. During the middle 1980s he left in pursuit of a new career, and like so many former members of RPC Transport he is probably in another job, still remembering the good times.

Now in fourth ownership, and still on its original Gardner 150, AUE 543J dates from December 1970. It started life as a bulk cement tanker at Chinnor Works, Oxfordshire, where it stayed for 13-14 years. It is now over 43 years old and was photographed at the Great Dorset Steam Fair in 2006/7. Superbly painted and lined out, it represents a fantastic era in road transport, now sadly gone. The cab and chassis are 100% original. My friendships have developed with most of the showmen and their families who bought ex RPC ERFs initially from one of three sources at the time of disposals, namely

Charlie Watts (scrap man), Cossington Garage at Leicester (ERF and Gardner agents), or the Company themselves. Starting in earnest around the early 1990s, one of those I met was the late Joe Merrin.

Shown above, Young Joseph Merrin was aged 4-5 after his dad bought BWD 703J F/N 703 from Cossington Garage Leicester in the early 1980s. Joe Merrin and his family were to keep 703J for a total of 16 years. His comments to me before he sadly died in 2005 were – "It only cost me three fan belts in 15 years use, apart from the purchase price". Joseph is now married with a family of his own. He travels juveniles including a toyset and his father's former cup and saucers ride. Joe's former ex RPC / ERF in chassis cab form is shown below at the Welland yearly show in 2005. It was up for sale at the time, and was eventually bought for preservation by a gentleman from the Eastern Counties area. Where is it now? The well-remembered L/V ERF cab structure remains crack free. This chassis is ripe for restoration and is now well over 38 years old and, again, still on its original Gardner 150 no less!

There is intense concentration as the driver reverses on to the weighbridge prior to loading up. The Bunyard family were to give many years of service as drivers with Albert Bunyard, starting in the 1950s. He later transferred into the garage after serious illness, where he stayed until retirement. Peter followed his father as a driver. He stayed on as an owner / driver until the middle 1990s, but is now retired. Barry Bunyard, shown here, was a night driver. He left, I think, before redundancies came along, to start his own business delivering vehicle off road spares for Volvo. He too retired due to ill health and lives in the Rugby area.

I am never surprised, these days, to learn from various sources, both within the fairground and elsewhere within the old vehicle network, of former RPC chassis still in regular use, but I was absolutely delighted to know, after a visit to Rod Jesson's house in Redditch, that Mason's Fun Fair, who travel in and around the High Wycombe area of Buckinghamshire, operate two ex Rugby lorries, which have, between them, a total age of 73 years from new.

Shown in the above photo is BUE 330J which started life as a bulk tanker 8 wheel chassis in March 1971. By my own reckoning, this lorry is now 43 years old, plus a little bit more. It had the same driver from new, in that Ken Wright who, like his lorry, was never off sick. Nor was he ever late. This combination of man and his machine lasted for a total of 13 years delivering bulk cement from Rugby Works before the chassis/cab was sold out of service in the middle 1980s. Purchased by AJ Barker & Sons Amusement Caterers of Selby, Leicestershire (who were, over a period of years, to buy several ex RPC chassis), Barkers built the half box open sided bodywork and added charging engines and other necessary equipment in keeping with their amusements. 330J, after painting and lettering, served the Barkers faultlessly for a period of many years or more, before it was resold on. I then lost track of it for a few years, but I'm reliably informed that it has since emerged from within the Mason's Amusements stable, still fitted with the Barker's open half box bodywork, superbly painted and lettered in a very traditional way with simple red colours interspaced with colourful lettering. This lorry is still on its original Gardner

150 and it remains a credit to its third owner, and its makers – ERF Ltd.

Just a few years younger, in 1974, GAC 585N is just as impressive in Mason's ownership, particularly when you, the reader, realise that this chassis started brand new as a 6 wheeler bulk tanker, again for a time based at Rugby Works, driven by Brian Stretford, a young driver whose energies for looking after his lorry earned him the respect of his colleagues and management alike. Dating from November 1974, GAC 585N is now, as we speak, 40 years old or more. Sold out of fleet service in possibly the late 1990s, it was bought originally in 6 wheeler form by Joe Rose Senior and his family who lived at Bloxham near Banbury. Joe and his three sons, Joe Junior, Jack and Tom, removed the trailing rear axle and fitted the box body work and sold this lorry soon afterwards to another Oxfordshire based part-time showman who I got to know also. Thanks to his kindness, I was allowed to drive this lorry in its 4 wheel guise. I found the experience a whole new ball game. In Mason's ownership, along with 330J, these 30 year old plus classic ERFs may well serve the family for a good few years yet. Solid British engineering at its very best – the likes of which have gone forever.

We should be grateful to all showmen, whose efforts over many years have allowed many lorries, considered by their original owners to be finished, to be recreated with self-built bodywork and mechanical innovations, and to be transformed from chassis once considered only for scrap. Showmen don't do colossal mileages. This, together with relatively slow travelling speeds whilst moving their equipment between sites, means that these lorries may well be seen for a few years more.

Brian Peeps started his employment as a driver with Eastwood's Cement in April 1961. His job was to continue on for very many years, certainly after the buyout of Eastwoods by RPC in 1963. Fortunately for me, Brian took his camera everywhere he went during his RPC Transport career, and so many previously unseen photos of transport activity at South Ferriby are now here for everyone to enjoy.

Brian is shown below with his nightly charge, ERF L/V artic NUE 112F coupled to the bulk tanker trailer. Two nightly delivery runs to Leeds Depot with stock loads occupied some nights.

Delivery of bags, or bulk to a certain extent, depended upon whether thick fog was prevalent in the Lincolnshire Wolds, which meant the runs were cancelled. It was fitted with a 5 speed David Brown gearbox coupled to a 180 Gardner engine. I remember in early 1969 some days whilst working bags out of Southam Works, seeing both 242 and 243 being used for bulk loads to Turner's Asbestos at Tamworth who had the capacity to accept these bigger loads. George Trotman was the driver of 243. He did not like anyone to know how old he was, and tried all sorts of ways to avoid being told to produce both his driving licence and birth certificate when required.

More memories come flooding back for me from the early 1970s, or maybe a bit later on, when an individual was running back late from being asleep somewhere? On the return journey he lost control of one of these artics in Long Itchington village, some 3/4 of a mile from Southam Works, whereby he ran out of road, smashing into the village duck pond and tearing down the perimeter fence. Both the unit and bulk trailer then fell into the pond on the driver's offside. What made this situation just that bit more serious was that the families of swans, so coveted by the villagers, were about to hatch their young cygnets. He was sacked immediately for

gross misconduct. His rapid exit from Southam Transport caused a huge sigh of relief from Clive Mumford (the garage foreman) plus many of the drivers and fitters alike. His uncouth language, together with total and often relentless rough usage of all the lorries he drove, was therefore at an end. To this day I don't actually know what caused the accident, and so cannot say. After this incident, and when the whole lorry and trailer had been recovered and checked for damage, one of the best remembered individuals became involved with F/N 243, the sister ERF artic NUE 113F.

Arthur Harris started with RPC Transport in March 1975. He was destined to stay with the company until redundancy forced him, and many others, out of the job he loved in 1988. Arthur, or "Fruity" as he became known, looked after lorries as if they were his own. He was one of the most popular drivers at Southam, shown here in his younger days with summer uniform trousers and little else. Arthur transferred onto bags with Dodge K 6 wheelers and artics. He and his wife Rene became very good friends with myself after us Rugby bag men were transferred to Southam in 1982, along with another Southam bag man, the late Kevin Billingham (so tragically killed on the Rugby Southam road by an uninsured foreign driver). The three of us were the best of friends. Arthur's talents as an experienced digger-driver saw him work for both Priory Plant, Southam, and Rugby Plant Hire before final retirement.

How many ex RPC drivers recognise this individual? His name evokes laughter. It's Arthur Harris, no less!

When I went for my driving test at Rugby Cement Works in May 1968, I was given ten minutes tuition by Ray Lowe on his 1969 registered ERF L/V 8 wheeler bulk tanker PUE 309F which carried F/N 289. This lorry was virtually brand new at that time, but the combination of a huge engine and a long thin gear stick was totally new to me then! I found my initial driving experience of this ERF during my trial a bit of a handful, and lack of proper gear changing in a David Brown 6 speed gear box was noticeable for the examiner. But I did get the job on the proviso that my first few weeks with RPC Transport would be spent getting used to changing gear properly. My admiration for the L/V ERF cab design stems from both my experience as a confirmed former lorry driver and enthusiast alike, and as a scratch build model maker. The LV design remains a favourite of mine. The two photos, above and below, both black and white, portray to the reader exactly my comments. F/N 281 was new to one of Southam Cement Works' character drivers, Piggy Collins. He drove it on many occasions when I was seconded to work 8 wheeler (bags) for Fred Williams – Southam's despatch manager. Piggy lived at Norton Village, midway between Daventry and Whilton Locks. He had a small-holding at Norton where in his spare time he kept and reared pigs – hence the nick name! My memories of him as an individual are based on the fact that he was a jolly person, always good for a laugh, but at the same time, he would do anything for anybody.

A scene which was perfectly acceptable to all members of the travelling public, certainly from the early 1960s onwards, is shown by Rugby based driver, Mick Dietrich's L/V ERF bulk tanker en route through Evesham Town Centre, long before the bypass was built.

Mick was an Irishman by birth. I had very little to do with him, but his inbred attitude and humour, such as it was, was accepted and metered out to his colleagues on the day shift. He was a bit of a private individual, or so was the impression I got. This was occasionally brought to the surface when someone else was on the receiving end of mickey-taking, which was part of the job. Mick Dietrich was a long serving driver with RPC Transport who, as far as I know, did not give much away, but did his job professionally and quietly.

The River Severn is very well known for the way in which it flows down through the Midlands area on its way to the Bristol Channel and elsewhere. What the ordinary person does not know, unless they work in riverside industrial areas like Diglis Dock in central Worcester, is perhaps better left unsaid. RPC Transport delivered almost twice a day, morning and afternoon, to RMC Concrete, whose truck mixer plant lay within a cluster of boat builder yards and the canal basin. Roy Bates a Rugby based bulk driver of many years service is seen picking his way through a variety of hazards driving PNX 532F carrying F/N 286. Registered in 1968 this was a standard ERF L/V.

Taken off the road, probably around the late 1970s, F/N 177 is shown discharging plant process dust within the quarry perimeters of Rochester Cement Works in Kent.

A mixed group of individuals, mainly Rugby based drivers, drove this particular vehicle at one point or another in its long life as a powder delivery lorry. It was given to Southam based Duggie Tombs who survived as its longest surviving pilot, before he transferred into the garage there as the resident tyre fitter. 177 passed to Dennis Garlick (alias Severn Valley Steam), a Rugby based bulk driver. Dennis kept that lorry until he received a new 6 wheeler square fronted ERF bulk in 1974. 177 then passed to Dave Cooksey when he started with RPC Transport.

The driver in charge of the ERF shown above is stripped to the waist, it probably being the height of summer. The versatility of the Edbro twin rams are shown to good effect. The blower would just be on a mild "tick over" as process dust is light, and would not require much pressure to assist emptying the tank. What a wonderful lorry this might have made, joining the ranks alongside three former RPC Transport lorries which

have survived into the vehicle preservation ranks.

TWD 201G F/N 658 was purchased by Barwell based Robert Lynch at some point in the early 1980s for second ownership duties within the fairgrounds. Fitted with Luton box bodywork in conjunction mainly with the family operated 'MOJO' ride, it was painted in a simple combination of crimson cab and loose panels, with the wheels and the box body structure in red. At some point later on, a flashing orange light was fixed to the Luton front, and a front panel from a later ERF model was fitted to give the old girl an appearance befitting her part in modern society. Many other showmen about this time operating former RPC L/V ERF 8-wheeler chassis, also changed their front panels for much the same reason. Taken off the road finally at some point during the early 1990s, 201G was to stay parked up in the family's Barwell yard in Leicestershire indefinitely.

It is shown overleaf in her new role as compact box bodied fairground lorry. Most showmen at this time favoured box structure construction, including lower areas known to enthusiasts and showmen alike as belly box storage. This method of construction doubled as extra storage, and was to present a neater, but streamlined finish, whilst presenting each lorry in a much more professional way. At some point, certainly during the late 1990s, after I

got to know Norman, and his late wife Phyllis and Robert, who was then involved with a showland young lady called Beverly Robinson, I advertised this lovely old ERF for sale with the REVS (ERF) Society's Newsletter. In 2000 Robert Wells from the Bedfordshire area of this country purchased TWD 201G for preservation.

Richard Nixon carried out much of the remedial and practical engineering work on the 201G, including a 100% total cab interior job which involved the already well known skills of Colin Pit and his staff. During the middle 2000s, I was contacted by Richard as he had experienced difficulty fitting a replacement blower, and so I arranged to visit his Amersham, Buckinghamshire premises, taking a former RPC fitter called John McDonnell with me as Mac's job at Rugby had concerned the discharge equipment.

I could not believe just how much attention and exact detail had gone into the completed work, and so took several photos of my own for posterity. Although much rebuilding and general repainting etc had been done, a tank body was acquired from the Barrington Cement Works near Cambridge.

Here, again judging by the completed lorry featured below the finished job ranks as near perfect, even to my own well experienced eye. The tank came from a B series 6 wheeler chassis, and whilst it still was of 15 ton capacity, the tipping frame has had to be modified slightly to fit the 8-wheeler chassis. Outwardly there appears to be little change other than that of a single Edbro tipping ram. Sheer elegance are two words which immediately come to mind.

Countless hundreds of former RPC bulk drivers will, I'm pretty sure, agree with my own sentiments, purely and simply because few, if any faults are visible. Full marks to both Richard Nixon and to Robert Wells for undertaking such an extraordinary feat and coming up with this beautiful result. There will be few, if any, people who will disagree with my thoughts. This superb restoration is testament to all ex RPC drivers, together with the Rugby Cement Company, which had such an effect on the roads of Britain for many years. These Vintage lorries are not going to amass great mileages so you can expect to see them in use and action for a while yet.

Another member of the ERF L/V batch of rigid 8 wheeler chassis supplied to RPC Transport is BWD 68J, one of three lorries registered in March 1971 for bulk tanker operation. The regular driver of F/N 700 was Pete Bradley, who was termed a "speed freak"! Not content to sit almost on your tail, at the first opportunity he'd get past you then slow down to the regulation speed of 25 mph before passing the one in front. 68J was purchased by Steven Stokes, and converted by him into an artic unit. Eight wheelers have, for years, provided the best base idea for use as fifth wheel operated chassis, but it took showmen to convince the general road transport industry what benefits could be gained.

Shown below, whilst undergoing modification the clean lines of the ERF L/V cab/chassis are there for everyone to see.

It's a rainy day as the Satellite ride, just visible, is moved on to the next ground. This photo was taken by the late John Crumpton of Brierley Hill, Staffordshire, who was well known to Anthony Harris, the Jones family of Cradley Heath and other Showland families in the immediate area. 68J would later be painted in a pleasing combination of red upper and crimson lower surfaces, including the wheels. Yellow lettering on bold capital letters advertises the Satellite ride equipment.

Every picture tells a story, as the saying goes! People who know me well will not be totally surprised when I say old Rugby Cement ERFs never die, they only gradually fade away. Parked out of use shortly after being last used in 1992, ex F/N 907 has not moved for close on twenty one years. Supplied new to RPC Transport at some point in 1969, it was one of eight similarly numbered 900 series' of L/V cabbed ERF bulk tankers, all of which were sent to Chinnor Cement Works in Oxfordshire between May 1967 and June 1969.

F/N 907 was destined to give between twelve and thirteen years service to Chinnor Works before being sold out of service use in early 1983 and purchased by Jimmy Wheatley and Son, who are showmen who work within the Leicestershire / North areas. They fitted box bodywork in keeping with their occupation. Later on, a Luton head was fitted to increase all over storage. This ERF was last used and photographed by Brenda Carlisle at the 1992 Truck fest-Peterborough event. This picture is by my own hand (author) and was taken by me in September 2009. By my own reference, this ERF is now upwards of forty years old, and still on its original Gardner 150.

Having been parked out of use for about twenty two years or more now, it is currently up for sale at £1,200 but Jimmy's son is rather reluctant to see the old girl go! Having seen for myself the cab is totally original, as is the underbody chassis, apart from a few missing lamp glass and bulbs. When I first started researching for part One of the story, I was pointed in the direction of Stapleton Lane (Showmen Quarters) at Barwell, Leicestershire from where I would eventually find five ex RPC ERF 8 wheelers. UNX 114G shown above is still at Barwell, patiently waiting.

Shown overleaf is former F/N 664 and registered UAC 560G. In July 1969, the ERF L/V 8 wheeler carried chassis number 17840. When fully fitted out with its bulk tank, and necessary blower / discharge equipment had been tested, this ERF, after the painting and lettering were complete, was delivered up to South Ferriby Cement Works in North Lincolnshire. Given new to driver George Castle, it carried a Murfitt built tank which had a nearside front mounted catwalk ladder. 664 was one of a batch of at least a dozen similarly fitted ERF bulkers. We had 666/667 at Rugby in later years. George drove 664 for almost twelve or thirteen years before the chassis was removed from fleet service and all re-usable parts were removed. The ERF cab/chassis was then disposed of via Charlie Watts, the Rugby based scrap merchant, who I know now was to handle more than 40 ex RPC ERFs, most of which were resold to showmen. UAC 560G was purchased by John

Scarrott, a Northamptonshire showman, whose transport continues to present itself to the public in the best possible sense, as it is an absolute delight to see and admire. 560G was fitted with pick up style bodywork and repainted in a dual cream/white, almost yellow livery with brown, red and gold stripes. Charging engines were mounted in the bodywork along with other items necessary for the travelling showman. The photograph shown on the right was taken in 1984 by Justin Glennon whilst the fair itself was on site at the Weston Favell car park on the outskirts of Northampton. Apart from the fitting of an A Series ERF front panel this 1969 chassis remained totally original. John Scarrott used 560G for well over eighteen years, during which time I visited his yard on two occasions over at Woodford Halse near Daventry. John's brother-in-law at that time told me that if John had asked him to take "The Old Girl" (as she was known to everyone at Scarrotts) to Scotland the old ERF 8 wheeler would have been perfectly capable of completing that journey. Sadly, in the late 1990s because of increased traffic numbers, together with really impossible conditions on the roads, the family very reluctantly put 560G up for sale.

She was purchased for £600 by Pete Smith of nearby Toll Bar Commercials, whose premises were on the Banbury Road, just three miles from Southam Cement Works. Later on, with Pete's agreement, I advertised this grand old ERF via REVs (Register of ERF Vehicles) in their newsletter for sale again at £600.

Alan Mitchell, of Weymouth in Dorset, then purchased UAC 560G for preservation. In the ten years or more since Alan acquired this grand old ERF a complete chassis change has occurred whereby UAC 560G has been rebuilt into a 24 foot platform lorry whilst still retaining much of her originality (as shown below). British engineering is therefore shown at its very best simply because other than the extended

chassis change, everything else remains 100% original. Over the past ten to eleven years of ownership Alan has sourced parts from around the United Kingdom in an effort to keep and present his ERF in its entirety. He is to be heartily congratulated for his efforts, which include a nice touch for those of us who are ex RPC drivers, in that the former fleet number is tastefully included as the telephone number seen on both quarter light panels. A simple effect of overall grey paintwork complements both the red wheels and chassis with a white roof finishing off a superb result. F/N 664 started life as a short wheel based ERF 8 wheeler bulk tanker. It had the same driver from new, almost until the end of its Rugby Cement service, which totalled nearly twelve years from 1969 possibly up until the 1980s. This ERF, in Alan's ownership, has since won many accolades at rallies in the South of England. I'd like to think in a small way that I (author) have had a hand in a success so richly deserved.

RPC Transport had more of its fair share of characters or individuals, all of whom had one thing in common, whether they worked days or nights. Whatever they did in connection with their respective jobs, the element of raw humour was always at the forefront of every occasion.

Jack Howell was a bulk driver on 8 wheeler ERFs based at South Ferriby. His real claim to fame started when he reversed into the toilets at the Sandtoft Tiles Plant at Goxhill. This was one of Ferriby's regular drops. Nobody was sure if the toilets were occupied when this happened. They certainly weren't when somebody went to investigate afterwards! Jack Howell took some time to live down his folly. Later on he received a 6 wheeler ERF bulker which he drove until his official retiring age; this was F/N 283. He then worked on for a year or two, driving the Ferriby minibus/van before finally calling it a day. When I qualified on to artics (author) in 1988, I met his son, John Howell, who was a bulk loader on nights, when I visited South Ferriby. We shared an interest in model cars, which in turn forged an early friendship. Needless to say, I have never seen Ferriby Cement Works during daylight hours!

Mick Lowe also makes reference to F/N 271. During his time on nights, travelling down to Rugby works one night, he had to stop at Swinderby and wrap the engine bonnet cover around his legs because he was so cold. His comments still ring in my ears, in that this was the downside of a Gardner, they always ran cold! Mick Lowe's own "claim to fame" happened one night later on when he was running SR bulk from Ferriby to Chinnor Works in Oxfordshire. He stopped for a break in the former long lay-by on the A43, not far from the American base at Upper Heyford. Not taking too much notice of a parked car at the end of a layby, Mick got on with more urgent needs of getting his flask and sandwiches out. Finally, engrossed in his newspaper, and with a full belly etc, he was interrupted by a sharp knock on the cab door. The reader must, however, be aware that this was the dead of night, on what then was a fairly busy road. Mick opened his door to find the car owner saying to him "Driver, you are far too early. The "Toms" don't get down here from Northampton until after midnight". Needless to say, Mick sent the man away with more than a flea in his ear.

Another South Ferriby man (on nights) was Albert Sillitoe, who thought rather absentmindedly that through his actions he could perhaps make extra money selling a multitude of goods from wherever, to his fellow workers. He stopped one night, on the way back from a second delivery to Leeds depot with bulk cement, to pick what he thought were turnips. "I can flog them to anyone at Ferriby" he thought. He was to be both sorely aghast and disappointed when he could not find any takers. What he thought in the dark were turnips turned out to be sugar beet!

Tony Foster started with RPC Transport at Leeds Depot in 1972, spending almost sixteen years on the night shift as a charge hand / relief driver before he left on redundancy in 1988. He informed me that Leeds handled a fair amount of cement in bags, something I was not aware of. He mentioned names from his past with Rugby, which included those of Sid Blackburn, Derek Heavysides and Chris Plowman. Derek was a former Pickfords bulk powder driver, and so fitted in well at Rugby Cement regarding pressure discharge etc. According to Tony, apart from the day shift / office staff etc, there were six night drivers and a yard man plus relief charge hands. Loaded bag lorries, as well as bulk tankers, which came in five nights a week from South Ferriby cement works, all had to be unloaded. In some cases, next day's deliveries in bags were reloaded and everyone mucked in to get the job done. Over many years, Tony and Mick Lowe, whose story follows, became good friends. I'm reliably informed since by Tony, however, that Mick Lowe's spending habits often came in for serious discussion. Tony also mentioned that one or two ERF 8-wheelers were also known for characteristics which faced drivers who were unfamiliar with them. F/N 202, a long wheel based bulk lorry, was known as the "Ghost Train". When you went over a bump in the road, the off side flashers flashed, and the engine bonnet cover lifted off. Side lights also flickered on and off until everything settled down. I remain indebted to Tony Foster for all of this information which, along with 70% of this second publication, is what RPC was all about.

Terry Golder

I started driving for Rugby Portland Cement at the Chinnor Works in early May 1970. I was then 24 years old. I had been driving a TK Bedford for a local joinery firm for four years previously. The first lorry I drove for RPC was a Commer 2 stroke 8 ton pressure vehicle. This was sent to scrap eighteen months later. I then drove an ERF 15 ton, fleet number 901, registration number LUD 679E for eight years. This is shown above right with me alongside taken at Benson Sands in April 1978.

This ERF chassis formed the backbone of RPC bulk vehicles and many clocked unbelievable mileages on their original Gardner 150 engines. These ERFs were destined to spend further years hard service in second ownership as fairground transport or heavy recovery units, before finally being cut up.

Five years later on, Terry switched to an S80 Foden 8-wheeler pressure lorry, fleet number 427, and carrying registration number CVC 182T. I had this one for five years, until one Christmas when we returned after the holiday to find that Rugby had exchanged 6 bulk tankers for 6 platformed lorries: two eight wheelers and four six wheelers. At that particular time, none of the regular drivers of the missing bulk lorries were pleased, but after a few weeks on bag lorries we enjoyed the change, as we had a lot more variety in our deliveries: from London to Bridport, Dorset, on the South Coast.

My lorry then was a B Series ERF, fleet number 551, with registration number MAC 316V. I drove this lorry until I went on the owner driver scheme in 1988. I enjoyed driving for RPC and am proud of the fact that in my eighteen years of company service I was never involved in an accident.

Two photos of Terry's Foden S80 eight wheeler are shown overleaf showing two different regular bulk delivery customer plants. Both photos refer to F/N 427, fitted with Foden's own twelve speed gearbox – for drivers finding themselves on these for perhaps a single day's work, the gearbox took a bit of getting used to!

Bradley's Concrete, within the Ashton Keynes, Gloucestershire, complex, was just one of several concrete / mixer plants which saw RPC lorries from both the Chinnor and Rugby works almost every day. Bradleys specialised in the production of kerbs and slabs and other concrete based items. Possibly two loads per day were likely to be delivered from Chinnor when the production of mixed items was at its height, whereby one in the morning would be followed by a late afternoon delivery. The strength of the single ram can perhaps be imagined in this excellent view showing the bulk tank almost empty of its load.

Almost at the same level of discharge by pressure, F/N 427 is shown below within the confines of the Redland Cement Plant at Denham in Middlesex. How long is it since we have seen Leyland lorries with the Boxer cab design in use as a concrete mixer? Equally so, the former Redland fleet livery is like so many good things of the past – gone forever.

In the earlier story of Terry Golder (an ex Chinnor driver), I described his adventures with CVC 182T F/N 427, sister to 428, shown opposite. Shown overleaf is a lorry line up. All bulk tankers seen are parked by the railway in Chinnor Cement Works. F/N 432, another S80 thirty ton chassis is in the lead, followed by an ERF 6 wheeler, F/N 427, plus two more Foden S108s and a second ERF six wheeler. This line up of loaded lorries was taken over a weekend, the lorries being ready for the off on the following Monday.

These photos give a better appreciation of these S80 Foden cabs remembered mainly by their dinner plate headlamps, which sorted this particular Foden design out from other models. The spaciousness of these cabs is shown here to good effect with a front view of Pete Bradley's Rugby Work's based CVC 184T, F/N 428, as it sits proud in this front row shot taken by Tony Higgins during a summer evening in 1979.

Personally speaking, when I was allocated a day on one of these twelve speed gearboxed mammoths I, like so many of my bag colleagues, played a merry tune trying to find the right gear!

Shown overleaf is a very different photo of DDU 541T after it was sold out of fleet use, possibly after the early 1980s. This is the same lorry at the head of the Chinnor line-up, DDU 541T, minus its rear axle, plus mirror glass and heads and the once famous Rugby Cement livery. Seen as Scrapyard fodder somewhere, it does look a sorry sight, but please note that the cab structure remains crack free. Perhaps someone could save it for the ranks of preservation! I do know that none of the thirty one Foden S80 bulk eight wheel bulk chassis which served RPC Transport survived into second ownership of any kind.

The kindness of everyone who worked in and around Chinnor Cement Works is remembered by me (author) during the many visits I made there, both with stock loads of bags, and later on when we were all involved with the M40 motorway construction. Close friendships were made with both John, better known to his colleagues as "Twinkle", and Chris Preece. John was typical of Chinnor's drivers, being one of the nicest and politest drivers I have ever met. In turn, he later introduced me to Vic Mulcock, who sadly died many years back. Between the efforts of these two gentlemen, I was therefore able to tell the true story of Chinnor Cement and Lime Transport. Almost every visitor to Chinnor remembers the sheer kindness of the staff as in the course of the job, nothing it seemed nor appeared, was ever too much trouble. If you, as the visitor, ventured into the Work's Canteen, the staff there went out of their way to attend to your requirements. Friendships sprung up with "the twins" Bill and John Ayre. I was later to build a C Series ERF bulk tanker model for John. I often wonder if he still has it, but more about that subject later. Much later on, the end for Chinnor came in 2008, when the entire works areas were dismantled. Like so many of

the Rugby Cement Works, the chimneys were local landmarks for decades. Ordinary people could tell how the weather was going to be each day by the direction of the steam emerging from the chimneys. Travellers on the nearby M40 motorway, along with local people used to seeing it every day, were like many, sorry to see it go. Almost one hundred years of cement and lime making finished for ever. Now there is nothing.

The first time visitor to Chinnor Cement Works could be forgiven for thinking "Am I on the right road?", as he or she coasted into the works on the approach road. If the railway engine was coming towards them the temporary misconception was caused by the parallel line of the road and the railway running alongside each other going further into the works.

The general approach and first time effect of the vastness of the site is better appreciated by the photograph shown opposite.

The prominence of the three works chimneys harks back to quite some years ago, but in evidence everything is where it should be. Memories for many drivers visiting, or indeed leaving Chinnor can be instantly recalled. Shown is a departing ERF 6-wheeler tanker with its driver barely recognisable about to enter the Transport office on the left hand side. The first two sizeable buildings visible in the centre of this superb illustration were the transport garage and workshop, and the attached building just under the silo on its left was used for many years as covered parking for Chinnor Transport lorries. This is a tremendous picture, remembering Chinnor Cement

Chinnor Cement Works 1979. Courtesy of the Railway Magazine

Works as it appeared to all visitors.

Graham Munday, a former Chinnor Cement works chargehand fitter in the garage, provides memories with a capital M when he shares an incident with you, the reader! Despatched to the MOT station at Launton, near Bicester, he'd entered the village of Launton on the back road where contractors were engaged in digging out the ditches and road edges in preparation for laying GPO telephone cables. Graham was piloting F/N 852 which carried registration JAC 479N, as shown on the right. Whilst negotiating the roadworks, 852 fell into the ditch as shown! I'm readily assured by Graham that 852 was towed out of her predicament by Fivealls Garage with little or no visible mechanical damage. It was washed down on site by the paddies, then Albert Church, the tyre fitter at Chinnor changed a wheel/tyre embedded in mud. Although the exhaust pipe had bent slightly on impact, after this was put right, Graham was able to continue with his journey to Launton MOT station, whereby 852 passed with flying colours. In the official fleet lists appertaining to all RPC Transport Sales Delivery lorries, 852 F/N carried JAC 679N. This error was carried by 852 for almost three years before someone in higher authority noticed. F/N 852 was one of the first batch of 30 ton bulk chassis which preceded the eventual use of ERF B Series. Ron Ludlow, a long serving driver at Chinnor, was the regular steering wheel attendant of this lorry.

Mick Lowe – South Ferriby Transport – Sept 1973 to Dec 1987

I started with the Company in September 1973 and was to be employed as a night driver, although the system then in place was that you started as a night driver until there was a vacancy on the day shift. Such vacancies, when they became available, were offered to the longest serving night driver, and if he did not want it it went down the list until someone said yes. My first week of employment was spent on being taught how to discharge (blow) a bulk tanker. I was put with a driver called Jim Burt whose daily lorry was ERF 8 wheeler NUE 116F. This carried F/N 246. This was for almost a decade. The basic 24 ton gross vehicle chassis allowed for a straight fifteen ton load to be carried; if you managed to blow 256 then as time went on you would learn to cope with most of the fleet. Of course, in just six days you only learned the basics, whilst making mistakes but if you listened and asked the old hands, you eventually became as good at it as the other drivers.

Being a night driver had its own merits, whereby you never had your own lorry, you drove whatever you were allocated for that night. Also, I was working with a good crew, plus the fact I saw more of my young daughter by being on nights than I would have done if I had been on days. At that time Rugby had a satellite depot at Cross Green in Leeds. Consequently, the main workload of a Ferriby night driver was keeping Leeds fully stocked up. Most weeks night duties involved two trips to Leeds, or one night going down to Rugby to do stock transfers or take lorries down for tank repairs or repainting etc. If you were on a later shift, you might also take time expired lorries back to Rugby and bring a brand new vehicle back up to Ferriby.

I spent almost fourteen years working for Rugby on nights, with the odd week on days at Bank Holiday time. During that time, one or two incidents of note took place, the most memorable being when I was involved in a serious traffic accident which resulted in me having several months off work. Rugby Cement, being the Company such as they were known for, did not forget employees off on long term sick or recovery. Consequently, if Mr Harvey, the RPC Transport Manager, or one of his Assistant Managers, visited Ferriby, they always made it a point to call on these employees at home to ask if things were going as well as could be expected. If you were off at Christmas, as I was, they left you a little something from the Chairman in an envelope. Such gestures are not forgotten.

At certain times, we found ourselves going to works or depots and consequently this work was shared between the different shifts so that all night drivers had a break from supplying Leeds Depot. Later on, we started running to Southam and Barrington Cement Works near Cambridge, and still later, we went to Birmingham on fairly regular trips. Visits to Chinnor Cement Works came later. This work came in earnest to these R/C works and depots mainly because Ferriby produced special cement not made at the other works. These trips involved stock transfers. Night work did not always involve bulk tank work. We also delivered bag loads to various works and depots where, unless it was a lorry or trailer changeover, it meant that the load had to be "hand-balled" off. This kept you fit! Other work consisted of delivering to concrete plants and sites where 24 hour working was the norm. All of this was my nightly diet of work which, on the whole I enjoyed. When Rugby brought in the ICH / owner / driver scheme, I took the decision to leave under voluntary redundancy, and left one of the best firms I have ever worked for finishing on New Year's Eve 1987.

After several years away from the cement industry, I am now back, driving at South Ferriby. But it is not Rugby Cement, instead it is Cemex, a global company, who acquired RMC/Rugby Cement – so in a way I am doing a job back in an industry I like!

My (author) years as a driver with RPC Transport produced many friends over the years, and since. Through redundancy from the company and beyond, I have made very many more, as it was always my serious intention to write about both the lorries and the people who made up RPC Transport and the parent company, Rugby Portland Cement, alike.

During my first winter season at Rugby Works, in late 1968, I was to become acutely aware of a character called Barney, who did a variety of jobs in the Yard Gang, but whose main job was to drive the mobile crane. His real name was Bryan Leslie Barnacle, but to his colleagues at Rugby Cement Works he was known simply as Barney. Fortunately he was blessed with a superb sense of both proportion and humour, two characteristics which, in later years, were to prove of enormous comfort to ordinary people. Although Barney started working for RPC in 1967, a year before I did myself, he was popular with colleagues, drivers and the works management, all of whom regarded him as a model employee and friend. In 1977 he was found to have arthritis of the spine, and was advised by his doctor to find alternative employment. It was about this time that Barney, after much consideration and thought, transferred into Crown House as the Commissionaire, as the previous gentleman had retired. Barney had voiced his thoughts about having to wear a suit and tie with his wife Shirley, mainly because he was an outdoor man. However, as time went on, both he and Bob Brown, another Commissionaire, shared varied duties. A change of direction by RPC was to dispense with Commissionaires, and so Barney worked in various other Crown House departments such as reception and the mail room. Later on, both he and Shirley were in charge of security. Over the years, I was to see and meet Barney while he was a patient in St Cross Hospital. Even when I was preparing Book One, I remember him shouting to me from his bed in the ward "I want a copy Mac please, when it's finished". Barney retired officially from the cement company in 1996, and although I was to see him and Shirley on odd occasions within the town, I and hundreds of other local and not so local people were to be extremely grateful to this man for all the correct reasons. In his capacity as a volunteer at St Cross Hospital his superb sense of humour and acceptance was to come to the fore when he put ordinary patients waiting for treatment or operations, completely at ease. Barney and Shirley, together with their son Neil, were only to share nine years of retirement, when he died in St Cross Hospital. The loss of Barney Barnacle to his wife and son was tragic in every sense of the word. Friends, work colleagues and the nurses and staff at St Cross Hospital, all of whom, including myself, attended his funeral along with Crown House Staff, proved beyond a shadow of a doubt that he was an individual who earned the respect and admiration of many. My thanks go to Mrs Shirley Barnacle for her assistance in producing this tribute to Barney.

Starting work in the garage at Southam Cement Works in the official capacity as night maintenance operator, Bert Perry was to become better known in later years, after being transferred to Parkfield Road Garage in Rugby Cement Works, as "Bert the Oiler". He was born Hubert William Perry in 1920 and he was a widower who, when he died, had two sons and two daughters. I, like many of my colleagues, often saw Bert checking lorry engines for oil and topping up radiators with water. Never one to conform to rules or regulations, Bert often came into confrontation with Ken Harvey (the Transport Manager) during one of his rare visits to Rugby Works, whereby Ken would suggest to Bert that cycling down to work in just a vest and overalls was perhaps not the right way to present Rugby Cement to the general public. Bert Kemp was an individual who had a preference for doing things his own way, and as politely as he was able to, he informed Ken Harvey that if he (KH) was not satisfied with the way that Bert did the job for which he was paid, then Bert would leave his employment with RPC Transport. Needless to say, Ken Harvey was, for the moment, both taken aback and speechless. Nevertheless, he told Bert that he wanted him to continue on with his job.

All drivers, from both the day and night shifts, had good cause to have Bert Kemp on their side, simply because he stuck to his guns and his priorities. He would not let anyone change his mind, even those from higher authority. For this simple, honest act of self righteousness, all the drivers stood by him with total respect. RPC drivers were required by Company law, in every 24 hours of operations, to check their lorries for oil/water/tyres etc. Somehow Bert got to know when your lorry was due for a service or MOT and he would inform you accordingly. I never forgot Bert Kemp's kindness to me in early 1976 after an appalling crash on the M1 when my KM Bedford Platform was severely damaged after a rear end collision which ultimately caused me to be off work for a few days. After the lorry had been repaired, and I returned to work, he came up to me and said "I am glad that you are OK. It's nice to see you back at work". Bert Kemp went everywhere on his old bike. His passion was gardening, and he managed two large allotments over Dunchurch way. Sadly, Bert was also one of the first redundancies at some point in 1984 as we, the Bag Men, had transferred to Southam Works two years previous. I only saw him now and then, still on his bike. Twenty one years in semi-retirement were to pass for Bert Perry before he was sadly knocked off his bike by an impatient car driver just by Rugby School playing field corner in 2005. He never really recovered from terrible head injuries, spending almost a year in Rugby Hospital before he died.

Bert Perry had a wonderful sense of proportion, he would do anything for anybody. As far as I know he did his job efficiently and without fuss. His departure from RPC Transport robbed the Company of an exceptional individual.

This photograph opposite shows all of Rugby Works colleagues with whom I was to work alongside between 1968 and 1982. I transferred to Southam with my fellow bag drivers when the Rugby Bag Shed shut its doors for the last time in July 1982.

Safe Driving Awards 1976

Each of the people shown in this photograph were individual characters and therefore it has been necessary to list each man's unique qualities separately.

Over the years since this photograph was taken at the Safe Driving Dinner / Awards Ceremony a good number of these individuals have passed away. This does not detract from explaining each individual's moods and attitudes over each working day during my fourteen years' service with Rugby Works.

Rugby Works - Transport Drivers
Back row, reading left to right

Roy Bates
One of the longest serving drivers, whose time with the company totalled nearly thirty years. His nickname was "Woofer". His preference for PV work stemmed from his early years on bags. He told me "sweating" was not in his contract.

Terry Turner
He came to us from Travis / Arnolds. Never one for hard work, he soon transferred on to PV Tankers, but his expression on a daily basis gave a hollow view. Sadly he died before the 1980s.

Johnny Cant
Another long server who gave many years service to RPC Transport. He was a darts and skittles player in his spare time. His death occurred whilst I was still at Rugby Works. He was very sadly missed.

RW Jenkins
Not a driver, but there to present the drivers with their medals. He was a Director of Rugby Cement, and a guest of honour.

Reg Coles
His head is just visible between Mr Jenkins and Harry Baker. Reg gave RPC Transport many years of service. He had connections with both the church and the village of Dunchurch. When the Central Garage opened he became a retained driver before final retirement. Never one for swearing or bad language, I often wondered how he coped there!

Harry Baker
Formerly Southam Works Manager, he took over at Rugby Works and completely turned it around. Something of a strict manager, he only had one eye, but never missed a thing!

Fred Saunders
His head is just visible behind Mr Baker. Rugby's longest bag driver with years of service, he could NEVER get up in the mornings. He only lived half a mile from the cement works. He and I became good friends, and remained so until he passed away in 2013.

Sid Cave
He always had a new joke to tell, and was one of the nicest drivers I've ever worked with. Both his lorries and his cars were always immaculate. Sadly he passed away in 2009.

Taffy Roberts
A lovely Welshman (one of three at that time), Bryn transferred into the lab where he stayed until voluntary redundancy.

Albert Kimberley
Better known to one and all as "The Fugitive", he was always on his own, never mixing with colleagues. Both he and his wife moved to Spain on "doctor's orders" for her as she required a warmer climate healthwise.

Chris Moon
Or Moony as he was better known. Well respected by both drivers and management alike, Chris' lorries were always immaculate. He was (and still is) my good friend. Always something of a joke player, wearing an old coat and wig he convinced supervisors and bosses alike that he was after a job at RPC Transport. There was Hell to pay afterwards!

Alan Caldwell
Son of Bob Caldwell, Alan did not stay long at RPC before leaving for pastures new. After 2001 I met both him and Bruce Linford (also ex RPC) at Asda Supermarket. They were still there in 2008 when I finally took retirement.

Pete Bunyard
Three members of the family were to serve RPC: Albert (Pete's dad), Pete and Barry. Peter served as an Owner / Driver before retirement. Pete's lorries were always smart and well looked after.

Bob Reynolds
His head is visible between Pete and Graham Woods. He came to RPC along with Alec Watts and others. They drove L/V ERF 8 wheel tankers. Mad as March hares!...up your exhaust one minute, and then creeping along in front at regulation speed of 25mph!

Graham Woods
He came to RPC in the early 1970s, but had gone before the late 70s to work as a painter of houses.

Ken Whyment
Almost forty years plus, most of it as a nights driver, were to occupy Ken's RPC life. In time he became the most Senior Driver. Now retired, and still living in Lilbourne with his wife, his days are spent caravanning.

Ron Sheasby
He looks fairly young in this

photo. When I began in 1968, both he and Pete Bunyard drove 4-wheel Maxiload Commer Tankers.

Still on the back row, we come to **"Bristol Smith"**.
Famous, as such, for smoking Bristol cigarettes. If your watch or clock broke down, he was magic with them. His memories of buying a "five foot wingspan turkey" one Christmas are never ever forgotten.

Brian Stretford

His head is just visible above Ken Wright's head. Brian came to us from the Post Office, and soon proved that he could look after lorries. Much of his service would be spent on 6 wheel square fronted (styled) ERFs after 1976.

John Hughes

He lived in the Nuneaton / Bedworth area, and always came to work each morning in a rush! He did not stay with us for very long, but was kept on 4 wheel bulk lorries for all of that time.

Tony Hall

One of the nicest, but funniest, drivers I've ever worked with. Like me, he was on Bags, and survived with all of us who transferred to Southam in 1982. Sadly into his second year with a Seddon Atkinson 6-wheel flat, he was to suffer a terrible accident at Bland's Builders in Rugby when he fell off the top of the load. Seriously injured, he never really recovered. An ex Redland Tiles driver, his humour was superb.

Pat Garrat

A member of Rugby Work's unique Night drivers, he was from a large family, but I always reckoned him to be a bit of a loner. Being on regular days, I never saw much of him. His Irish humour did occasionally come up trumps!

Alan Bloxham

Dougie Cleavers' next door neighbour for many years, he too was on nights, and blessed with regular moans and humour when the need arose.

Don Bell

Yet another night driver, though only for a short period. Married for a time to Charlie Bailey's daughter who worked in the Works Canteen, he was one of the first Owner / Drivers.

Dick Smith

Dick was the Despatch Office Supervisor. He was in charge of all drivers after Jack Brain retired. He and I got on better after differences were sorted out. An ex driver who knew all the fiddles, not much got past him. Retired more than twenty years, and in his nineties now, he remembers his years with RPC as extremely happy times.

Front row, reading left to right

Billie Jenner

One of the nicest drivers I ever worked with. Originally from the East Coast of "'ave you got a light boy" fame, Billie gave many years to RPC Transport. He also became an Owner/Driver before retiring. He and his wife have houses in both Rugby and Ireland.

John Heritage

Better known as "Buddy", and on bags with us for many years, John also became an Owner / Driver. Now retired, and still living in Rugby, he retains his sense of proportion and humour.

Peter Gudgin

Words can't express the humour which followed "Branch", as he was perhaps better known. Along with his fellow retained driver and colleague, Sid Cave. Both Branch and Sid, with many years' service, were each given a week's notice in 1985 at the start of redundancies. Peter Gudgin's life was RPC Transport, and he never got over being made redundant and died of a broken heart.

Billy Barber
One half of the union to Reg Price, both argued the toss with all and sundry. Billy left to run a Public House in the Wellingborough area.

Fred Seamer
Another long serving driver, and formerly an East Kent bus driver, he was well respected by everyone. Fred, Wooffer Bates, Dennis Garlick and Pete Gudgin all cycled into work for 6am starts.

Dave "Nobby" Clarke
One of the most charismatic drivers at Rugby. A bit of a fiddler in his early days, but well respected by all of his mates.

Charlie Smith
He was always pushing his glasses up. He stayed on 8-wheeler "bulk" right up to B Series ERF lorries.

Johnny Foster
A crafty ex-driver who drove the Cube-Van, mainly on behalf of the Work's lab, he'd wait at any of RPC's favourite watering holes, then you'd find him breathing down your neck pleading thirst.

Ken Wright
Never off sick, never late, Ken was one of those rare drivers whose life was RPC Transport. Long since retired, and still living in Rugby, he sadly lost his wife more than ten years back.

Bill "Happy" Alder
A more miserable looking individual you'd never meet. Hence his nick name! He drove the mail car right up to retirement. Smiling wasn't in his contract!

The drivers mentioned who'd opted for the Owner / Driver Scheme, did so after the eventual disbanding of RPC Transport in 1991.

I make no secret of the fact that after being transferred to Southam Works in 1982, along with my fellow bag driver colleagues, I personally wished that I'd done it before. The relaxed atmosphere in all of the areas within the works appealed to me greatly. One of the reasons, I think, was that Southam was ten miles away from Crown House and all the rest of the management.

From previous visits made by me in my capacity "on bags", I'd already made many friends, many of whom in their own way personified or contributed their own brand of twisted humour. The following selection of photos, taken unofficially by Tim Griffin, a chargehand fitter at Southam Garage, illustrate exactly why "work" with RPC Transport was enjoyable. The work always got done, but humour helped often.

In the photo opposite Bill Crawford is on the left. He was known to all and sundry as "Gladys"! Here he is shown at tea break in the old garage mess room, along with Maurice Golding, and Southam Garage's resident tyre fitter, ex driver Dougie Tombes. Maurice was one of those drivers whose normal temperament was dubious at times, but he looked after lorries in his care like nothing else. He was later to transfer on to nights when his family grew in size. His words to me were "I needed the extra money". Dougie Tombes on the far right was the tyre fitter. If he came out to your assistance when you had a flat tyre, his raucous type of laughter and his general approach to any situation had you doubled up with uncontrollable laughter. But in the end the job was completed and you went on your way. Jock Crawford and Titch Partington travelled daily from Rugby Garage to supplement the Southam Garage staff. When Titch took retirement he was replaced by Fred Adams for an indefinite period. This arrangement continued up until

Jock himself retired. Sadly, like Titch before him, Jock did not enjoy retirement long enough before he sadly died.

Another photo which came from Tim's camera shows Roger Sandford. Originally a driver, somehow over the years, certainly just before I joined the company, Roger engineered himself a job of filling up returning lorries at the diesel pump. All gallons were (or had to be) meticulously recorded in a book. Later Roger was put in charge of the vehicle stores. If you wanted bulbs or dusters he would give you just one so I personally soon learned to seek the assistance of the fitters. When he retired from the company Roger, who lived in the "model Village" opposite the cement works, could often be found walking into Southam "New Garage" most days to visit.

Clive Mumford (already mentioned within this story) had been garage foreman at Southam for more years than I could remember. Often being on the receiving end of Clive's misdirected sense of humour, he was never happier himself than when he was taking the mickey out of most of the drivers. He encouraged his fitters to do the same, or so it appeared to me. Clive's basic job as Garage Foreman was to supervise all work undertaken by his staff, both on days and nights. The hardest physical job he encountered every day was that of opening his sandwich box, and judging by the photo shown above this mild form of exertion exhausted his strength.

RPC Transport operated around twenty TSVs based on Ford Transit Chassis. They carried pick up body style designs with drop-down tail boards. Known as Transport Service Vehicles, they were used as garage fitter's runabouts. Tyre fitters attended puncture callouts with them. Most of them were fitted with bench seats, and Clive's after dinner nap is recorded here for posterity. Whilst we should be grateful to Tim Griffin for his achievements as a photographer, he cannot escape the written description of another comedian from "Mumford's Gang". Tim Griffin learned his profession of vehicle fitter when he worked for Jack Saunders Transport at nearby Long Itchington. When Saunders shut up shop Tim started at Southam garage in 1978. Previously mentioned in Part One, Tim and "Jock" Brown were forever taking the mickey out of each other. For whatever reason, it did not alter the fact that Tim was master of his trade.

Shown opposite in typical pose of "Hercules Unchained", the protruding belly shows a hidden capacity for beer, particularly if someone else was paying the bill. Tim Griffin, however, remains a very good friend of both myself and his night shift counterpart fitter Tony Higgins who was also often on the receiving end of Tim's jokes etc. By far the most popular individual on Southam Works about this time has to be Danny Burke (real name Terry) who sadly is no longer with us and merits more than a casual mention in this story. He was the Canteen Manager who, along with his long suffering assistant Henry King, looked after the needs of the day shift workers and the drivers.

When he got to know me a bit better, during which time both Chris Moon and Fred Saunders had pre-educated him about my spending habits, plus my "in-bred" Scottish aims to get value for money, he once said to me "I am not going to make my fortune out of you McBirnie", to which I replied "I come to work to make money, not to put it in your pocket". I tried exceptionally hard not to enter "Danny's Domain" as it was called, but when I did, out of sheer necessity, this unique man's superb sense of (often twisted) humour, came to the fore. Danny never missed an instance, like Clive Mumford, where he could niggle or annoy the drivers. He once referred to me as the biggest tight fisted Scotsman who walked this earth. I once picked up a newspaper in the canteen which had been left by a night shift worker, before I had time to open it Danny shouted at my saying "You did not pay for it, leave it alone. If you're not spending, leave the premises!". These ribald

remarks, and often serious sounding comments directed towards me were taken in the spirit of mickey taking, but to other individuals within earshot, I often wondered what they thought of "dear old Danny".

The late Kevin Billingham, me and Fruity Arthur Harris were the best of friends, but Kevin and I always appeared to be on the receiving end of Danny's tongue, so one day we decided to do something about it. One late afternoon, after we loaded bags for an early start the following day, we were roping and sheeting our lorries outside the canteen, which fortunately for us had just closed. The usual catcalls and impudent remarks about our ability to unload came from Danny at the canteen back window. I said to Kevin "You keep him talking" whilst I was out of sight of Danny around the corner. During this time I tied a piece of withered sheet rope to the rear of Danny's bike which was propped up against the canteen wall. I then tied the other end to the down pipe junction which carried excess water of the canteen roof. We then swapped places. I tidied up my lorry sheets for Danny's eyes, whilst Kevin turned his bike and saddle right round the wrong way. I then wiped cab windows and rear lights to waste a bit more time before the pair of us took our lorries down to the wash to fuel up ready for the next day.

Danny usually pushed off for home at around 4.30pm, or earlier if he could wangle things. We'd done and finished both jobs certainly by then, as I was in the garage talking to Tim Griffin when Danny came cycling and wobbling all over the road. He had a basket fitted to the front of his bike and I shouted that it was "only poofs who rode bikes with baskets". He damn near fell off, and almost collided with the kerb, but he shouted at me, "I've just had an accident and pulled half the roof off the canteen". It was a real effort for me to keep a straight face, but I learned later that Kevin got most of the blame! I shall remember Danny Burke for many things, best of all for his supreme sense of fun and laughter, so absolutely necessary when different types of men worked alongside one another.

Later on, when John Winfield's "crane crashed to the ground" in the new Bag Shed some years later when the cables holding his forklift crane snapped, I've since learned that Danny was one of the first on the scene comforting John as best he could before medical assistance arrived. At one of the last Town and Country Festivals I had Danny and his wife Sheila laughing so much as we remembered the good times at Rugby Cement. Danny died shortly afterwards. Perhaps he has since found his vocation in heaven, humouring the angels with his perverted sense of humour!

John Bousefield came to RPC Transport at some point in the 1960s. He was a Geordie by birth. His friend at that time was Ted Bean, also by then well trained in bulk cement delivery procedures. However, the point I am making concerned two very different individuals whose attitudes differed vastly. Ted Bean was constantly laughing and playing jokes on his fellow drivers. He also played in a band as a drummer. This in effect, was to have a disastrous effect on his RPC career as a driver, which I shall tell later in this story. John Bousefied, on the other hand, like the weather, could be both miserable or mildly happy, depending. Ted Bean began his time at RPC Transport by going out for a test drive on an ex Eastwood's Foden S18 cabbed 8-wheeler platform TLO 103 which carried F/N 491. This was fully loaded with fifteen ton of cement in sacks, and Dick Hudson accompanied Ted on his trial run. This started off straightforwardly enough in the direction of Rugby from Southam Cement Works, but on the return journey, a switch was made when coming down the Straight Mile (A4071) to Princethorpe crossroads. Ted passed muster and so began his bulk training with Ken Whyment, a long serving driver of many years standing. Ted remembers other names from more than forty years ago, like Monty Lloyd, Cliff Underhill and Les Timms.

Another driver who started about that time was John Baskot. John Bousefield and Ted Beam drove identical Murfitt bodied high cone backed bulk tankers. They had front mounted catwalk ladders and discharged cement powder a bit easier than the flat backed versions at that time. They were fleet numbers 666 and 667.

Shown below in his younger days parked outside his sister's house in Coventry, John Bousefield has a smile on his face, whilst UAC 882G shines! When I got to him later on, both him and Godfrey Noon were on bags together, and were very good friends. Later on, this pair had the first two Seddon Atkinson 557 and 558 palletised flats. Certainly, by 1982, John Bousefield opted for the Night Shift and was in charge of Southam Despatch Office. John Baskot, mentioned earlier, could never have been taken for a cement delivery driver because he was immaculate in both his personal and vehicle presentation. His same attention to cleanliness and presentation was lavished on all RPC Lorries under his care. Like John Bousefield did later on in his RPC Career, John Baskot started more or less straight away on nights. After his initial bulk training, he remembers working with George Greenaway. They were detailed to take a pair of loaded bulkers to Gloucester Depot. In those long forgotten days, the route was Southam, Stratford, Bidford, Evesham, on the A46 heading for the M5 just outside Tewkesbury. Once on the motorway, John exited at J12 for Gloucester and headed down the Ring Road to Hempsted where the RPC Depot was situated. He'd changed over to an empty lorry, and had a cup of tea before George Greenaway arrived. He'd had to carry on down to J14 Stroud before he could turn back for Gloucester.

One of the characters John Baskot came into contact with whilst on nights was the late John Ellis. John Ellis (before his untimely and tragic death within

the confines of Gloucester Depot) was the instigator of what would become the RPC Caravan Club. Both he and his wife convinced Harry and Dora Ryder how good caravanning was, so much so that Harry and Dora were to purchase their own van. Because of this joint enthusiasm and the fact that they wanted to interest other RPC people whose interests were in a similar vein they founded the club.

Names from these early years were to include Bill Izzard, the Night Garage Foreman at Southam. I remember he brought two different wives to RPC Caravan sites! Another member was Ken Whyment a long serving Rugby work nights driver. Alf Measy worked nights, both as a bulk loader and doubled in the despatch office. He had a Volkswagon camper with CHP on the registration. He was nicknamed the "Chips Man". Later on, with advertising within the company, more new members came forward. Roy and Rosemary Allen, Doug and Barbara Johnson. Eva Scales, who worked in Crown House, became a regular member with her husband. John and Chris Preece from Chinnor also appeared. Much later on a decision was taken to attract non RPC members but this was not acceptable to some. Dave Cooksey and his wife joined, as did Pete Walkins (a Travis / Arnold Driver) and his wife, also Dennis and Bett Garlick and their son Graham. I was destined to meet all of the RPC Caravan Club members at the Town and Country Festival events during the 1970s and 1980s.

John Baskot transferred on to the permanent day shift in 1971. At Southam he remembers Alfy Butler's horrendous accident at Harvington, near Evesham. Dougie Tombes, "the reincarnated tyre fitter" at Southam, nicknamed Alfy Butler as "Springhill Jack" on account of his bouncing step, which everyone could not help but notice. When Ted Bean learned bulk procedures, him and John Bousefield ran together for a short while. When John transferred onto bags, Ted stayed on bulk until his downfall which came later on. Both he and his wife Valerie have always been busy with their interests. Valerie is an amateur painter, whilst Ted rates music as his forte by playing in a rock band. He remains an accomplished drummer.

Bulk deliveries from both Rugby and Southam depended very much on reliable drivers turning up on time. John Baskot would remain on nights for around six years before he switched to regular day shift hours. During that time, however, Double Gloucesters were a basic night shift chore, but he also drove 801, a 30 ton platform lorry, taking stock bag loads, also to Gloucester. Later still, night bulk delivery runs to Sharpness Docks from Gloucester Depot made a nice change. I got to know John Baskot very much better after 1982. His nickname was "Stumpy" on account of smoking his cigarettes down to the last little bit. Both he and his wife, Mary, remained very good friends but sadly John Baskot died in 2013.

Ted Bean's real claim to fame concerned his love of playing the drums. Getting up very late from an early morning finish at 2.30am Ted, knowing that he had a 6am start at the cement works, did in fact not arrive at Southam until well after 7am that morning, having only been in bed for just under four hours. Sent off to the Redland Tiles plant at Leighton Buzzard, Bedfordshire, which for both Rugby and Southam bulk drivers was considered to be a good number, Ted arrived there possibly before 11am. After the usual booking in and coupling up the delivery pipes he was told to wait before starting to blow. So, as we all did, Ted went to sleep. Twenty minutes were to elapse before the sales attendant woke Ted up and told him to start blowing, which he did, raising the tank up two rams high. These were ordinary, everyday procedures for RPC bulk tanker captains at that particular time. Nothing was amiss, but Ted was quite simply overtired, and perhaps physically exhausted by the previous night's activities of band playing, and so went back to being sound asleep. The resultant "folly" was that he blew the top off the silo, and half of his load of bulk cement powder over the surrounding Redland Works before being woken up by a frantic silo attendant. The resultant mess was tremendous, for which there was no excuse, ie "sleeping on the job". Ted returned to Southam Works to find Albert Southam (Assistant Transport Manager) and Fred Williams, his boss (and Southam's own despatch manager) waiting for him. He was sacked on the spot!

Ted Bean went to work as a mixer driver for Smith's Concrete at Bubbenhall Plant near Coventry. He also worked, for a time, at Barford Plant near Warwick. Both plants were regular customer deliveries for Rugby bulk cement tankers and Ted was destined to remain with Smiths until retirement. He still plays drums in his spare time, and has lost none of the humour which has followed him around at both Rugby Cement and Smith's Concrete.

Both F/Ns 666 and 667 were moved to Rugby Works, where 666 was given to Owen "Taffy" Thomas, whilst 667 became the daily responsibility of Brian Stretford. When these two ERFs were finally removed from fleet service, 666 was cut up, but 667 was bought by a showman called Rennie Crick from North Derbyshire. UNX 668G is shown below in second ownership carrying box bodywork, which itself has a generating engine and other showman's necessary equipment. Painted with a pleasing red cab and chassis with front and rear box ends supporting cream sides, this ERF was destined to serve Rennie Crick faultlessly for a few years further (Chassis number 17729).

As previously said, many employees were to notch up tremendous periods of loyal service with Rugby Cement, none more so than Jack Skelcey, who started as a driver with RPC Transport in 1955, driving Thornycroft and Commer bag lorries. The photo of Jack shown right was taken by his daughter Maggie, on the last day of his service in June 1980. I have two black and white photos showing Jack with Commer bulk lorries in 1962. By the time this second book of mine on Rugby becomes available, Jack Skelcey would have been retired for twenty nine years or more since he last wore the RPC uniform. He was now in his early nineties, with failing eyesight, plus other factors of growing old gracefully which did not stop him and his wife Peggy from enjoying their double passion of rallying their Morris Minor car. He was

generally put in the centre of local Morris Club members when out on the road en route to rallies etc. (Sadly, Jack Skelcey passed away in 2010).

Shown below, F/N 825 given new in 1974 to Billie Jenner at Rugby 151N managed a very creditable eleven or twelve years on bulk duties before being sold out of service around 1986. Bought in chassis / cab form by Roger Tuby, a showman from the Yorkshire area who fitted both a transverse generator and fifth wheel arrangement over the back bogie, this ERF, with a blue cab, pulled an Automatic Arcade Trailer.

RPC Southam Drivers 1970s

Dayshift and nightshift bulk and bag drivers, plus office staff, in the middle 1970s at Southam Cement Works.

Back row, left to right
John Bousefield, Stan Reader, Pat Kelly, John Brunt, John Baskot, Oscar Jayes, Arthur Harris, Pete Timms, Monty Lloyd, Mick White (Despatch Office), Gilbert Bennett, Mr Sear (Southam Works Manager)
Front row, left to right
Gordon Hill, Malcolm Thornton, Ian Mackie, Frank Linnell, Malcolm Clark, Kevin Billingham, Lew Smith

The first 30 ton operated pressure bulk lorries were very adequately described in Part One.

However, additional photos of others have emerged within the last few years. Shown attending to F/N 789, one such venerable lorry is the former night-shift Southam garage foreman Bill Izzard in his well remembered flat cap and overalls. I got on alright with "Izzy", as he was probably better known, but a few other drivers with different temperaments found that he argued the toss. But, at the end of the day he was Night

Foreman at Southam Garage, and his word was law.

FN/851, registered HKV 981N dates from January 1975, and was based at Rochester Cement Works in Kent. Its regular driver, for a while, was Jimmy Deville. The difference in the RPC Livery and lettering between both these identical ERF 30 tonner bulk 8 wheel chassis is very plain to see.

Personally speaking, the simple black lettering on the reddish background served the company over many years, the new white crowns emblazoned on tank / cab sides, together with script lettering on tanks, appeared to be something akin to a Public Relations exercise which, had the late Sir Halford Reddish still survived beyond the late 1970s, would not have been considered at all.

This photo is also included to show a Rugby based thirty ton ERF L/V purely and simply because it was the only heavy goods vehicle capable of being able to travel through the ever rising flood waters when the river Avon burst its banks close to the main Rugby to Leicester road, the A426.

The late winter and early spring in 1980 saw monsoon type rains, which swelled rivers and streams alike. These were to join the Avon up near to the top side of Rugby. Shown in the background is the former English Electric factory, now long gone.

The Rugby ERF is in three inches of flood water; another half mile away and the depth of the water would be up to the top of the wheels. F/N 806 was driven by Dougie Johnson, based at Rugby Works and it carried registration number OAC 422M. Only one of these early thirty tonne bulk chassis

survived into second ownership. Perhaps it was because 2 or 3 of the 800 series of these particular lorries capacity bulk chassis were fitted with thirsty Cummins 220 diesels, but they provided Rugby Portland Cement with an entry into twenty ton load operations prior to the introduction of the ERF B Series in 1974. Noisy in extreme, particularly when discharging their loads, I've known glass windows to shatter because of the scream of the blowers, but they did their job efficiently in the seven years of fleet use.

DNX 725K, carrying F/N 711, was delivered new to Rugby Works in 1971, and given to me as an 8-wheeler replacement for my scrapped Foden S21. I was only allowed to keep this lorry for a year, mainly because demand for bags from Rugby became less, whilst at nearby Southam the demand increased tenfold. 711 went to Southam and was to stay there until sold out of service. First it went to Toll Bar Haulage in Coventry. It was then offered back to Les Clark Transport, and finally ended up with a fourth owner, delivering both steel plate and cement in bags, before it was finally scrapped in 1990 after nineteen solid years in use.

Within most of the main cement producing mills of Rugby Cement, with lots of men working in close proximity there was always going to be a combination of comedians or miserable individuals whose daily exertions would impress their fellow workers whatever the situation. We had our fair share of such drivers at Rugby and at Southam in later years. Equally so, ordinary workers became involved in situations which, in every day terms "rocked the boat" or to a lesser extent upset the local communities. Two ex South Ferriby based members of the Transport based there very definitely fitted into this category. Ken Brien, a former Transport

Despatch Supervisor, who was better known to all drivers as "Moonshine" or "Blakey" ran off with a female cleaner much younger than himself. I would meet him at some of the early RPC Caravan Club meetings, not really knowing about his folly until many years later.

Stan Petit, a South Ferriby based driver, was well known for his strong Labour views, and on occasion he shared his opinion/feelings when the opportunity allowed. In the driver's ready room he had his own red painted chair. Although I never knew this individual I can well imagine his rants and wishes. Something akin to a "Red Rag to a Bull" must have seriously been the result when he was given a brand new B Series ERF 8 wheel bulk tanker with an interior which came in blue!!

I have since been readily informed, by Mick Lowe, that RPC South Ferriby supplied bulk cement deliveries for cable anchoring plinths when the Humber Bridge was being built. By prior arrangement, in the early part of 2010 when Mick Lowe managed to arrange a load to Rugby Works, we met for the first time on the Leicester Road just over the M6 at Junction one. A very memorable forty five minutes were spent discussing RPC Transport in great detail. This was the beginning of serious contact and exchange of material, plus an ongoing friendship which continues unabated, along with Steve Hastings of Gillingham, Kent, who's father Jim was a bag driver at Rochester Cement Works in Kent.

CHAPTER 7

Rugby Portland Cement Transport 1970s and early 1980s

It was the building boom of the 1960s, together with the increasing demand for more and more bulk cement deliveries, which constituted the immense growth of RPC Transport. Replacement lwb 4-wheel chassis for cement in bags came firstly in the shape of K Series Dodge wheelers. Some Perkins engined variants, particularly with the 4-wheeler chassis, appeared in RPC Transport carrying a straight 10 ton load at 5 ton unladen wt. Air assistance for braking was standard, and bag drivers, including myself, took some time to exert sufficient pressure on the dash mounted handbrakes to effect release.

Shown above is Rochester based F/N 796 with a full load. These K types were fast, and weighed less than 5 ton unladen. We had 736 at Rugby with "Mr Cement" in charge, alias Mick Shepherd. The year was 1972 and RPC were not keen to depend on one particular chassis, so three different bag chassis appeared within Rugby works about this time. Chris Moon received ERF GWD 465K, whilst I got HUE 738L, a 1972 KM Bedford. These latter two were purchased purely for evaluation, although several more KMs came into Rugby Cement and were dispersed around the Group.

Thankfully, now looking back over these years, only one "A Series" 4 wheel ERF was bought. Fitted with a Gardner 100, David Brown 5 speed plus and Eaton 2 speed axle, it was classed like the others for 16 ton operation. But, it's main disadvantage for any unfortunate driver finding himself on it for a day, lay in the fact that Power Steering was not fitted. If Arthur Alcock, the former Central Garage foreman had his way (which thankfully he did not when purchasing new chassis!), he would have replaced all 4 wheel chassis with these 4lw Gardner powered ERFs. My KM carried fleet number 738. I drove it for five and a half years solid with absolutely no problems. One very long delivery to Weymouth in Dorset with piling cement, then made at Rugby Works, more than proved to "Jock" Henderson (RPCs well versed Fleet Engineer) that even with a journey of almost one hundred and forty miles or more in each direction and with an expected night out at Swindon, and after arriving back at Southam Works' diesel pumps it still had 4 gallons left. RPC Transport engineers worked out that even at 40 mph (or slightly more) with a full load, the Bedford 366 diesel returned 16 mpg, which in 1972 was unheard of. RPC purchased more platforms as well as sub chassis for bulk operation. Almost all of the KM tanker versions went to Chinnor Works, although I'm reliably informed by Jim and Steve Hastings that two were based at Rochester works for a time. Shown below fully loaded for a regular 3am start for a 7am Cardiff Builder's Merchant delivery is Kevin Billingham's former KM flat NWK 968P carrying F/N 395. We had F/N 404 and 407 at Rugby. Jack Smith drove 404 for most of its working life. He drove very fast whereas I treated 407 differently. Looking back, I have to say in all honesty I'd just as soon have had my old 738 back because of what I found out from Day One. P, R & N registrations were by this time in evidence within the Group. The Ns were centred on the then new Dodge H1 Liners which had replaced all Commers. My second Bedford KM 4-wheeler flat SKV 874R F/N 407 given to me in 1977 started life with an annoying but seriously overlooked problem by the dealer's Pre Delivery Inspection (PDI), in that I soon found out starting from cold either loading up in the yard or running to the first delivery of the day, that the electrical system fitted would not hold the charge. Having mentioned this alarming situation to Arthur Alcock the Central garage foreman, I was rather taken

back when he said 'you drivers leave the lorries to us'. After that outburst one day returning from a Birmingham delivery I purchased half a dozen 17 amp fuses from the Coventry based C/E Motors Bedford agents just off the Fletcham Stead highway. Each morning from then on I replaced a 13 amp with a 17 amp alternative knowing that I would at least not be inconvenienced by breakdowns.

However one morning I was detailed to take a bulk tanker out to the Steetley Mixer Plant at Shawell near Rugby as its regular driver was late and my KM was later to be loaded for a fairly long distance delivery the next day. In my absence Vic 'Dinger' Bell the yard shunter loaded my KM and found to his absolute horror that the engine would not start. I'd replaced the 13 amp fuses the night previous and so he summoned the garage fitters to sort it out. Me being out of the way fortunately saved me from another roasting from the garage foreman who saw me later that day, and said "where are the more powerful fuses". I replied by saying "your instructions to me earlier were crystal clear in that we drivers have to leave the lorries to you", I then added "its not the batteries or the engine at fault its the fuses", it was made clear to me a second time that day by Mr Alcock that breakdowns of lorries were not the drivers concern.

The next morning with a 5am start, I left Rugby Works at 5:25am with an 8am delivery for Shrewsbury County Council Atcham Bridge depot 6 miles South of Shrewsbury on the A5 still with the 13 amp fuses fitted. After outlining to Fred the depot foreman just what would happen, we unloaded the off side bags, I then turned the lorry round and switched off the engine and we unloaded the near side of the load. The complete load was off in just over half an hour. Numerous cups of tea followed and the delivery sheet was signed. Knowing that the lorry would not start and totally refusing offers of a tow, I waited until 9:30am until telephoning Central Garage for help. Mr Alcock did not start work much before then, and in the meantime a police sergeant friend of Fred's pulled into the yard for a regular chat and a cup of tea. Fred told him to get hold of the extension telephone as I started to explain to Mr Alcock about the problem. This police sergeant asked me for the RPC transport managers name, the late Ken Harvey. I am not aware of the subsequent conversation which took place between these two gentlemen - whatever it was resulted in Central Garage sending two fitters out with our veteran Foxden S21 6-wheel fleet recovery unit to fetch me and my KM Bedford back. That breakdown would neither pull you out of bed nor pull up your socks, but they arrived between 1:30pm and 2pm, and towed me back to Rugby arriving there at 4:10pm.

Next morning I asked to see Mr Harvey at Head Office where I explained in detail what the problem was and how all the inconvenience could have been avoided. I also told him I had been informed twice by Mr Alcock that all lorry problems were the responsibility of the workshop staff, and that drivers should not be concerned.

Shown on the right is perhaps a better photo of SKV 874R on relaxed carnival duties, by which time the annoying fuse problem had been sorted out. This photo dates from 1978 during the Rugby Carnival when I was driving for Rugby Play bus and carrying young children dressed as Space Cadets; their mothers walking alongside were dressed as space women. Whilst building up in the morning earlier before the Carnival, most RPC drivers who'd volunteered, or were nominated, for such duties were fed and watered by the people concerned.

I was never a fan of the Dodge Hi Liners chassis which replaced the Commers, however, they served the company well enough in platform, bulk and tank and box tipper form. The use of SWOP BODY operation was a complete disaster and discontinued completely after the complete collapse of the loaded bodies in Southam Works yard. The principle, however, of dropping loaded flats is shown here for the benefit of the reader. The driver concerned is Pat Kelly.

The use of SWOP BODIES was a joint arrangement, initially between Bostock/Barsby Ltd and RPC Transport engineers.

Loaded Bodies seen in Southam Yard. Fleet Number 965 Dodge dropping loaded bodies in Southam Yard

Legs down prior to driving vehicle away

Lower rear end before driving vehicle away

Shown on the left is the now infamous Dartford Tunnel Blocker, formerly in Jim Hastings' charge from Rochester Works. NVC 286P carried F/N 379 and is fully loaded with 10 ton (200 sacks) of cement in bags. Supplied at some point new in 1975/76, these Hi Liner Dodges lasted for around seven to eight years before they were removed from fleet operation. These Dodge Hi Liners also came in for possible use in Carnival duties.

Here, shown left is Chris Moon's immaculate platform under the equally capable hands of Dennis Garlick, shown tying on a banner whilst members of Tyntesfield special school offer helpful words of encouragement. YVC 249S carried F/N 480 and was supplied new in May 1978.

Some idea of the faith that RPC Transport had in the Dodge Hi Liners can be imagined with this superb night-time photo taken by Tony Higgins in Southam Works' yard. Thirteen Dodges, fully loaded and ready for the next day's deliveries, stand in line.

Les Clark terminated his employment with RPC Transport in the middle 1980s to start up on his own as an outside contractor, and his antics of using Fred Saunders' former 8 wheeler ERF platform are described earlier. Not content with one lorry, he was destined to purchase several more ex RPC chassis.

Shown below, and carrying his preferred, and attractive at that time, cream and brown livery is Dodge Hi Liner platform ex F/N 970, carrying registration number EKV 882T. Pleasing to the eye, this was a delightful combination of colours. Les was also to increase his share of both the surviving area space in Southam Works' yard areas, whereby his attempts to service his growing fleet did not endear him to fellow drivers, RPC staff, or indeed the Works Manager at that time. Further purchases of two identical ERF B Series 6 wheel tankers, namely BHP 289P / F/N 360 and OHP 291P F/N 362, completed his fleet.

Both are shown on the left with Les Clarke and Carole (née Stephens), who later joined Les with her own 8 wheel bulk cement tanker painted in two shades of blue. Les Clarke began with good intentions, but by the early 1990s it all disappeared. For a time he was offered the use of DNX 725K, a former ERF 8 wheel platform given new to the Author, but which was transferred to Southam Works when demand for bags at Rugby was slack. This carried former fleet number 711, and was destined to have four separate owners before being scrapped in 1990.

After the Rugby bag drivers were transferred permanently to Southam and things settled down amicably between all drivers, I remember going on a fairly regular basis with early morning bag deliveries to Colliers of Gloucester. Before the transfer, we'd done this trip from Rugby Works when Southam despatch staff conveniently forgot to remember this weekly order. Colliers were a family of the father and his two sons. They asked for a 7am delivery. Their yard was between terraced houses, just off the ring road. I used to ask for this trip because it only took 20 minutes to unload (10 minutes per side), even after turning round.

Harry and Nora Ryder lived on the other side of the ring road at Tuffley. I'd got to know them through the RPC Caravan Club initially and after unloading at Colliers I'd nip over to Nora's house for tea and toast. Harry was a driver on bulk at Gloucester Depot and so was "out of the way". Consequently, it was not long before some of the wags at Gloucester Depot got to hear that an RPC fleet lorry was parking outside Harry's house in the mornings on a fairly regular basis!! I was a perfect gentleman (always), coupled with the fact that an open invitation from Nora for tea and toast and nothing else justified crossing the Ring Road! I was always back at Southam Works in time for a second load of the day. The delivery to Colliers was to continue when we went to Seddon / Atkinsons 6 wheelers, but the family preferred 10 ton loads as opposed to 15, and so private haulier 4 wheel lorries took care of this once popular run. Harry and Nora Ryder remained good friends, although in the years since the disbanding of RPC Transport both Harry and Nora have suffered with innumerable health problems. They still enjoyed caravanning with the assistance of neighbours and friends. Harry Ryder passed away some years back. He is very sadly missed by all RPC Transport friends.

One amazing, but hilarious, incident concerned my second KM Bedford shortly before I lost it for good. It happened in 1983, some twelve months after we'd been transferred to Southam Works. Despatched early one morning to a Somerset council yard which involved a 3.30am start, I began a journey to Clutton Hill, not far from the Bristol boundaries via the A38, or so I'd been told. Fortunately, at that time of the morning, and with the M5/M32 motorways, which between them meant that I didn't meet a lot of traffic going through the centre of Bristol at 6.30am. Even with a ten minute stop I arrived at the council yard at 6.55am. The load came off in half an hour thanks to the joint efforts of both SCC employees and drivers alike, and I sped back up the M32 now against rush hour traffic going the other way. My five and a half hours were up at 9am and I managed to get back to Michael Wood services at 8.50am. After the customary Thermos of coffee and surviving sarnies, I got my head down. I must have dozed off almost immediately as, in my semi-conscious state, I dreamt some father was hitting me with a cricket bat hard on my backside after I'd spent an hour or so in his daughter's bedroom. In actual fact, the bang I'd just experienced in my dreams was caused by my mate Chris Moon reversing his ERF 4 wheeler flat up to the back of my KM Bedford. He then lifted the clutch and the two back ends met! The impact shot me off the seats and down on to the cab floor-well, whereby, having just enough strength remaining, I managed to open the passenger door and more or less fell out of the cab in a heap! A burst of applause brought me to my senses as I turned round to see all of the night stop drivers, and my mate Chris Moon, vigorously clapping their hands at my predicament. I returned to Southam Works in time to manage a second load to Travis / Arnolds at Rugby where the hilarity continued. Well known for their half hour tea breaks, the load came off in ten minutes flat. I finished at 3pm later that afternoon after a very eventful day.

Chris Moon was a born comedian, he was also well known for his practical joking. Care of his lorries was excellent and he was well respected by all of his colleagues and transport management alike. At the same time as me saying this, as an individual turning your back on Chris Moon was not an option!

Having said all these things about him, I have to add certainly that in all of my twenty two and half years with RPC Transport, up to December 1990 when we were all made redundant, Chris Moon and his wife Joan remained very good friends with both me and my wife Diane. Shortly after I lost SKV 874R for good. It suffered a broken crankshaft in early morning rush hour traffic on my way to a Wolverhampton Builder's Merchant. I was not sorry to see it go!!

Building departments at both Rugby and Southam cement works relied upon Karrier Gamecock 4 wheeler dropside lorries for years in keeping with using several hundred Commer 4 wheeler chassis of both forward control versions and later Maxiload types fitted with 2 stroke (horizontally opposed pistons in each of the three cylinders) power engines, in use for bulk/bag deliveries within the group. When Peugot purchased the Rootes Group, the RPC company continued to buy Dodge lorries, but discontinued purchase of lighter chassis by going back to Ford. The works lorry at Rugby Works for many years was based on a D Series Ford of five and a half ton capacity. This worked mainly for the estates department and its regular driver was a Mr Miller. Registered VAC 662X F/N 647, it was the victim of an unplanned accident at the bottom end of what is known locally as the Straight Mile on the B4453.

I'm not aware of what caused Mr Miller to go for the ditch, but knowing the road, it suggests to me that he came round the corner and met two vehicles coming towards him, one on either side of the white lines. F/N 647 was not seriously damaged, and after being checked over was soon back on the road. Just behind the tree on the right, and bordering the small tree, is the drive leading up to Mitchell's Potato packing premises – still there in active use today in this new century. With detatachable body sides and the visible bolster, this Ford was one of "the Stars" a few months later when it appeared in the Rugby Carnival. The photo shows the preparation by the people concerned for the "hire Job" putting on the balloons along with the finishing touches to a fantastic transformation of our works lorry into what was basically a castle.

These events happened well over twenty five years ago – perhaps more. Since these days I've still not found out who hired the Rugby Works' lorry. When RPC ceased to exist in the early 2000s, VAC 662X was auctioned off. It can still be seen working around the Rugby area these days, still carrying that well known reddish colour of happier times. Although the

D Series Ford has technically been around since 1965, over the years the model has been improved with better suspension and more powerful engines etc.

Human error, or indeed lack of judgement, could have been blamed for this roll over accident of the former Rochester Works Sweeper, itself based on the D Series Ford. These lorries were universal across the Rugby Group, doing a boring but very necessary job, trying to present each works' in a cleaner, better environment by battling cement dust in all hidden corners. These sweepers, as they were referred to, carried several gallons of water to assist their daily tasks, so perhaps the weight of water contributed to the roll over – perhaps not!

The earlier reference to the use of Karrier Gamecock lorries, which supported both Rugby and Southam cement works many years back did not prepare me as either an author or an interested spectator when I was informed that the remains of the former Southam Works Karrier was purchased at an auction in Coventry for £100 some years back by Dick Stuart, who was a very good friend of mine. 345 EAC dates from 1963 and I remember this lorry was still in service in 1968 when I started with RPC.

Looking at the immediate task facing any would be vehicle restorer is enough to put many seriously like-minded souls off. Dick Stuart gave these remains to his grandson Daniel, hoping to keep him away from undesirable people. In his own words "the wrong crowd".

I watched young Daniel spend many weeks attacking the rust with a simple wire brush. Over an eighteen month period the transformation became obvious. I gave Daniel a rather worn out Perkins front grille badge to which a prolonged rubbing down brought the required shine. Some time later, when the cab and chassis had been treated, holes re-welded and rust preventative sprayed all on the underside of the lorry, I arranged with Ken Barsby (whose former father and grandfather's coach-building/painting business painted most of the RPC Fleet) for the full re-spray and lettering of Daniel's Karrier. During the drying-off period, when the re-spray was complete, Ken also had the Bostock / Barby sign-writer come back to take care of the lettering in full RPC livery. Later on, open dropside bodywork was constructed and fitted to the Karrier. A sheet was found to cover rally equipment and up until 2001 this well remembered colour was admired

at rallies both locally and further afield.

Sadly, for all the wrong reasons, Daniel left the family home and returned to a life of uncertainty. He is now in regular employment and a married man, but with little time to maintain his interest in the Karrier.

Dick Stuart was a long term outside bags contractor who came into Southam works. Over many years I forged a friendship with him and his daughter, Jennifer. Between their two lorries, they delivered cement in sacks over many years. Later on, Willy Flomer came on the scene through his friendship with Jen. He was, in relative terms, Dick's son-in-law. Willy's life has centred around lorries and road transport for most of his years. During his progressive and well-intended approach to most things, particularly servicing and improving his everyday lorries, as well as vintage items, he often met with disagreement from Dick. As a bystander, I regarded my friendship with them all as tremendous. When the disagreement took place in good part, Willy would not back down as Dick stuck to his guns! In the end, however, a form of compromise was reached. Visit their yard, however, and you were soon involved in "transport folklore" of all kinds and the kettle for tea / coffee became second nature. Sadly, for all the wrong reasons, I lost my friend Dick Stuart two years ago. Lying on his back in his early years servicing his lorries did him no favours at all. His last journey on the back of the RPC Karrier, driven by Willy Flomer, is shown in my photograph taken as the RPC Karrier makes its way into Canley Crematorium, Coventry, decked out in black ribbons on the front of the cab and the body sides.

Dick would have approved wholeheartedly. Later on, at the reception, the regard and total respect from everybody was evident, as was the tribute given by Willy for his father-in-law.

Dick Stuart spent a lifetime in road transport and embodied hard graft in all weathers. His dedication to his customers was paramount. His mechanical know how was gained through service with the RAF in the desert, where he kept the wheels turning at all costs. I

remember Dick Stuart building an 8 wheeler platform from two chassis – the pundits said it would not work, but it did, and it earned its keep twice over.

Kevin Billingham was one of the best remembered bag drivers at Southam Works. He was a very good friend of mine, and also to Arthur Harris. Both of us, now in our early pensionable years, remember the jokes and the laughter which surround "Billy", as he was perhaps better known to his mates.

F/N 385 is shown loaded with a load variation design which kept all the bags in their proper place. Not used all the time, it was (I think, but don't know for certain), put on lorries going to a new customer with the first load. Of particular interest to former employees are parts of Southam works before the new Bag Shed was built. The old Bag Shed is recognisable by its sloping roof.

This was where, at times, you loaded white or masonry cement in bags. Also of note is the earlier constructed storage building, which had a well weathered roof over bricks which came from a decade ago. The old summer uniform with prominent CROWN badge on the pockets, plus the "Beatles" haircuts are also reminiscent of happier years, now long gone!

Long before computers, mobile phones, ipods or whatever came along, customers of Rugby Cement Works were visited regularly by company sales representatives who reported daily to the sales department at Crown House with the orders. The importance of keeping the customer happy in the knowledge that he received his order, be it bags or bulk cement, was the dominant factor in the mind of the Rugby Cement Chairman the late Sir Halford Reddish. As far as I know, some of these sales reps may have lived near main cement producing works. Others worked directly

from Head office. Visits were made on a monthly basis to builder's merchants and orders were placed. This information was then passed to the Sales Department at Head Office, whereby each area's orders were totalled up and despatched to the nearest works. This information came directly to the Transport Despatch Offices from the main teleprinters at Head Office to each separate area. Drivers were given a loading sheet detailing all the types of bags to be loaded. This ticket was retained by the bag shed foreman and kept for reference. Bulk loads were often received much in the same way, but certainly at both Rugby and Southam Cement Works. I know from personal memories that ready mix plant despatchers dealt directly with Despatch Office Staff, when at busy periods they ordered additional loads by telephone. This meant that speed was the order of the day, particularly when large pours occupied all their mixers and the mixer plant staff did not want their silos getting low.

A six sheet teleprinter order form was the basis of all orders. Sheet One was kept by Sales. Sheet Two was given to the loaders. Sheet Three was kept by the customer after signing. Sheet Four was retained by Transport Despatch and Sheet Five was kept at Crown House for proof of delivery. This system worked 100% perfectly for years. Whilst I forget the sheet numbers in order of priority, the basis was that service to the customer was paramount.

I am indebted to John Winfield (and his wife Josie) for the following information regarding names from long before my time as well as those who I was to see on a daily basis within Southam Works Bag Shed.

Packers who worked the chutes before the advent of the Palletiser Shed, included the following: Martin Habel, Henry Sherwood, Jack Cheney, Denis Long, George Nichols, Robert Gaskins, George Webb, Dave Askew, Ken Gardiner and Pat Scandrett.

I started on 8-wheelers (Bags) in October 1968, and often remember suddenly being switched to working out of Southam Works. This happened to me for two reasons. Fred Saunders, Rugby's longest serving bag driver, could never get up in the mornings, and so was late almost every day at Rugby, even though he lived less than a mile away. Also, his preference for wanting to stay at Rugby, as opposed to being transferred, meant that I was next in line. This opportunity, in these early days, was to create friendships with almost all of the Southam Packers / Loaders which remain to this day. Consequently, the fun and hilarity which abounded elsewhere within RPC Transport often came to the full in Southam Bag Shed, where every opportunity presented itself. Here, again thanks to John Winfield, are all of the individuals who made up the two shifts of packers / loaders. Where known, I have also given the impression each character made upon the casual observer.

Harry Neal was the bag shed foreman. He and his daily partner, Ben Saunders, could load an 8 ton load of bags in twelve minutes flat. So neat and tidy, without one bag out of line, they had been doing that for years and knew it off by heart. When Oldham's of Barford starting coming in late on Monday afternoons with clapped out BMCs and Morris / Commercial 4-wheeler platforms covered in cow dung from Rugby Market deliveries in the early morning, I well remember both of them telling the Oldham's drivers to get the lorries washed before they came to load cement. Numerous rows erupted later on when the Oldhams brought in other 4-wheel chassis which had damaged platforms with cracked/holed bodies. This was wholly unacceptable to the Southam Packers who included Billy Beck, Charlie Wilson, Les Groves, John Winfield and Derrick Rolfe, whose nickname was "Stingray" on account of the magnifying lenses in his glasses, along with "Big Arf" (Arthur Basely) and Dave Fisher, aka "Blink" because his eyes would blink all the while he was talking to you.

Steve Driscoll's moods changed like the weather. He lived next door to the Nelson Club in Stockton Village, and rumour had it that much of his spare time was spent on those premises. Derek Sutton was another miserable individual, whose general attitude to RPC was that smiling was not in his contract. Pat Ryan and Dave Hatfield were later made up to charge hand packer / loader levels. Pat, I could always get on with, but "Hattie" was always trying to give bosses a better impression of himself. He is still employed at Cemex in Rugby Works. Ron Beechey, Southam's undisputed King of the Bulk Loaders, along with his wife, is passionate about old time dancing. I'm told that his house in Elm Row, Stockton, boasts many presentation cups and trophies. Ron always had a smile on his face, no matter what the weather threw at him. Joe Scott, who was better known as "Gypsy Joe" spent much of his time in local pubs and was the other supposed bulk loader. Many is the time, after a heavy drinking session, he'd be found sleeping it off at the rear of the bulk silos in the warmth of the Packer's Huts. Pete Ball, or "Teggy" as he was probably better known (as he had virtually no teeth) was the nights bulk loader. Something of a character, who I got to know a bit better after I qualified on artics after 1988, he lived on the caravan site up at Princethorpe.

Bill Minnet was the Supervisor in charge of all Packers / Loaders. He could always be seen in the late afternoon scurrying across Southam Works yard with his clipboard full of bulk / bag loading tickets in an effort to get back to his office alongside Southam Despatch whereby, with the aid of an adding machine, daily / nightly tonnages would be worked out. Very much a quiet and studious individual, Bill Minnett was an extremely clever and gifted man. He was also very polite, and a more conscientious employee you could never hope to meet. He was, in my estimation as Author, the Southam Cement Work's Harry Potter.

From memory, just before the advent of the new Palletiser Building coming into operation at Southam, I seem to remember that both Gypsy Joe Scott and Derek Sutton were to die suddenly, also the Packers received a brand new spacious cabin positioned at the rear of the new building. Most mornings at break times either Big Arf or Blink would saunter across to the hot water tap by the front of the Canteen to fill up the billy Cans. A torrent of good natured abuse would greet the Packers from Danny Burke's lips.

When the new Palletiser building operations started in earnest, loading of all flat lorries became much easier and quicker. By then Seddon Atkinson 6-wheelers were in use alongside the two ERF C Series and Dodge Hi-liner 4-wheelers. Together with a multitude of private contractors' lorries, the often remembered fun and laughter was to continue but, as an individual you had to be extremely careful. Big Arthur Basely was six foot of bone and muscle. Give him some lip, and you risked having both your ears twisted back. The pain lasted for days!! Billy Beck, having loaded bagged cement for years was not that much bothered by normal mickey taking, but if the individual's sex life practices came into the conversation, one swing of his powerful arms was enough to silence the perpetrator. Harry Neal and Ben Saunders had both retired a little before the operation in the old bag shed finished. Neither of these two individuals were to be allowed a long and happy retirement. Ben Saunders lived in one of the houses at the end of the Southam Works drive. From memory, his death occurred some four years after finishing at the Works. Ben and his mate, Harry, were often referred to by the flat drivers as "Bill and Ben, the Flowerpot Men". Harry Neal and his wife used to live in the Model Village opposite the Cement Works. When he retired they moved into flats in the Pendicke Street development in Southam. I've since been informed that Harry died some years later.

This picture is a rare shot of George Scandrett in front of the Fluxo Masonry Packer. His beer belly is of prominence as he concentrates on the job of placing each bag on its spout. His capacity for beer would, I suppose, come to the fore particularly when someone else was paying for it. When the new Palletiser shed came on stream in the 1980s, maybe the late 1970s, George was far enough away, high up in the old Crown Packer, from any drivers or other individuals who mouthed verbal abuse and obscenities to him via the Voicebox connecting the packer. George, and various other members of his family, were to give loyal service over very many years to Southam Works. Knocked off his bicycle, George was sadly confined to walking with two sticks, and I was informed by several ex RPC friends that his general state of health deteriorated. Sadly George passed away in 2013.

His humour of earlier years, which often came to the fore when required, now remains as a memory. The seriousness of George's concentration whilst pushing empty paper sacks on to the spoon filler for Masonry is perhaps in keeping with an official photographer nearby also concentrating on doing a good job. Gypsy Joe Scott, mentioned earlier, who was officially the second day shift bulk loader was, I've since been told, an expert at knitting. Many pullovers, cardigans and scarves were produced on Joe's knitting needles inbetween his drinking and work commitments. I did not come into contact with Gyspy Joe Scott, but I'm reliably informed that he was "Magic" at knitting!

Les Cage was a fitter in the garage at Barrington Cement Works near Cambridge. Known to his colleagues as Budgie, his typical style of RPC humour prevailed throughout transport in all areas. Being ex Welchs Transport of nearby Stapleford, Budgie was, I think, very set in his ways, although judging from his comments when we met at the last Open Day activities at Barrington Cement Works in 2007, he fitted in admirably in the workshop during the time he was there.

He remembers another character from years back called Dave Day, who, buying a few things in the Works Canteen handed over a £10 note to make payment. Not the kind of thing that was expected in those days. Another time, the same individual wanted to lessen the weight of a large collection of small change in his pocket so handed it all over to the canteen staff to pay his bill of just £1.20. I don't think his popularity would win him any Brownie Points from the Canteen ladies, certainly not at Barrington.

The photograph shown here gives a splendid view of the ramp exit from the Barrington Garage / Workshop area. Shown centre stage is a K Series Dodge 6 wheeler bulk tank JNX 953L F/N 752. Leading into the works area, several Commer Maxi Tankers are in the background (flat backed rears), plus one platform shown on the far left next to a Foden S21 cab. To the visitor such as myself during my early trips with internal bag stock loads, I found the easy going, sometimes rebellious attitudes to Rugby and Crown House rules difficult to accept, but on the whole friendships were made and the jobs got done.

On later visits to Barrington, I found that the workshop staff were always eager to assist you if you were in trouble. Their favourite saying to visitors was – "Go down to the canteen, and we'll call you when it's ready"!

This photograph demonstrates the resourcefulness of the Barrington Works fitters. The picture shows a former Eastwood's Cement Bulk Tank, altered slightly with the provision of a pump and delivery hoses, in its new role as a water tank for use within the Works to keep the dust down in the working areas as well as the reception, offices, pathways and roadways. The former lorry chassis, less cab and engine etc, was modified to be towed either by a Landrover or Tractor.

Les Cage remembers an incident which was to cause a combination of rage and amusement for the people concerned. He walked past one of the pits in the garage where down below Tom Cook was working on a lorry brake drum. Les picked a 1 inch drive and bar and hit the opposite brake drum as he walked by. The bang was followed by the thud of Tom's head hitting the drum plus lots of swearing. Tom's reaction was to leave Budgie in no doubt that, given the opportunity, he

would attempt to get his own back. Budgie swore to Tom that he hadn't realised anyone was down there, but anyone would have done the same thing.

Budgie could not stop using his twisted sense of humour to make life in the garage unbearable for his companions. One day Brian Williamson the Supervisor got a can of drink from the canteen. Budgie broke the ring pull off and put a small hole in the bottom of the can, turned it upside down and put it back on the bench. When Brian went to get his drink he found it had no drink pull and its contents dribbled all over his feet. Had he drunk it from the hole in the bottom he'd have been okay, but he didn't see the funny side, and threw the can away in disgust.

Trips to Chinnor Cement Works taking new lorries from Central Garage often called for volunteer drivers on Saturday mornings, invariably with a 5am or 5.30am start. I remember one particular occasion when I, as a regular 8-wheeler (bags) driver knowing the best ways to Chinnor on account of inter works stock deliveries, was asked by Dick Smith if I would lead half a dozen other drivers. From memory, it was myself, Chris Moon, Wilf Childs, Jack Kenny, Bob Hare and Dougy Cleaver. Jack Kenny opted to leave our convoy as we entered Towcester en route to Bicester, saying he knew a better way. Before we got clear of Bicester, Wilf Childs started flashing his headlights frantically. I stopped and it transpired that his bladder was full to bursting and he demanded to know why we hadn't stopped earlier! In the event we were then about twenty five miles from Chinnor and were to stop again before we reached our destination. We pulled into the works just before 8am without seeing anything of Jack Kenny. After delivering our lorries to Chinnor Garage we headed for the works canteen for our statutory half hour break which we all decided to take before starting the return journey. It later transpired that Jack Kenny had gone in search of some scrap items in exchange for beer money, something he was well known for at Rugby Works. Arriving at Chinnor so much later was to make him later still getting back to Rugby, but no questions were asked. Jack Kenny preferred his own company, and so, like similar characters who are best left to their own devices, the majority of drivers kept out of his way, myself included.

As explained in Part One all new drivers starting at RPC Transport were put with an experienced bulk driver, usually for a three week period of training. Apart from being shown all the procedures of discharging bulk loads, together with reloading at depots or works, new starters drove the lorry during the instruction period whilst the tutor drivers took notice of the learner's attitudes to other road users, as well as their general standard of lorry driving. Most new recruits to RPC Transport, including myself, were probably not made aware of the purpose of the black looking clocks affixed to the rear cab bulkheads of company lorries. It was therefore to be some time into my own Company Service before I learned just why they were there. Basically, they recorded all unofficial periods of when the engines were switched off. Given that most daily transport operations ended on Saturday afternoons between 2pm and 2.30pm each week, these Service Time Recorders were regulated to include all non weekend working hours. A basic time clock was matched to a magnetic pointer which recorded time to the exact second. Even when driving time adhered to Road Transport rules and regulations, whereby drivers were required to take a half hour official break after five and a half hours, all periods of non engine running were recorded by these time clocks irrespective. Cards were changed in these clocks at the discretion of the Transport Department managers if they thought that an individual was attempting to break the rules. Various adaptations by drivers were tried to offset the magnetic pointers, whereby womens' hairpins, drawing pin or paper clips etc were inserted into these time clocks. Such offenders were initially given a warning, but as far as I know no one was sacked or lost his job for tampering with the time clock. Most of the company drivers obeyed the rules and did the job. Consequently, when Tachographs were introduced much later on, RPC drivers throughout the fleet adjusted accordingly with little or no fuss.

Drivers based at Chinnor Cement works near Oxford always presented their lorries in exemplary mechanical condition. Previously explained in detail, a two shift system ensured bulk lorries (ie box tippers) were each looked after by two drivers. However, when times and methods of delivering cement improved, the drivers at Chinnor continued to keep their lorries immaculate. When John Ayre received a brand new Dodge Hi-Liner 4-wheel bag lorry in 1979 he continued the practice of keeping it tidy. Looking back upon my own experiences, keeping flat lorries clean was a nightmare!

Des and Andy Clarke were private contractors on bagged cement at Chinnor Cement Works, and so on recommendation from John Ayre when RPC Transport

Lorries were about to be sold off, they bought DDU 540T for their own regular use.

Des Clarke takes up the story. "Prior to us buying it, 540T had had a brand new engine fitted. With a few modifications, including changing the livery, we worked her out of Chinnor until the ten and a half ton bag loads ended. We then sold the lorry to a driving school in Exeter".

DDU 540T was new to RPC Transport on January 1st 1979 and carried F/N 983. She was one of twenty similarly bodied chassis, all of which were platform bodied supplied to the fleet during the first three months of 1979. She carried bagged cement for twenty years under two owners. The photo shows the lorry in the ownership of Des and Andy Clarke (father and son). All remnants of RPC ownership have been removed; the addition of the Michelin Man atop the o/s mirror bracket, the radiator paper bag "muff" plus windscreen stickers all signify private ownership. On reflection for a lorry touching twelve years ownership in 1991 or more when this photograph was taken, the overall presentation and condition were truly remarkable.

Des and Andy were later to purchase a second RPC lorry – a 6 wheeler ERF B Series Platform MAC 321V which went initially to driver Ken House.

This was new to RPC Transport on the 1st June 1980 and bodied as a 15 ton platform lorry carrying cement in sacks. Taxed for 24 ton GVW she carried F/N 554. Several years were to go by with the regular driver until that awful word "redundancy" became part of many RPC Transport drivers lives in the middle 1980s.

Prior to being sold out of fleet service with Rugby, a new Gardner 180 engine and rear suspension was fitted, with all the work being done in the Chinnor workshop. The Clarkes then worked it for a number of years.

The photograph overleaf shows the lorry devoid of previous RPC ownership, a white roof, plus the front panel also edged in white completes a wild transformation. Andy and his father Des sold MAC to another contractor from the High Wycombe area in 1990. She survived for ten years at Chinnor Cement Works, also under two owners. On information since received from Andy Clarke 321V has again been sold to someone from the Farnborough area.

Sold out of service to a gentleman called Alan Pearce

toolbox kept in the passenger well of the cab of Alan's lorry, and it transpired that this toolbox was behind a completely unexpected catastrophe. The lorry had been parked within the workshop overnight whilst being serviced. With the cab tipped up completely the already mentioned toolbox slid out of the open cab area, and caused a short circuit with the fuses whereby a spark engulfed the fibre glass structure, this in turn blacked out the interior of the Chinnor garage workshop. Apparently the workshop remained out of use for sometime as all interior equipment was cleaned and

who was an outside contractor at Chinnor Cement Works "on bags" and repainted in a simple fleet colour of blue lower surfaces and white overall, this ex RPC ERF B series lived on.

Graham Munday, a chargehand fitter at Chinnor works garage, rebuilt the engine completely on 322V just six months prior to an awful accident which was to involve this lorry. Alan Pearce was another gentleman and a contractor on bags, he was then owner of MAC 322V. The fitters remaining at Chinnor were to be concerned with servicing remaining company lorries plus those of outside contractors. Concern had been earlier voiced about a heavy

made ready, along with tools etc. Whilst this was going on the workshop staff relocated to another building within the cement works. Shown earlier are the remains of 556's cab looking very forlorn after the damage caused by the fire, which on balance could have been avoided by the person concerned. I remain indebted to Graham Munday for supplying the information and the photo evidence for this story.

A similar lwb 6-wheeler platform registered MAC 324V had F/N 555. I'm not exactly sure of its base works, but Rochester Cement Works in Kent springs to mind before it spent some time at Chinnor. Sold out of fleet service in the early 1990s, fitted with both a new cab top and swop body equipment, painted firstly in an all over white livery with black cab roof and lower panels, it was first photographed at St Giles Fair, Oxford, several years back. Still with its white box body, the cab and wheels had received a coat of red paint. No second ownership details are known.

Looking back now, it's almost more than 40 years since the introduction of new 30 ton B Series ERF 8 wheeler chassis, which were fitted with blower equipment and the bulk tank

Chassis number 43375 ex 15 Ton platform 6 wheel chassis

bodies. With this wholly new concept of ERF design, like its predecessors, the B Series ERF was to contribute wholeheartedly to the daily and nightly operations of RPC Transport. Shown below is F/N 417 registration number WWK 619S being driven away from Gloucester Depot by Stevie Leonard. Supplied in March 1978, this photo suggests that this lorry is not very old. I can't remember who had 417

regularly, but Bill "Cassius" Clarke, a Rugby based driver, had it new. These lorries had the 180 Gardner engine, plus a six speed David Brown gearbox, which between them aptly provided power and acceleration pulling thirty ton loads. Attractive to the naked eye, these bulk 8 wheelers more than proved the justification for their introduction on deliveries nationwide. With well over two hundred and fifty chassis swelling the ranks of RPC Transport from the mid 1970s onwards, one chassis appeared very similar to another. Unwary bag drivers like myself were concerned, however, as the rear end controls for discharging differed slightly on each chassis. The B Series cab was ERF Limited's first tilt cab design. This was to prove very handy for the garage fitters after years of dealing with fixed cabs.

RPC lorries did not break down often, owing to the strict maintenance and servicing procedures which were laid down. MOT preparation, including chassis steam cleaning, involved a three hour session on the ramps beside the old wash at Rugby Works. The convenience of both the tipping tank and the cab can perhaps be appreciated in this interior shot of Southam Works' new garage taken by Clive Mumford (the foreman), showing Sandhu Singh, a Hindu fitter who was always smiling, no matter what! He is attending to F/N 447 prior to its MOT test. Note tins of black paint and the job sheet attached to the cab door handle. Any part of the engine can easily be accessed with tilt cab design.

Tim Griffin has already been mentioned in this story. Both he and Tony Higgins, who worked the night shift in the garage, were forever taking the mickey out of each other. Higgins went out of his way to fill Tim's saddle bags with all manner of

broken spring hangers, brackets and other heavy condemned bits of metal. This was done so that Tim struggled up the hill into Stockton every night when he went home. Occasionally, Tim managed to get his own back on Higgins. How, I don't know! What I do know, however, is that both men remain good friends, and it is fair to say that when they meet up with each other at local events "devilment" in one form or another is never far away!

Danny Burke, the former canteen manager at Southam, almost got more than he bargained for one day when a day shift worker took out his dentures to extract a food particle which had caused him to choke. Whilst cleaning his bottom set in the toilets, he'd left the top set on the table, just for a second. In the meantime, Danny came up quickly and poured a small measure of cooking vinegar over the unattended dentures, then bolted back behind his counter waiting and looking innocent. The owner of the dentures came out, satisfied with his work, picked up his top denture set and put them back in his mouth. I can only report what I've been told, not having been there at the time, but apparently he almost choked on his own sudden vomit and rushed back into the toilets at a fast pace. Unfortunately, ten minutes later when the day shift worker regained his composure

he heard from the toilet Danny say out loud to customers "That'll teach that bugger to be impatient when I've got a queue at the window". The day worker rushed out of the toilets, grabbed Danny by the collar and said, quite definitely, "If I get the sack for what I'm going to do to you, then it'll be worth it". Fortunately it didn't come to that as the two men were dragged apart by others. The fracas finished just as a supervisor entered the canteen, and Danny skulked into the back room of the servicing area, well out of the way.

Photographs of drivers and lorries are as much a part of this second attempt to portray the well remembered RPC Transport fleet, and shown below is a version of just such a daily partnership.

John Brunt was based at Southam Works for all of his company service. He was a bulk driver and is shown in this photo a few years back when his hair was grey, looking fitter and very much younger. He is standing alongside his "daily steed", at that time PWK 439R F/N 367 which was new in October 1987. Licensed for 24 ton operation on six axles, these replacements for earlier 6 wheeler square fronted ERFs were powered by Gardner 180s, coupled to a 6 speed D/Brown gearbox. They were destined to serve the RPC fleet admirably for fifteen ton loads of bulk cement. Normal discharge time with these 6-wheeler chassis

varied between twenty minutes to a full half hour, depending upon both the skill of the driver and the available storage space at many of the customer's plants where we delivered on a fairly regular basis. After slogging along for years with slower bulk ERF 6-wheelers, these 180 powered versions were like a breath of fresh air.

Shown left, in second ownership with Les Clark Transport (a former RPC driver who set up on his own), and from the same batch as F/N 367, this former B Series 6-wheeler ERF carries his pleasing coffee and cream fleet colours. New to RPC in July 1976, OHP 291P carried fleet number 361. I have a distinct feeling that this particular 6-wheeler went to Chinnor for part of its working life. We had 364 / 365 at Rugby. Charlie Jones had one, which one I'm not sure, and the other one was driven by Albert Kimberley for an unspecified time. These 6 wheelers were operated primarily for access to customers premises where they manufactured slabs, kerbs and other concrete products, where access for larger lorries was difficult to say the least. Even using all their delivery hoses, where necessary, these 6-wheelers were to fully justify their purchase by RPC because of their supreme manoeuvrability in confined spaces like the premises mentioned earlier. Causing their ultimate downfall when sold out of fleet, however, was the fitted trailing rear axle.

OHP 291P may have carried other colours other than RPC Transport, and for an unspecified time was operated by Les Clark Transport.

However, its basic function and design was to last until the middle 1980s, whereby the lorry delivered bulk cement powder over a wide area from Southam Cement Works for its two owners from new, before being disposed of some time during 1989/90 at the grand old age of thirteen. Like a mixed collection of ERF 6 and 8 wheeler chassis it went for scrap – unless of course any reader knows otherwise!

Since I was a small boy, growing up in post-war Scotland, I have harboured a very serious interest in Fairground and Circus transport. My particular favourites come from the early years until the 1950s, although thanks to the kindness of endless showland families who purchased ex RPC ERFs, my interest spans all ages of vehicles up to the 1980's.

Shown on the previous page, discharging into bulk storage at Lewes Cement Works, is F/N 464 CVC 185T. This was a B Series 6-wheeler tanker. It was driven for quite some time by Brian Newman, a Rochester based bulk driver who was better known to his colleagues as Bootsie. Needless to say, Brian is shown reading his newspaper in defiance of RPC Transport instructions that drivers remain at the rear of the tank whilst discharging. Despite this ruling, because of the vastness in storage capacities within the RPC and Group works and depots and, as previously referred to, these 6-wheeler ERF B Series' could, and did, unload fairly quickly, and without incident. The single ram stability is shown to good effect in this photograph, together with coupling pipes at the various points on the building wall. This particular 6-wheeler is shown a few pages further on too, in company with an 8-wheeler B Series at Lewes Cement Works during unloading. 464, as far as I know, did not survive into second ownership. Unless of course it remains in some scrapyard, or indeed, in Malta.

CHAPTER 8

Fodens and ERFs
A Driver's Own Story
Crashes and Conversion – More Memories
RPC Transport in Miniature

The trials and tribulations experienced by RPC Transport regarding their eight Foden S39 6 wheeler chassis, which entered fleet service on bulk deliveries at some point in the late 1970s, are well known in respect of regular mechanical breakdowns. Other operators, along with RPC Transport, had for years used Foden chassis produced at Elworth-Sandbach in Cheshire. These were very popular because of their excellent reliability in harsh conditions and were exported worldwide.

Shown above right is F/N 452, one of these Fodens just three days into use and registered YWK 550S. This was one of two similar lorries based at Barrington Cement Works near Cambridge and was photographed by Peter Davies to whom I record my own personal thanks. Presumably on its way to a customer, it is compact in both design and appearance. This photo, however, does not show the reader any visible signs of it not being up to the job for which it was designed. Fitted with a Gardner 180 engine, or according to the pundits who have the combined mechanical knowledge and experience to know otherwise, a 6LXB power unit was matched to Foden's own well tried 12 speed gearbox. If you were like me and suddenly found yourself in charge of one of these bulk lorries despatched to deliver a load, you'd have been surprised by all manner of noises coming from the gearbox as you made multiple unsuccessful attempts to get the right gear in the right range. I personally found that only after much exertion, and by using the second and third middle or top ranges, you could keep both the wheels moving and the engine running the compressor so that you had air for braking. I make no secret of the fact that I (and perhaps other drivers) did not like these cabs, mainly because of the low headroom. You would regularly bump your head on entry and exit and whilst there was enough room for your legs to reach the pedals, space within the cab was at a premium. The small capacity diesel tank was also a worry on long delivery runs, and the two Rugby based S39s regularly almost ran their tanks dry.

Right across the Rugby Group, after all the mechanical inadequacies of these Foden 6 wheelers had been noticed and experienced, they were kept on reduced mileage delivery runs from whichever works they were based at for a time prior to their removal from regular service within the fleet. Quite a few years have passed since the four Fodens were sold, and I presume by now that they have been scrapped or disposed of. Shown below is one of these which were kept by the company and rebuilt into fleet recovery units. F/N 454 was the sister to the lorry already described. Fully fitted out for recovery duties, it is shown parked in front of the main bulk loading silos that can be seen in the background at the Barrington Cement Works. This is the business end of these well-equipped and totally rebuilt Foden S39s showing the A-Bar, together with enough flashing, reversing and rear cluster lights plus the covered workshop area. Sadly for all the wrong reasons, their role as recovery units ended when RPC Transport was in the throes of being disbanded, which came in the late 1980s. Of the four former S39 recovery units sold off, I have been able to trace the former Rochester Works' recovery unit, now owned by JP Whittaker. Another similar recovery unit was photographed some years back at the Bloxham Steam Rally near Banbury, owned by Sheppard Services (not pictured). Both of these Fodens were still in recovery mode.

However, by far the best possible restoration carried out, certainly since the start of this new century, has to be that of BHP 505T. Whether this was one of two former Rochester based tankers, or not, I am not sure. However, both Tony McGovern, the North London bulk refuse contractor, and his chief garage foreman have used their mechanical expertise to admirably transform this former Rugby lorry into a box tipper, keeping it simple whilst

retaining its well known design features.

My own photo, taken at the 2007 Classic Lorry Show at Gaydon, Warwickshire, shows 505T taking centre stage within the Foden Society's stand at this event. This lorry is kept purely for old vehicle rallies and it fits in superbly with other classic restored tippers in the McGovern stable.

The following three images show the extensive damage caused to F/N 486, a Barrington based Foden Haulmaster bulk tanker when a night bulk loader reversing another tanker on to the loading weighbridge was talking to a bystander rather than paying attention.

In this picture the near side is completely full of impact damage, I would politely suggest (not having been there) that the culprit must have been reversing and caused the damage with the pointed tank end of a sister tanker. As shown, there is extensive damage to the cab of the lorry, including broken windows and the cab structure itself, which even the inexperienced eye could see would need a complete new cab, rather than just a repair.

Closer inspection of this second picture shows the extensive side impact damage, whereby the whole cab structure is twisted out of shape. The roof of the cab is cracked, again through impact. The nearside quarter light window remained intact, a surprising fact considering all of the other glass which had shattered and broken.

The third, and final, picture, shows the extent of the damage to the whole of the nearside of 486. The catwalk ladder is twisted totally out of shape, and is virtually useless. The rear mudguard and wing assembly is cracked. Les Cage, aka Budgie, a Barrington garage fitter of some repute, was detailed to steer this damaged Foden on the bar behind the Barrington Foden S39 recovery unit back to Rugby Central. He had to wrap himself up in all manner of protective clothing behind the wheel, as there were no windscreen or cab windows. Because of the extreme damage to the cab and near side door, which would not shut properly, the whole of the cab had to be roped around and tied securely to the tipping rams for the journey.

Joe Taylor, a Rochester based driver, was given a new Haulmaster bulker F/N 424 WWK 623S. Much to everyone's surprise, he did not crunch the gears. Bill Gordon got another one, F/N 431 DDT 541T, new on a Friday, he polished it until it shone. Sadly, he was taken ill the following Sunday, so 431 passed to Roy Gaddich, the next driver on the list.

Bill Gordon ended up as the tyre fitter at Rochester, but retired due to ill health. To the uninitiated readers, the Foden Haulmasters' 8 wheel chassis supplied to RPC Transport as well as other users, had two visibly different front panels. The first one was the chromed enclosed space carrying the Foden Kite scroll. This version is shown to good effect by Rochester based driver Kenny Smith's Foden, discharging at a concrete plant. EDU 442T carried F/N 489 and was supplied new in March 1979, licensed for thirty ton operation. The driver is shown at the rear of the cab in the required position whilst controlling discharge procedures.

The cluttered premises of a typical mixer plant were, to some extent, a daily nightmare for Rugby drivers as they manoeuvred into the correct position without getting in the way of other users. The fact that this photo includes the

RPC driver in question is of paramount importance to this story. The smaller silo on the left was used for the storage of additives for manufacture of ready mixed concrete, whilst the taller of the two silos contained cement powder, sand and gravel etc which was brought in by conveyor belts to that structure

and mixed with cement before being deposited in truck mixers.

Whilst 489 did not, as far as I know, survive onto second ownership, a sister lorry did.

Shown below is EDU 448T ex F/N 490, supplied in May 1979. It was reported to be

229-14 24/08/00. Foden S108 Haulmaster 8x4 1979. Location: A50 at Normacot, Stoke-on-Trent. Still going strong 20 years on. ©BillClowes2000

still going strong as a tarmac tipper some twenty years later up in the Stoke on Trent area. By removing the tank blower parts and fitting a tipper body, most other chassis parts would remain. The addition of an orange flashing light on the cab roof was so necessary when operating in confined areas. This, with a pleasing all over dark green livery interfaced with red wheels, chassis and front grille, makes this ex Rugby Foden adequate for quite a few years use yet.

Having myself spent time driving these Fodens with their Foden 8 speed range change gearboxes, I can fully justify their longer lives in other jobs.

MAC 318V was new to Rugby driver Fred Seamer, and carried F/N 544.

This is my own photograph, taken whilst I was in charge one day of discharging at the Deniff plant at Shawell, near Rugby. The strength of the single ram is shown to good effect here, as is the old mixer plant structure and conveyor belts. Now and again excess water would be pumped away, hence the large wet ground area at the rear of the Rugby lorry.

HDU 913V carried F/N 503 and in the beginning it was given to driver Taff Roberts. He did not keep it for very long as he transferred to the Works Laboratory where he was to spend the rest of his company service before taking redundancy. 503 then went to Roly French for a time. Roly

was small in build, and for a time found it a bit difficult to enter and leave the high cab, so Chris Moon presented him with a set of small steps to make life a bit easier. Roly, however, did not have much of a sense of humour, and didn't react as well as he could have, so the steps were forgotten. Roly French and Bill Clark were brothers in law.

After 1982 the transfer of Rugby bag drivers to Southam Works together with their platform lorries took place because the Rugby bag shed was extremely old and not considered suitable for any sort of rebuilding. For me personally, this move was to take on a complete new meaning as I'd made many friends within Southam from previous years working for Fred Williams. Also, being ten miles down the road, and away from prying eyes at Crown House was, for all of us another good reason for the transfer. Lorry drivers, by the very nature of their job, prefer their own company than that of their colleagues. Sadly, due to the passage of time, plus constant changes over many years in terms of transport law and legislation, lorry drivers will never be the same again. Characters and individuals and so many different souls abounded within the ranks of RPC Transport.

Shown below, is a display of raw twisted humour within Southam works; Johnny Isham, a driver of very many years standing, on the left, vies for the position of best comedian with Dougie Tomes, the resident tyre fitter. Both are wearing fancy hats in front of F/N 543, John's Foden Haulmaster tanker. Sadly, John Isham passed away a few years back, taking his fantastic sense of proportion and humour with him to the grave. All of us who were privileged to know and work alongside him miss his presence. Dougie Tombes has since died. Before Dougie became ill, myself, John Baskot and Dougie organised a visit to see one of Southam's Night Garage comedians. Now confined to a residential home, not far from his village of Ashorne, Tom Mockler used to check lorry engines for oil and water at Southam Works for many years. His sense of perverted humour and laughter was typical of his Irish birthright which supported Clive Mumford's efforts on the night shift. Mocklers real claim to fame came about whereby with so many lorries to check each night, and with a long walk to the canteen tap, walking down to the canalside each evening was a quicker option, and in Mocklers mind did the same job. Not so. The stagnant water attacked the copper head gaskets used in the build of Bedford 466 engines. In my case, very early one morning on

my way to Jim Hales (a builder's merchant) in the Forest of Dean Gloucestershire, with the engine working at full whack climbing another hill, my KM Bedford suffered major head gasket failure. Tom Mockler was also responsible for suggesting the prank with Danny Burke's bicycle. Sadly Tom Mockler passed away a few years back.

Shown above in a typical pose, Ian Mackie's stern look did not include any form of laughing in his contract. Never a man to show much in the way of humour to his colleagues, he worked nights with George Greenaway loading bag and bulk lorries. Somehow, like a few others, he engineered himself into Southam Despatch Office looking after despatching early drivers off with their loads. F/N 884 A614 HVC shown behind Ian Mackie was Barrington based, but I don't know for sure. This is the second cab design showing the plastic front grille design.

Both the headlamp and sidelamp cluster and flasher units were re-planned into a design which was practical, if not as attractive as the first design. Front towing eye brackers were incorporated into the bumper bar, as opposed to earlier versions which were in the lower areas of the S106 cab structure. Cab interiors in the second design also came in for change, in that they were slightly more luxurious. Bearing in mind, however, that RPC, when receiving new chassis for fleet use irrespective of bodywork initially stripped them of both cab radios and the small Union Jack front grille badges. The reason given at the time was so ridiculous, apparently it was to cut down on unladen weight!

Later on, however, many bulk drivers had their own radios and, for a time, CB equipment. F/N 884 was based at Barrington Cement Works. Its regular driver is unknown to me. What is known, is where 884 went when sold out of fleet service. It was purchased by a member of Smiths, the Leighton Buzzard family of Showland fame. Easily recognised by its Warwickshire registration number and blacked out company name, this former bulk tanker cab chassis looks comfortably at home in its new role as a fairground frame lorry. I would be interested to know if A615 HVC is still in the ownership of the Smith family, as I have no doubt whatsoever that this Foden will have outlasted some of the family members.

Pictured below beautifully painted and lettered in traditional showman's style, these two former Foden S108 Haulmaster ex bulk chassis 8-wheelers formed the basis of an old time Galloper ride, probably more commonly known to fair goers as The Galloping Horses. The overall presentation of both these lorries is absolutely 100% first class, and both of them are a credit to Showman John Armitage. Registered A739 JAC, this carried F/N 887 and I think, but don't know for certain, that it may have been based at South Ferriby Cement Works. The Foden on the right is A21 MKV, it's F/N is not known. It is expected that these two Foden Haulmaster eight wheelers will outlive their usefulness for quite some time. Both are suitably painted and lettered in the true traditional styles of the travelling showman.

Many drivers based at Southam Works, including the former Rugby bag drivers, should, and probably do, remember the absolute mayhem and hilarity caused by Chris Moon when he dressed up in an old dirty frayed coat and an equally dirty woolly

wig and pretended to apply for a driving job at Southam Works one afternoon by confronting an embarrassed Fred Williams. Dougie Tomes at that time met this scruffily dressed individual crossing the yard and remarked to Arthur Harris walking alongside "He's got no chance of driving our lorries". Later on, Chris ducked into the worker's toilets and removed his smelly gear, but it was not until some time later that the truth came out. Chris later used those same clothes on the bag

unloading staff at Birmingham Depot with devastating effects when he posed as a time and motion study engineer. He tied both Wally and Shirley in knots when he quizzed them about their coffee breaks. When the truth came out weeks later, both Big Slim and Charlie, the two Jamaicans who never stopped laughing, nearly lynched Moony when they found out. Chris Moon got away with it twice, but I don't think that a third time would have worked, certainly not at Birmingham Depot. It took Fred Williams quite a bit of time to recover – such was life at RPC Transport.

B763 DKY was new in late 1983, being fitted with the revised Foden 106 front panel – ie a plastic Foden kite grille badge. It was given to driver Stan Fryer at Rochester Works, who I have never met. He is shown tipping the tank upwards to its fullest extent. The controls for both the blower and tipping the tank were fitted under the driver's seat. Not knowing too much about whose premises this is, I would imagine that this was a fairly easy blow.

The lower parts and wheels etc and the underside of the tank bodywork appear to be in urgent need of either a good wash or are ready to be re-painted. Most of my regular bulk colleagues, at both Rugby and Southam, over the years made do with a ten foot length of delivery hose. "Tanker Captains", as such, were not known for using extension pipes unless it was absolutely necessary. Their idea of physical exertion was rolling the pipes up and getting the delivery ticket signed so as to get quickly to the nearest transport café. As previously mentioned, some of these second series Foden Haulmaster ex RPC 8 wheeler bulk chassis were to join the ranks of contractor bulk haulage companies for an unlimited time until the life span insurance ran out on the tank bodywork, thereby eliminating further use. This, in effect, would render the chassis to be used only as a tipper lorry, or instead it would be put up for sale. Quite a few of these Gardner S106s were to find favour within the fairgrounds, and so yet again, thanks to the camera of Rod Jesson, we can see the fruits of his labour.

Shown above is a re-numbered F/N 211, which carried registration number A597 LWK. Seen at Hampton Court Fair in June 1993, this ex bulk tanker chassis began life some ten years earlier in 1983. As to where this particular lorry was based, I don't know. Judging by the obvious weight imposed on the chassis by Mr Ayres, and presumably expected to pull a trailer or living van, A597 LWK is to be worked even harder. This lorry has been minimally altered to provide its owner with a double deck frame bodywork capable of carrying various sections of a ride. In any respect, it's nice to see the Rugby Crown logo remaining on cab doors.

Too many drivers (myself included) when they first started driving for Rugby Cement, or indeed either of the sister companies (Chinnor or Eastwoods) were to find the rules a bit irksome. Those that could not, or would not, abide by them, invariably fell by the wayside and left. Others, like myself, soon settled down and got on with the job. Many of my own colleagues, at both Rugby and Southam Works, notched up very many years of service. Chinnor and Eastwoods drivers would, after the Rugby buyout of both companies in the early 1960s, spend many more years delivering cement in bags or bulk

One such individual was Alan Holland, a Chinnor based driver who started in 1961 when he was 24 years old. This is his story:

"I started bulk tuition at Chinnor Works with one of the best remembered characters (Ron Ludlow) who taught me all about the controls and how to discharge an eight ton bulk load of cement. The lorry they gave me to start off with was a BMC FFK Morris 8 tonner, fitted with a four speed gearbox. Quite some time after this, Chinnor decided that with modifications to the gearbox ie the addition of a 5th gear, they as a company, might see an improvement of a few more miles to the gallon. The Morris was dutifully sent to a dealer where a fifth gear was fitted. I was bringing the lorry back to Chinnor Works when I realised that going into fourth gear was a higher ratio than the new fifth. Over the next few weeks I just loaded up my Morris tanker and drove it as normal in fourth gear. After going on holiday for a couple of days, I returned to find that the replacement driver on my Morris Tanker had complained about the gearbox to the garage foreman. This resulted in the Morris being sent back to the dealers for a replacement gearbox to be fitted.

Transferred on to an 8 wheeler Albion tanker fitted with a Bonnalack tank I found, upon investigation, that as a flat back tank, a small ledge was fitted inside the rear of the tank to stop the cement blocking the discharge outlets. As a driver on bulk deliveries it was essential to remember your training. Exactly how many drivers tipped these tankers up too quickly, rather than allowing for the cement in the tank to remain at a safe level I'm not sure. The purpose of this ledge, fitted to Chinnor's Albions was, quite simply to allow the cement to flow underneath it and straight to the delivery outlet. If a lot of cement powder lodged on this ledge, then lowering the tank became very difficult, and caused trouble. By 1965 the old Albion was completely worn out. The clutch was slipping badly, and the prop shafts were just about at their last gasp when I was instructed by the Transport Manager to drive her down to Basildon, which I did. Afterwards, I was collected by the Manager himself and brought back to Chinnor.

One of the worst things for any driver at Rugby Cement was to be classed as a spare driver, and I found myself in this position for about a week. I covered for any driver who phoned in sick. One day, after clocking in, I got a call from the Ticket Office to take a Foden 15 ton tipper bulk cement S20 model down to Universal Asbestos at Watford. My first reaction was that I'd never driven one of these lorries before, but I did know that "flat out" their top speed was just 30mph. Fitted with a Gardner 120 engine and a 4 speed gearbox, I managed to get down to Chorleywood and saw a sign for Watford. Mistakenly going down that road was to land me in trouble. It had a very steep hill called Salt Hill. At the bottom I got into bottom gear, and with my heart in my mouth, the last gasp of that old Gardner finally managed to get the old Foden over the hill. That episode in my life taught me a basic lesson – plan your journey before you leave the depot!!"

It would appear from Alan's personal adventures that fun and laughter, often at the expense of others, was as much the order of the day at Chinnor as it was at both Eastwoods and Rugby. One of the regular tricks guaranteed to annoy the shift drivers at Chinnor was for "Somebody - Mr Nobody" to put some small stones in the front hub caps. The noise this made when the lorries were on the move caused the regular drivers to report to the garage workshop complaining about a noise in the front wheels.

I had been a spare driver for a while when the Transport Manager called me into his office one day and said "Do you think you can manage a nice new lorry?" My reply was that it should be a lot better than the old Albion, but in reality I was to be proved horribly wrong! This new Foden, based, I believe, on the S21 Mickey Mouse cab, arrived fitted with the original Bonnalack tank (off the Albion). It had a five or seven speed gearbox, and proved to be an absolute "cow of a lorry" to drive. I drove it solidly for about two years, and then left the cement works in pursuit of a job with an engineering firm. A period of perhaps five or six years went by before I returned to Chinnor Cement. During my absence, Rugby Cement had taken over, and so I applied for a driving job. I was given fleet number 864, a Dodge Commando 4 wheel platform on bag deliveries, shown right.

It was to take me a very long time to get used to unloading bags off the deck, so to speak, but after quite a while I became very fit. These Dodges had the revised 6534 Perkins, coupled to what I think was a Turner five speed gearbox. Taxed at the sixteen ton GVW, they carried a ten ton load with comparable ease. They were kept for around seven or eight years before being disposed of.

Chinnor's lorries were kept spotless by their drivers. JWK 382N dates from June 1975 and carried chassis number 752407. Two or three years were to pass with me and my trusty Dodge bag lorry, when all of a sudden, two or three ERF B Series 8 wheeler platforms were sent to Chinnor works from Rochester Depot in Kent. I was asked if I would transfer on to one of these. LDU 653V was a March 1980 registered ERF B Series Platform lorry taxed for twenty ton operation. It had a Gardner 180, a 9 speed range change gearbox, comprising of 4 ratios in each range (ie low/high), plus reverse in both. They were an absolute delight to drive, and quite a jump in both comfort and speed from my old Dodge Hi Liner 4 wheeler. Carrying fleet number 548, it could legally carry a twenty ton load.

Shown "at rest" these 8-wheeler flats were to prove capable of more than their fair share of work during RPC Transport ownership. Prior to the introduction of palletiser operations, company vehicles, particularly rigid chassis vehicles, were brought into service with aluminium based palletiser bodywork, which, in general terms, became mobile pallet chassis.

One particular experience, whilst in charge of Fleet number 548 concerned a twenty ton load on pallets for a Bournemouth customer. This journey involved a 7am start from Chinnor Works. I managed to get down to the Handy Cross roundabout, but the traffic lights were on red. When they changed to green I pulled away in bottom gear (low range), but by the time I made it to the middle of the road, the traffic lights had changed back to red. Needless to say, several drivers behind me were a bit upset. Eventually, whilst going down the Marlow bypass, I looked in the mirror and saw that "Mr Plod" was following me. At the Marlow junction he pulled me over. When I got out of the cab I asked him what the trouble was. He said "I think that you had better follow us up to the Weighbridge because I think that you are overloaded".

I answered "I think you had better check my delivery ticket and the plate in the cab. Both of these will tell you what weight this lorry can legally carry". After conferring with his mate, he said that I could carry on with my journey. When I returned to Chinnor I informed the ticket office about my ordeal with Mr Plod. They had a good laugh about it, simply because they had one over on the law. After that episode, Chinnor Works reverted back to 18 ton loads on their 8-wheeler ERF platforms.

The versatility of these particular 8-wheeler chassis is shown in the photograph below carrying a twelve ton load of cement in sacks (240) on eight wooden pallets loaded in the centre of the platform body. Both the front and rear parts of loaded pallets would be strapped down (as shown) before the lorry sheet covered the load and roping took place.

The scene of this photograph is the main yard of Chinnor Cement Works. Fun and laughter was never far away when loads of men spent their working hours together. Out of sight somewhere, is a wellington boot being thrown by the driver on the ground at his mate!

These B Series platform lorries more than proved their worth at each of the Rugby Cement Works where they were based. They paved the way for endless stock loads, delivered in this case from Chinnor to Southampton Depot. Barrington Works' long serving driver, Keith Collett, who became a

close friend, always had an 8 wheeler platform of one sort or another. His company service started during the Eastwoods Cement days, and progressed into Rugby's ownership. When we met initially, I had just delivered sulphate bags (15 ton) to Barrington one Saturday morning in 1970, reloading later with masonry (15 ton) for return to Rugby Works. During the following seven or eight years, we would continue to meet one another somewhere between the two works.

Shown here with his brand new B Series 8 wheeler flat fully loaded with Masonry Cement, Keith Collett is trying to look serious for the photographers.

KRW 75V was new on the 1st March 1980, and was licenced for 20 ton use. It's gvw was rated at 30 ton. Power came via an 8 speed range Fuller gearbox with reverse in both ranges. I never drove one of these lorries, so cannot comment.

This photograph shows KRW 75V in all her glory. Fully loaded within the confines of Barrington Cement works, this was a publicity shot taken to show the carrying capacity of these new chassis. In fleet service for around seven years, 75V was later sold out of service, probably around the late 1980s.

Tony Higgins, in his double capacity as night shift fitter at Southam Garage, plus enthusiastic road transport photographer, always managed to take photographs of great magnitude which reflected activity at night in all of the RPC Transport workshops. Shown above the reader is spoiled for choice. On the left, two tipped ERF B Series cabs are receiving attention of one sort or another. F/N 920 was, I think, brand new, and it was given to Dougie Cleaver, one of Rugby's best. Dougie knew all the quick ways to jobs. He also knew all of the best cafés, where he was equally well known in return!

Next to 920 is one of two Cummins 220 powered 8 wheeler bulk tankers. F/Nos 849 and 850 shown here were both based at Chinnor Cement Works. Just in front of F/N 850 is a ten ton based Dodge Hi Liner Platform carrying F/N 965, which was driven by Chris Moon at Southam for a time before he transferred on to F/N 872. This is a really tremendous picture of the night time activities in which the capacity and scope of Central Garage repair and servicing facilities reigned supreme.

Mick Lowe, one of South Ferriby's finest night drivers, was informed one night by his Supervisor that after unloading at Rugby he was to bring back some garage spares. This was to involve him being on the receiving end of Night Foreman Mick Hennesey who loved to play tricks on visiting drivers. After unloading at Rugby, and having his official break, he drove up to Central Garage to be informed by Mick Hennesey that a blower was the intended spare for Ferriby Garage. "Bloody Hell Mick" was the obvious response! "How the hell are we going to get that weight on to the passenger floor?" Seeing Hennesey struggling out with the blower on his shoulders, Mick Lowe positioned himself on top of the engine cover, sitting down ready to relieve Hennesey of the heavy blower. Looking back, after many years, it's very hard to know how Mick Hennesey managed to keep a straight face and not give the game away. This is a miracle known only to him!

The blower in question was a fibreglass model made especially for all RPC garage fitters to see where the holes were. Grasping for the expected weight from Hennesey's shoulders, Mick Lowe was suddenly propelled over the engine bonnet, where he landed upside down in the driver's seat area. Mick Hennesey was laughing fit to burst as he returned inside Central Garage.

Determined to get his own back on his next trip to Rugby, a Leeds' Depot night driver was to do it for him. On three sides of Central Garage, large windows were set into the walls at about shoulder height. These were opened in hot weather by a bar which allowed a half section to raise. During an official tea break in the Central Garage, the man from Leeds positioned his ERF tanker alongside the west side, facing the railway parallel to these windows. He then donned a plastic horror face mask, climbed onto the tank ladder and yelled for Mick Hennesey to come and sort out a problem. Mick grabbed some tools and went racing out of the end doors, looked up and saw this figure making a frightening gesture. He quickly bolted back into the safety of the workshop frantically shouting "I've just seen a ghost"!! When it was all sorted out, it took poor old Hennesey quite some time to get over it, but he always managed to get his own back. I personally always found Dave "Nutty" Hazel and Mick Hennesey eager to please and oblige any driver who had a problem.

Although Rugby Cement was to remain loyal to ERF for more than fifty years using nearly all the models which came out of the Sandbach company and getting 100% reliability from the hundreds of chassis used over these years, a company policy of using just one make of lorry was not an option.

A photograph taken by Steve Hastings, whose father Jim spent many years as a a bags driver at Rochester Works, shows three separate platform lorries in use in about 1982.

Shown from left to right are F/N 714, an ERF L/V cabbed 8-wheel platform, new in November 1971 and taxed for 27 ton of operation. Load weight was 17 tons of bags. I have no record of 268K being used in second ownership. F/N 749 started life as a 6 wheel bulk tanker in November 1972, carrying 15 ton loads, but taxed on the 24 ton rating. They came with V8 Perkins engines, and were very thirsty on diesel. Purchased initially for London area bulk deliveries, they did not stay very long in use as pressure vehicles. All were removed from service. Several were sold and the remainder were stretched into 6 wheeler platforms. This change of use was not a successful experiment for these KT Dodges

as nearly all of the weight was to be concentrated at the front end when the lorry was empty, meaning that drivers had to concentrate just a bit harder. We had 753 at Rugby Works which, for an unspecified time after his horrendous accident with F/N 710, Alan Burdett drove. Even he found driving this stretched K Type Dodge 6 wheeler something of an experience.

Those which were converted to 6 wheeler platforms retained their original fleet numbers. Their period of use with bags was equally limited, and all were to be sold for scrap eventually. I am never surprised, even in this new century, where after more than twenty years have passed by since I left Rugby Cement due to redundancy, I am suddenly confronted by a photograph of a former RPC Transport chassis and registration number which is Warwickshire registered.

Shown below, in its new role under second ownership, is KRW 75V. Shown on the previous page in its original form as a 30 ton platform for the carriage of cement, this particular lorry was, as earlier mentioned in the care of Keith Collett at Barrington Works.

This photograph was taken by Tony Maynard, a good friend from the Yorkshire area. He and I, along with another good friend of many years, share a serious interest in Showland transport of the post war years. Looking at this photo, the reader is immediately reassured that the showman owner has used the length of this former platform lorry to his best advantage by building an enclosed box bodywork which incorporates fold down opening panels for easier access when loading or unloading as shown. Fortunately, the owner has also kept the cab as near original as possible, other than repainting it and the body in an attractive red over crimson with white flash. These 180 Gardner powered flats were extremely comfortable to drive, so I'm assured that this lorry will be on the rounds for quite a few years. The standard ERF bumper has been replaced with a more manageable towing eye arrangement which, when required, will assist in pushing other trailers into position on the fairs and elsewhere.

Rugby Portland Cement Transport in Miniature

When I built my first model L/V ERF 8-wheeler model P/V tanker over forty years ago (1970), I never dreamed that this one model would one day inspire and interest the general public as well as RPC colleagues right across the group. I well remember the heartache and the stress of mind and body, trying desperately to get both the cab and tank bodywork as near perfect as I could, having plenty of full size lorries at my disposal to refer to every day during my early years of service at Rugby Works.

The general impact and sheer delight of visitors over many years at the Town and Country Festival, held every August Bank Holiday until 2004, at seeing these models of mine, have encouraged me to enlarge my miniature fleet over the years. Ten years after I completed my original 8-wheeler ERF, I was approached by Ken Harvey's granddaughter and her then boyfriend who would ultimately become her husband, with a view to selling them my ERF. When I asked why they wanted the ERF, it transpired that Ken's 80th birthday was not far away, and they'd decided that my ERF would be the crowning glory on the birthday cake! It would, however, really delight Mr Harvey, he being the former RPC Transport Manager.

Whilst my ERF was my own doing, because it was being bought as an 80th birthday present for my former manager, it had to undergo some drastic rebuilding. The entire rear of the L/V cab was removed and rebuilt exactly, with the sloping fibreglass panelling in place. The tank was also removed, rubbed down and repainted and relettered. When refitted, all the lights, front and rear, together with flashers and reversing lights etc, were touched up as near 100% perfect as possible. The model was then paid for at £30 by the young lady.

I've since found out, that when Ken Harvey was presented with the ERF model on his 80th birthday, he was very close to tears!

Built within the past twenty years, RPC Transport in Miniature now numbers a dozen different models. With the exception of a Sentinel Steamer 4 wheeler, I drove most of their bigger brothers during my twenty two and a half years' service with the Company.

Shown on display at the 2010 Peterborough Truck Fest Model Show, my entire RPC Transport fleet includes five of our Associate Companies' lorries. RPC Transport is

shown represented by a dozen models as follows: *left – right* ERF K/V 8 wheeler bulk, ERF L/V series 8 wheeler bulk, ERF C Series artic bulk (die-cast), Foden S21 8 wheeler bags and smaller model (both die-cast), Sentinel Steamer (bags), Foden S20 recovery (part die-cast), ERF L/V artic bags (die-cast), Commer Minibus body wagon (die-cast), Bedford KM (scratchbuilt) bags, ERF L/V artic bulk (scratchbuilt), ERF B Series 8 wheeler bulk (scratchbuilt).

Shown in the above photo alongside each other, left to right, are: Eastwoods Cement Foden S18 3 pot bulk, Chinnor Cement 8 wheeler Foden (bulk) and a Rugby Cement ERF K/V 8 wheeler bulk. Other models shown in the first photograph include an Eastwoods Cement "O" type Bedford (bags), plus a Chinnor Cement Foden S21 box bodied bulk 8 wheel tipper and a Leyland Comet flat bags.

All of these are further complemented by an enormous private photo collection, depicting RPC Transport and Rugby Cement over the years, which continues to grow.

The models, together with the photographs and my first book published in 2002, continue to remind the general public and former employees of Rugby Cement, just how good it was to work for the company. Fortunately, however, I am no longer alone in remembering these happy years. Visit Jim, Beryl and Steve Hastings' delightful house at Gillingham, Kent, and you will find what amounts to an RPC Transport "shrine". Using a well tried system of beg, borrow or take on long term loan, Steve has obtained the former builders merchant's signs. By cleaning them up and mounting them "in situ" at the rear of the house, Steve has his own RPC grotto. Go a bit further down the back

garden and you will see former front grilles from Seddon Atkinson RPC palletised bodied flats together with numerous publications referring to the days of Rugby Cement, a growing photographic collection and an equally representative amount of die-cast Rugby based model lorries.

Mick Lowe spent almost fourteen years as a night driver, based at South Ferriby cement works in Humberside. Whilst he is perhaps the junior member when it comes to collecting former RPC literature in all forms, his enthusiasm for everything relating to Rugby Portland Cement Transport knows no bounds. Mick is still driving at South Ferriby, working the day shift for the new owners, Cemex. Combining the respective energies of the three of us, each in a different part of the country, means that ordinary members of the public can be rest assured that Rugby Cement will never be forgotten.

1982 was the start of a very busy year for me. Gathering photographs and other material for the book research project involved most of any available spare time over a period of ten years between 1982 and 1992. It did take me fourteen months, but during my busy ten year research period I did also find time to construct a replica model of a B Series ERF 8 wheeler bulk tanker model. It was based on one such lorry which I saw nearly every working day, the one which was given new to driver Wilf Childs 'always on earlies', F/N 914 KRW 888P.

Shown here is an example of F/N 924, which was driven nearly every day by a Southam Works driver who was something of an individual and who gave the impression of thinking he was better than everyone else I personally kept clear of him as he was of the view that Rugby drivers like me, and others who had transferred to Southam after 1982, were not in the same league as himself. On his own for much of the time, he did always get on with his job, but several accidents attributed to him in Southam Works' Yard did not endear him to a lot of people.

Something of a compromise in size and shot is overleaf with my model of the B Series ERF. It is shown the other way round, but in essence it's all there, even down to the cab and opening front panel. This tank body was replaced in 1989 with a better, stronger material when it bowed bent in the car during a hot day in 1989.

A similarly bodied 8-wheeler B Series ERF thirty ton flat began life at South Ferriby Works in North Lincs. It is shown here

fully loaded within the confines of the works. LDU 654V was new to RPC Transport on the 19th March 1980. It carried chassis number 42576 and was classed as a twenty ton delivery chassis platform. F/N 549 was given to driver Keith Lacey and, as far as I know, it stayed in fleet ownership for around seven or eight years. These 8-wheelers were up to the usual standard of the ERFs. Twenty ton of bags could be loaded and transported without any bother at all, but pallet loads were limited to seventeen and a half ton. These lorries more than proved their worth at Chinnor, Rochester, South Ferriby and Barrington, where long delivery runs were the norm. When sold out of service, LDU 654V was to be bought by Robin Clack Transport. I'm readily informed, by both Jim Hastings and his son Steve, that this man was something of a character.

Shown opposite is the same lorry, but with all of the RPC lettering painted over. Silver or white edging lines painted on the wheel steps and on the diesel tank, are the only changes. This lorry was collected from Chinnor by Robin Clack after purchase.

Another recently traced member of the LDV batch of thirty ton chassis was found and photographed by Mrs Brenda Carlisle as long ago as 1992 at the Great Dorset Steam Fair.

LDU 658V dates from May 1980, and carried F/N 552. It was bodied as an 8-wheel platform for use with bagged cement, and might have been

based at Chinnor Cement works near Oxford in later years. It has been completely transformed with simple box body work, and painted cream all over with a green flash on the body and cab. Additional storage areas on both the chassis frames resulted in underbody storage structures. These present a neat but very practical change. A Gardner 180 engine was standard power, plus a 7 speed gearbox. This combination would be absolutely ideal for any showman. The addition of twin roof mounted orange flashing lights is the only non-standard fitment.

Meeting Alan Holland and his charming wife way back at the 2005 Town and Country Festival when they came as visitors, was both a surprise and a sheer delight for me. It was not long before RPC reminiscences came to the fore, and I had both of them uncontrollable with laughter as we remembered happier times at Rugby Cement. Alan Holland managed a creditable twenty five years' service - even though it was broken. He was blessed with a superb sense of fun, coupled with utmost loyalty to the Company. These are the things that I shall remember about this jolly individual. Before Alan and his wife left Stoneleigh, I asked him politely if he would find time to put down on paper some aspects of his Company service as a driver. His own story, which you have read earlier, sums up almost 80% of driver individuals who would spend almost the whole of their driving life with RPC Transport amid the constant fun and laughter which abounded in the ranks of Chinnor, Eastwoods and Rugby Cement alike.

Looking back to the late 1980s, when some of these ERF B Series 8-wheeler flats were sold

into second ownership, the full load potential was achieved with little or no fuss whatsoever.

The individual mentioned earlier at Rochester, alias "Catweasel", might have made new friends had he got the paint pot out and given the front grille ERF letters a white coating, rather than just doing minimal improvements. I have since been informed that these particular 8 wheelers did not survive too long under second ownership. What they did achieve with Rugby Cement, however, was that they assisted the Company with the fifteen and twenty ton delivery loads nationwide, as well as any remaining building site deliveries before the total transformation following the introduction of the palletised pack operation. This came about after the installation at the various cement mills of automatic packing and loading facilities, coupled with the introduction of the new Seddon Atkinson 6-wheeler pallet bodied lorries and the later C Series ERF 6 wheeler chassis.

CHAPTER 9

The Simple Ideas Are Always the Best
New Chassis for Bags and Bulk
S/Atkinson ERF C Series
Artics Introduction
Sold Out of Service

A previous Atkinson 8 wheeler DNX 253 platform lorry which was not fitted with a starter motor was the only connection with this well known commercial vehicle manufacturer when it carried Crown Cement colours. Thirty six years were to pass before new Seddon Atkinsons were purchased following the amalgamation of Seddon Atkinson with their mechanical engineering development capability which was owned by a foreign power namely International Harvester of America. The actual buyout took place in 1974 and six years later the appearance of the Seddon Atkinson 300 Series 6 wheelers with their simply designed castellated bodies and mobile pallet base, took the transport world totally by surprise. This design concept was down to RPC Transport engineers themselves, whose forethought in simplicity has to be admired. The Seddon Atkinson chassis were ordered new through Vee / Inline Diesels at Daventry S/A Agents whose base was just off the the A45 in Northamptonshire.

They were later delivered direct in this form to Cossington Garage in Leicestershire, who were the ERF main dealers and were to be responsible for building the aluminium styled black bodywork. The following two photographs show the complete lorries, fully equipped with flat metal plates which fitted into the slots when building site deliveries necessitated. Fortunately, this was not very often.

As time went on, early in the 1980s these plates were removed from use completely, because many sites, as well as building premises, used fork lifts for unloading. Five Seddon Atkinson 6 wheeler platforms are shown in the sunshine outside Central Garage. The second photograph shows these same five lorries taken from the near side. As earlier mentioned in Part One of RPC Transport, this simple style of loading and unloading was to revolutionise the delivery of bagged cement. The simple ideas are very often the best.

The first two Seddon Atkinson 300 Series went to Southam Works, and were given to Godfrey Noon, who took charge of RDU 616W, and John Bousefield who had 558 SKV 75W. How long John remained on bags I don't know, because not long afterwards he took over on nights at Southam Despatch. My memory does not recall 558 staying at Southam, but then again, I may be wrong. These revolutionary chassis assisted the fitters in as much as the tilt cab made their job easier all round.

More information came from Mick Lowe up at South Ferriby concerning some of these Seddon Atkinson issued to his colleagues. He says that 572 went to Graham Lewis and 573 was the responsibility of Dave Peacock. They also had 592 whose driver's name was not known. Gordon Avell drove F/N 712, an ERF L/V 8 wheeler platform, DNX 726K from new. I received the sister vehicle new in August 1971, DNX 725K, F/N 711, but it was taken off me twelve months later because Southam Works' demand for bags was larger than Rugby's at that time.

Henry Knight's tanker was loading bulk masonry at the far end of the packing plant at Southam one day quite some years back. As he was always to be found either criticising someone or stuck behind the steering wheel reading the Daily Telegraph, either option may have resulted in someone shouting. Henry immediately drove off the loading point. The trouble was that the masonry was still being blown into the tank. Southam Works' Yard was three to four feet deep in masonry cement powder within seconds before Henry could be stopped further up the Yard. There was no real damage to either the loading point, nor to Henry's lorry, and most of the mess was carted off down to the quarry. Needless to say, Danny Burke, the canteen manager, reprimanded Henry the next day for his impatience. True to form, Henry shouted back "This doesn't concern you, you nosy sod!". Both of these individuals were constantly at each other, but everything was usually taken in good humour.

 Rugby Cement

One of our specially designed lorries being loaded.

Far right
Off loading at site and a member of our sales staff with a demonstration load explaining the expendable pallet system.

Handling cement on an expendable pallet in a store.

Already described in earlier pages, this leaflet shows a close up of the fork lift movement placing the cement pack on to the special bodied 6 wheeler Seddon Atkinson.

Photos of drivers and their lorries are an author's gain because they show man and machine as things were. Believe me, when I say that RPC Transport, like so many other well known and less well known firms of years gone by, had its own characters.

Derringtons, the Birmingham based builder's yard, had moved to a new yard just off the ring road near junction 6 of the M6 when this photo was taken. Godfrey Noon, Southam Works' longest serving bag driver, was given the first Seddon Atkinson 300 flat with the castellated bodywork - basically a mobile pallet chassis. He is shown putting the sheet on top of the load. It was rolled up and tied down on the head board ledge. We've all done it hundreds of times.

Two characters, different as chalk and cheese, are shown in Southam Works' Yard. They worked as loaders. George Greenaway, standing on the lorry, never stopped talking or laughing, whilst Ian Mackie, in the cab, appeared at times to be rather serious. Drivers all over are their own worst enemy, and when Ian Mackie doubled up as night despatch clerk, his attitude to all drivers changed overnight, as he assumed rather wrongly that his word was law. His actions did not really endear him to the drivers, myself included. After all, we were being paid to do a job which at that time we all loved doing.

Another posed driver is captured on film with this shot shown opposite. Brian Hazelwood, a Rochester Works based bag driver, is about to exit the cab of his Seddon Atkinson 300 F/N 559. The well remembered front end of these popular bag lorries is seen to good effect. RPC S/A 6 wheeler flats were classed as 300s, whilst future 8 wheeler bulk chassis were known as 301s. The Seddon Atkinsons worked alongside Dodge Hi Liners and ERF C Series 6-wheelers. The whys and wherefores of these particular bodied Seddon Atkinson 300s and their ERF Turbo cabbed 6-wheeler lorries with their special bodywork, have been explained in detail.

In all of the major Rugby Cement mills at that time, modernisation of all of the Packing Sheds (Bag Operations) was underway, certainly in 1979 – 1980. In most cases, extra long buildings at South Ferriby, Southam, Barrington and Rochester were in the process of being constructed.

The photograph shown on the next page shows in detail the Southam Works overhead driven forklift cranes used to load these new style delivery lorries. Godfrey Noon's Seddon Atkinson 300 is shown almost fully loaded with three more bag packs still to be put on. The reader should, however, be aware that the original Fluxo packers which existed at each of the above five RPC Cement works still packed each individual bag of cement. The change of getting the bags down into these new storage buildings was made possible by extension conveyor belts, all under cover, which joined the packer to the new storage sheds. The bags were brought down singly and fed into the central enclosed machine, which was similar to a butter pat. 30 bag packs emerged every sixty seconds, and were automatically diverted either left or right, dependent upon demand. Chinnor bag shed loaded both pallet and cement

packs (30 bags) together. Their bag loading shed was extended, but at the four remaining Works already mentioned, separate buildings, although connected as mentioned, were built from new.

Seddon Atkinson 8-wheeler bulk tanker chassis entered fleet service during February 1982, although F/N 576 YAC 37X came twelve months early. I am pretty sure that the photo shown of a brand new Seddon Atkinson 30 ton bulk tanker is taken within the confines of Leeds Depot on the former Cross Green Industrial Estate. The individual holding on to the door is John Todd, a driver with many years' service. He spent forty one years at South Ferriby

Works. 576 was probably being used for test loads from either Rugby or South Ferriby at that time. The difference of outward front panel design, together with cab interiors, can be judged between F/N 576 and that of F/N 992 shown discharging a stock load at Southam during the hours of darkness. The dual orange painted silos of Leeds, are similar to that of this newly painted lorry. The apparent absence of any other RPC lorries suggests that this new lorry has been brought in to

get bulk drivers' opinions and to gain familiarity with discharge operations.

Seddon Atkinson 8-wheeler tankers were classed as 301 chassis and F/N 992 has the revised front panel. This particular chassis came too late into the RPC fleet to be included in part one of this story, hence there are no registration or fleet number details. In fact I think, but don't know for certain, it was snapped up for owner/driver operation after 1990. Both these bulk tankers appear similar in a visual sense, however, F/N 992 was fitted with oil pump discharge equipment.

Note the electric fan fitted to the offside second front axle mudguard, and the oil storage tank positioned aft of the lorry's main diesel fuel tank. Single rams were introduced on all 8 wheeler chassis when the Rugby Cement Company started operating thirty ton lorries.

Accidents within RPC Transport were few and far between, purely and simply because 60% of the fleet, certainly from 1964 – 1974 onwards, barely made 26mph fully loaded. Even on empty running, you were lucky to make 30-32mph. Before I came off 8 wheeler platform lorries, I was plagued by silly bumps and scrapes off road, either on building sites or in merchant's yards. Each of these incidents prevented me from achieving accident free driving, and so consequently I never qualified for a medal from 1968 onwards until a few years' later.

Shown below is F/N 584, driven by Jim Hastings, a Rochester Works bag driver, which suffered slight damage to the offside front when a Mercedes driver found himself in the wrong. Rather than hit the coned off area of road-works, his car collided with the front of Jim's lorry, causing the damage shown. Although work would be required to fit a new front bumper and an effort made to straighten out the cab step and surrounding areas, I have no

doubt that the Rochester garage staff may have had this lorry back in regular use within 36 hours or less.

This Chinnor based Seddon Atkinson bulk tanker shown right had suffered a very serious front end shunt on the offside and centre. The impact has sheared off the front bumper, the silencer box and damaged all the lower areas of the chassis. The offside front side panel, lead light and flasher areas will all require extensive repairs. Also shown in this picture is Chinnor fuelling island and the main works' office. I have since been informed that this lorry collided with a nearby railway wagon hence the front end damage.

This picture of two Seddon Atkinson lorries which survived into second ownership is now also in my possession. These I'm told, soldiered on after being sold around 1990. The first of these is Alan Burdett's replacement lorry after his terrible crash with 710. He changed from bags to bulk when he was given DKV 870Y, shown parked out of use on the Shennington, near Banbury, premises of Sea Bea Transport, and fitted with a bulk corn and cattle feed body. It was photographed by my late, great friend, Roland Parry when on a visit to these premises. Traces of RPC paint are still visible on the mirror arms and the rear wings. An illuminated headboard's claim to customers is typical of this transport operator, plus a hasty repaint, initially on the cab and wings. Since this photo was taken the lorry has been scrapped.

Found and photographed as long ago as 1997 by the late Rod Spooner of the Fairground

Society of Great Britain, A130 MDU, a former 301 ex RPC Bulk Tanker chassis, is shown under second ownership at the Newcastle Town Moor Fair of that year.

Belonging to a Keith Turner (Showman), it is fitted with box bodywork and tastefully painted in a pleasing green and white livery with yellow lettering to match. These Seddon Atkinson 301s suffered terribly with gearbox problems when owned by RPC Transport.

Two former Seddon Atkinson 6 wheeler platformed lorry photographs supplied to me as late as early 2011 need to be included in this story. Both were originally based at Rochester Cement Works in Kent. XRW 191X, carrying the original F/N of 578, was delivered to RPC Transport on the 1st April 1982.

The significance of this photo, of the two identical lorries owned by Clugston Distribution in second ownership, is that 191X has the driver in position. Also, the orange centre border between white and blue is in a lower position. The background buildings show the newly built bulk and bag site at Rochester some years back. Sadly, since these two lorries worked for Clugstons, cement making and distribution from the Rochester area has finished. The works and surrounding buildings were demolished in 2011. The second photograph shows BWK 203Y, which carried F/N 597, also Rochester based, and presents a well sheeted and roped load

in similar surroundings. This is a better interpretation of the Clugston livery with the orange cheat line separating the blue and white fleet colours. Equally, the white fleet number shows up against the blue background.

203Y was supplied to RPC Transport on the 1st August 1982 and was sent direct to Rochester Cement Works. It is very sad now remembering better times under RPC Transport. This period of second ownership began at some point in the late 1980s after the disbanding of RPC Transport, when all former company lorries were advertised for sale to outside contractors on both bag and bulk operations. The Rochester site will soon be cleared of all cement related buildings etc, and made ready for new housebuilding.

Pre-fleet publicity photographs were also taken in later years of both the Seddon Atkinson and the C25 ERF 6 wheeler platform chassis in front of the Central Garage by the former Company photographer Robin Palmer. He later emigrated to the island of Fiji, where in between visits to the United Kingdom to see family members, he still lives to this day.

This pre-fleet introduction photo was taken in August 1983, shortly before all the lorries were dispersed throughout the fleet at the various factory locations. F/N 904, 5 and 6 are shown here prior to leaving for points unknown, which, some 28 years ago, may have been either Barrington Works in Cambridge, South Ferriby in North Lincolnshire, Chinnor near Oxford or Rochester in Kent.

A close up scene, opposite, shows the impact of the then recently introduced alternative Rugby Cement livery on the offside cab door of a new ERF C Series. Facing the camera is F/N 906, ready to go to pastures new. There is no doubt in my mind, even after all the time that has passed since the introduction of the B Series ERF in 1974, that the gradual improvements in the basic original design eventually resulted in the C Series design shown here – superb!!

I was one of possibly ten former Rugby Works based Bag Drivers who were to find ourselves, and our own lorries, in June 1982, being transferred permanently ten miles down the road to Southam Works. This happened because the Rugby Works Packing and Loading

bag shed was old and not then eligible for refurbishment. At that time, Jack Smith and I had our Bedford KM 16 ton platforms. The rest of the Rugby flats involved ERF and Dodge Hi Liner lorries. Not all of my former bag colleagues were to be enamoured with the change in our working days to be based at Southam. Mick Shepherd opted for voluntary redundancy, and left accordingly.

Jack Kenney, a bag driver, was to leave RPC employment on medical grounds.

I soon settled into the Southam Works' routine, as I'd often worked eight wheeler bags for Fred Williams, the Southam Despatch Supervisor. The easy going atmosphere in the whole of the cement works there was a complete revelation. My younger brother Gordon had married Kath Alcock, the daughter of Arthur Alcock, the foreman at Central Garage. When Clive, the Southam Garage foreman got to know about this, he made it his business to tell everybody. Fred Saunders, the man who could never get up in time for work at Rugby, was faced early on with a decision, which in time almost cost him his life. Fred, like most of us required to clock on at Southam, had to completely revise his getting up habits. He had his own car, which he used for a time to get to Southam and home again, but this idea didn't go down well with him so, much to everyone's amazement, by getting up at 5am he tried cycling the ten miles to Southam

Works. Bearing in mind it was the summer months when we transferred, the weather was fairly reasonable, but early morning frosts were visible. I was then 44 years of age, but Big Fred was older. No-one had an inkling what he was doing until Chris Moon, giving a lift to former postman Roy Allen better known as Telegram Sam, passed a lone cyclist in RPC uniform near The Boat canal pub one morning at around 5.47am. Both Chris and Roy said together "That's Saunders!". They carried on down to the Southam Cement Works, clocked on respectively at 6am and did the same for Fred Saunders. Clocking on for someone else was a sackable offence, but for the moment it saved Fred from showing as being late. Chris had parked his car in the works car park, found his own lorry, done his vehicle checks (as you did) and was on his way to Southam Despatch to pick up his delivery tickets when Fred Saunders made his way down to the Transport Office around 6.15am. Fred was RPC Transport's longest serving bag driver, starting initially in 1950. He was to give the Company just over 37 years' service before he was redundant in 1987. He was then 63 years old. I have since learned from Fred why he started cycling to Southam after we'd all been transferred there in 1982. Gordon Brown already mentioned had agreed with Fred that he would cycle alongside him, but on the first day in question Gordon Brown dropped out for whatever reason. After Fred's initial first attempt to cycle the eleven miles from home to the cement works at Southam, his nickname became Reg Harris, after the famous racing cyclist. What a large number of the drivers did not know was that Fred cycled each way for nearly a fortnight before he packed it in permanently, mainly for two reasons. One reason was that he was not getting enough rest at night, and the other was that his working days occupied twelve hours or more.

After the reallocation of the Seddon Atkinson 6 wheeler platform, I was to be given YAC 39X F/N 581 after Ted Shoebridge, who'd had it from new and moved away from the Southam area. Roy Allen, Fred Saunders and Tony Hall, alias Captain Pugwash, all took on a Seddon Atkinson platform.

The transfer of the Rugby bag men to Southam was, for me, a salvation and revelation in respect of being away from officialdom and the nearby presence of Crown House. I wished I'd transferred permanently months before. Fred Williams, Southam Depatch Supervisor, was still there in 1982. His second in command, Mick White, would take over not long after we arrived, as Trevor Griffin, the original 2nd in command had been appointed Transport Supervisor at Chinnor Cement Works in Oxfordshire.

Early in 1983 the first two C Series ERF 6 wheeler flat platforms arrived at Southam Works. Initially they were given to Kevin Billingham who became the permanent owner of F/N 871 EHP 939Y, whilst 872 became the responsibility of Gordon Brown. The two drivers were the best of friends, and seemingly went everywhere together. Both had done their time earlier on KM/Bedford flats. These two ERFs, fitted with the castellated palletised bodywork both entered fleet service on 1st March 1983. I have since been readily informed that Kevin and "Jock" Brown more or less ran together with their new lorries on more than fifteen deliveries, mainly to the Bristol areas.

Totally exhausted after tipping at Bristol Sand and Gravel's dockside yard early one morning, Jock Brown is shown overleaf in classical pose – fast asleep – and parked underneath the Bristol Suspension Bridge where there was a good café which was a regular haunt for RPC lorries and other customers. Gordon Brown is shown stretched out in his C Series ERF cab with suitable levelling on the driver's seat, plus the use of a headrest as a pillow. Whether this was an official break, or otherwise, I'm unsure.

Gordon Brown and Chris Johnson ran the TGWU for Transport drivers at Southam Works. Their combined approach to the individual was a complete reversal of the tactics used in the past at Rugby Works by Reg Price and Billy Barber. There were very many drivers and individuals who'd been with Rugby Cement for longer than myself, many at Rugby, Southam and elsewhere within RPC Transport who, when Union membership was offered, would and did remain dubious. Halford Reddish, who had guided the fortunes of Rugby Cement for many years, was totally opposed to being told how to run his Company by a Union. His views on Trade Unions with regard to all of his employees, was that nothing was to be conducted inside any Rugby Cement Works or depots.

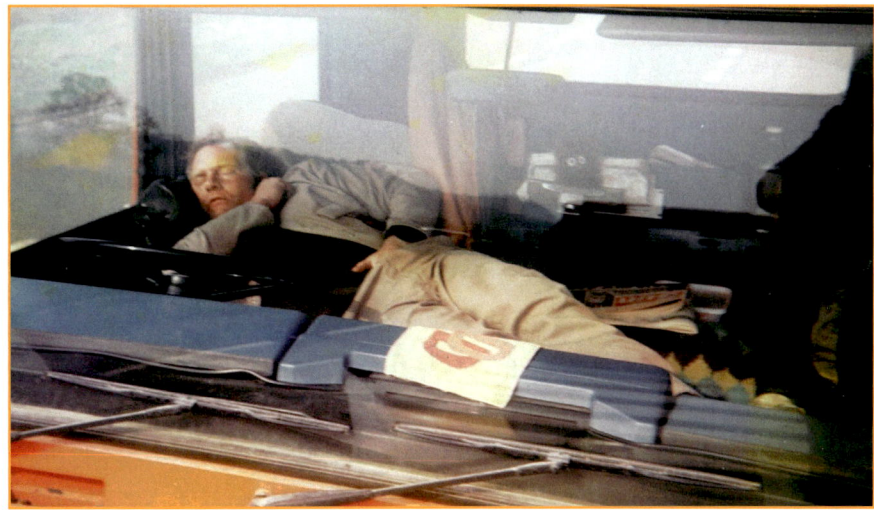

The picture shows Gordon Brown's F/N 872 receiving attention on a pre carnival build up for Rugby Electronic Organs, alias The Flintstones. These 6-wheeler pallet bodies carried a set of flat plates which, along with the Seddon Atkinsons, covered up the gaps on the castellated platform, giving these lorries a solid platform base, which as you can imagine, on Carnival Day was an absolute necessity. Most RPC drivers who were asked to do this voluntary job, would paint the wheels black and give the lorry in question a thorough wash and brush up in preparation. Looking at 872 in this photograph, this lorry is immaculate in every sense, and

represents the company well whilst in drag. Almost all of these ERF C Series 6-wheelers were to see second ownership within the fairgrounds of Southern England. More about that later.

The sister lorry to 872 was Kevin Billingham's 871. These two individuals stuck to each other like glue, and appeared, on balance, to go everywhere together. Kevin was a really lovely character to work with, always laughing and blessed by being able to see the funny side of life. If there was any skulduggery or a funny incident, either in the bag shed or elsewhere, these two always had something to do with it.

When regulations were relaxed somewhat with requests from charitable associations to do with the Carnival or whatever, invariably 871/872 would be involved. Later on artics were to be used. In the photograph shown right Kevin can just be made out laughing, as ever, behind the wheel of 871, carrying Admiral's Court residents. Not much in the way of decoration is shown, but certainly they are a very happy lot of people riding on the back coaxing the general public to part with their money. When Gordon Brown relinquished 872, it passed to Chris Moon. Redundancies unfortunately had become a part of all the drivers lives at Rugby Cement in the middle 1980's. Consequently, it was worked out on the basis of last in/first out, and Kevin Billingham left Southam Cement around 1985-6. For a short time, he worked for a brewery in the Wood Street area of Rugby. Later on, he obtained a job as a porter at St Cross Hospital. A little while later, he drove out-patient ambulances. Knowing Kevin as I did, often being the butt of his humour, aided and abetted at times by Fruity Harris, I have no doubt that this infectious style of humour would find immediate favour with all of the staff and patients at the hospital.

I keep an album full of ex RPC Transport lorries in their second ownership roles, but so far F/N 871 is not amongst them, unless of course the readership knows otherwise.

When Kevin Billingham worked at the Cement Works he lived at Willoughby, near Rugby, and had done so for a number of years. During his time working in and around the hospital, Kevin was to strike up a friendship with a lady called Sue who worked in a senior position within St Cross Hospital. This friendship deepened into romance, and so they eventually married and set up home in Rugby. Kevin's humorous nature would, I am double sure of now, have complemented Sue's own upbringing, because her father was Mick Hennesey, one of two of Central Garage's night

foremen, whose own fame and notoriety for skulduggery was well known to visiting drivers. His own sense of perverted humour, would I'm sure be familiar to Sue. Sadly, however, for all the wrong reasons, Sue and Kevin along with Sue's son were not to be allowed to stay together in their shared happiness. Kevin and Sue's son were killed outright in a head on crash in their car coming back from Southam one evening. A foreign driver, with neither license nor insurance, and also who had no reason nor right to be in the United Kingdom, had caused this collision in the most horrendous way by being on the wrong side of the road whereby he ploughed head on into Kevin's car at a ferocious speed. The double loss of both her husband and son was horribly tragic for Sue, and totally unforgivable given the terrible circumstances. For those like myself and other drivers who'd worked alongside Kevin Billingham in happier times, his loss cannot be imagined or accepted in any way. Kevin took to the grave a fantastic sense of proportion and raw humour, the likes of which we shall never be allowed to enjoy again. Billy, as he was perhaps better known, even now, years after his passing, is still fondly remembered and will not be forgotten.

Eleven former ex RPC ERF C Series 6 wheeler chassis were destined after the disbanding of RPC Transport in later years, to enter the fairgrounds of Great Britain. Four of these, included Jock Brown's ex 872.

Some idea of the extensive maintenance and servicing given to all RPC Transport lorries, can perhaps be imagined and appreciated by this superb view of the Barrington Cement Works Garage Workshop areas.

Four or five inspection pits are visible, and both a C Series ERF 6 wheeler platform, and what looks like a brand new Foden Haulmaster 8 wheeler bulk tanker, are seen receiving attention of one sort or another. Well lit pits and surrounding areas, plus ample room to work between them, present an environment of safety that was pleasant to work in. I remember,

many years back being both impressed by the eagerness and the kindness of the garage staff there when I had brakes sticking on an S21 Foden 8 wheeler fully loaded with S/R bags.

Looking very forlorn and forgotten stripped of its RPC lettering and its fleet number (919), is LRW 316P new in October 1975.

It is parked amidst other redundant chassis all awaiting an uncertain fate. Mechanically and visibly in good order, these B Series ERFs did not have colossal mileages. The 8-wheelers were fitted with double drive, whilst the 6-wheelers were not.

Most of the showmen who bought 6-wheeler B Series ERFs opted to cut off the rear trailing axles. These lorries were parked at the rear of the new garage at Southam. A complete revelation in both visual appearance of a former B Series ERF and general effect which are pleasing to the eye, supplied new in August 1979, F/N 510 was eventually to be given to Johnnie Overton, whose passion was golf. Eventually offered for sale around 1986, it was bought by Philip Read of the well-known Reads family of Longhope Gloucestershire. Beautifully presented in crimson, with a white centre cheat line and front bumper, HDU 910V survived for a few years more, working out of Southam and Newport Depot in South Wales.

Several in and out cab improvements, such as horn, a sun visor and chromed upright exhaust stack, really transformed this former standard RPC 8-wheeler bulk tanker into a class of its own.

My last statement, concerning these beautiful C Series ERFs is borne out by the second of these two photographs.

I'm fairly sure that 699 Y is still in regular use. Photographed by Rod Jesson at the September 2003 Bridgewater Fair, A537 HAC now sports a cab roof and deflector, plus a super colour combination of all over grey interspersed with black and red cheat lines on both cab and bodywork. A generator of one sort or another is set into the off side rear bodywork. When in RPC ownership, this lorry carried F/N 900.

Almost certainly still in regular use, and again photographed as recently as 2010, the ex RPC ERF shown below was seen at Kingsbury Fair in London. Belly box storage, presumably on both sides, present this workmanlike lorry, whilst not detracting too much from the well known C Series ERF style. Named "Rebel", and painted in a pleasing grey on the lower areas, with upper bodywork in white, simple black lettering completes a practical showman's lorry. ERW 699Y in its Rugby Cement days carried F/N 879. Its base works is unknown. These turbo cabbed 6-wheeler chassis were everything the new Century Showmen wanted – stylish and thoroughly reliable with not rot cabs – magic in everything!

Another former C Series 6 wheeler platform bodied Rugby Cement ERF was photographed by Rod Jesson as recently as July 2009, proving beyond all shadow of a doubt that some of these ex Rugby lorries can still be seen in all areas of England.

A538 HAC was supplied to RPC Transport alongwith at least ten of her sister lorries in 1983. Consequently, when she was found by Rod at the Warrington Lanes Fair, this lorry was then thirty years old.

Shown here in an attractive cream and red combination, and fitted with the now accepted composite box bodywork, the fairground ride it transports is called a Round Up, and is seen built up at the rear of the lorry. The former F/N of this Rugby ERF was 901. Again its base works is not known to me. Very little of any major change has been done to the chassis by James Holland and the second owner, other than to fit flashing orange roof mounted lights. Consequently, the cab is entirely original. Numerous belly box storage areas are usable on the lower panels of the chassis.

One of the nicest and perfectly proportioned 8 wheeler bulk chassis ever to carry the RPC Transport revised fleet livery has to be F/N 231, which carried registration number B694 SHP, shown here in the confines of Southam Works yard before it was delivered to its own base works within the Group.

Powered, I think, by the Gardner 230, plus the Fuller 8 speed range change gearbox, many of these cab interiors, which came in a tasteful two tone brown, were thoroughly well balanced in terms of power, comfort and design. They were the last rigid 8 wheeler bulk chassis to be ordered in numbers around the Group.

Taxed purely for thirty ton operation, they very comfortably carried a full twenty ton bulk load with ease. To readers of this book, who may or may not know, the ERF B Series cab

shown with the lorry on the left, has been improved over many years, whilst still retaining the original shape. Powerful engines and gearboxes, together with more tasteful interiors put these C Series 8 wheeler chassis completely in a class of their own. Driving them, as I did on rare occasions, you felt as though you were literally "King of the Road". My own comments very early on in Part One of this story referred to positive steering and superb braking on the K/V ERF Limited's revolutionary design, even for the 1950s engineered 8 wheeler chassis put in fleet service by RPC Transport. Over very many years we were to be thoroughly mesmerised by the L/V cab, which itself underwent numerous front panel design changes over a 12 year period. Many former company drivers, including myself, spent our entire life with RPC driving ERF chassis, and many of these self-same drivers, all individuals in their own right, much preferred ERF chassis to other makes in the RPC Fleet.

Our drivers were no different from countless hundreds of other drivers in the industry. They were not interested in what engines or gearboxes were in their lorries, what their daily and nightly priorities depended upon was whether their particular lorry was warm and comfortable. Various adaptations were put to the test in order to get a good sleep on official breaks. Speed was never an issue, because all of the Gardner engines in the fleet were set via the injection pumps to get the best possible miles per gallon.

When the ERF B Series came out in 1974, Gardner 180s were standard in both 8 and 6 wheelers. The tilt cab design would greatly assist the garage fitters, but it was only after then, more or less on a permanent basis, that speeds were to be increased a bit. Although the first square fronted thirty ton ERF 8 wheelers were brought out in 1971 / 72, both Gardner and Cummins engines brought higher speeds denied to RPC drivers for years. I make no secret of the fact that as a driver on bags for eighteen years out of twenty two and a half in total, driving the ERFs always gave you a feeling of complete confidence, simply because you knew, however slow, you always got home. We qualified on to ERF artics in 1988, by which time redundancies at all of the cement works in the Rugby Group had reduced the fleet drivers perhaps to less than forty overall. I drove rigid lorries for over twenty years at Rugby Cement before I, along with remaining colleagues, all of class 2 qualification, were informed by Transport Management in 1988, that we would be trained up to HGV class 1 artics. For me personally, along with a few of my friends, it was to take two bites at the cherry before I passed with flying colours on my second attempt in June 1988.

Shortly after June 1988, when I finally qualified as a Class One artic driver, the remaining Company employed weekly paid drivers were split into groups on a six week (days) and a three week (nights) shift system. Cost effectiveness were two words which, from then on, were to ring in our ears right across the group.

Readers must be aware that by this time nearly 60% of all drivers who had left the employment of Rugby Cement did not want to have anything to do with an Owners/Drivers scheme which had brought about this situation.

Drivers on artics were also not interested, and so constant use of the artics on both night and day operation became the norm, and the wheels never stopped turning.

Shown here is a photograph of F/N 240 taken by its driver at that time, Roy Allen, alias Telegram Sam, who was a former postman. The location is the former Mixconcrete plant at Torrington Avenue at Canley in Coventry. The constant ravages of hardened cement dust particles show on both the unit's cab roof and on the top of the tank, which itself looks as though it is in need of a thorough wash. This plant was typical of most Mixconcrete premises, whereby you, the cement drivers, bound by company rules to watch the pressure at the rear of the tank, had constant dripping water falling on you from a great height. This was bad enough, but if the wind was blowing in the wrong direction whilst you were there, and the sand and gravel was tipped into the bins, you got blasted by grains blowing into both your hair and face. I found, rather early on whilst driving these artics with the bulk trailer behind you, it was rather bumpy loaded or empty, but with twenty tons of bags on you did not know it was there. Constant verbal instructions from the transport office, both within Southam Works and at Head Office at that time telling us to go faster, did not go down well either with myself or my remaining colleagues. By that point we

had all served the Company loyally having been trained from day one to drive both safely and legally in accordance with Company instructions and the law. Therefore, none of us were prepared to break the law by going faster.

Shown here is the same artic unit B839 TAC with me, the author, having my official half hour break parked at the former Crick Stop Transport Café. This was later the former Eddie Stobart Transport workshop and parking area. I was on the way back to Southam cement works after a bulk delivery to the Steetley Deniff plant in Nuneaton.

Photos of workshop staff are extremely rare, but the one shown here was orchestrated at Barrington Cement Works near Cambridge. Whether it was an official request or not, I don't know. Shown left to right are Brian Williamson (Garage Foreman), Alan Dorman, Andrew Teige, Ray Wing and John Gallacher. Ray and John were ex works fitters who transferred to the garage. On the far right is Tom Cook. They are all standing in front of ERF C Series C770 WDU F/N 254. I was later to photograph this unit in second ownership in 2009 being used to provide power for a Wall of Death, a motorcycle stunt ride, at the Stoneleigh Exhibition Centre that year.

A year after myself and several RPC colleagues qualified as HGV Class 1 artic drivers, I returned to Southam Works one afternoon after dieseling up at the pumps, only to be confronted by a police car and accident ribbons across the front of the Palletiser Shed. Needless to say, something very serious had happened, but being near my going home time it was to be a couple of days before I found out what the trouble was. Bear in mind that this happened almost twenty years ago, and because of the nature of this particular accident I needed to find out the exact truth for this publication, so here it is.

John Winfield – reference my accident – June 1989

"I'd just relieved Arthur Bazely on the afternoon shift at 2.30pm on crane number one in the palletiser shed. Having placed a loaded module of cement on a lorry, I was collecting a second module when, suddenly, the cab of the crane I was operating crashed to the ground. I was knocked unconscious for quite a while, and therefore know nothing about what happened during the period of time whilst I was out of it. Eventually I came round, and although I was in extreme pain from my lower back region, I went and sat on a pallet of bagged cement. Looking back, this was probably not the wisest thing to do! An ambulance was called for, and I was blue-lighted to Warwick Hospital, where I was diagnosed with a crushed and fractured vertebrae in my spine. I spent three weeks in hospital, and after being discharged I had to wear a specially made brace for six months as I had restricted bending of my back. Unfortunately, this ended my time in the Packing Plant, but I am still here to tell the tale".

John Winfield transferred to the Works Laboratory in Southam Works after returning to work, where he remains as a Cemex employee.

Derek Biddle and Rodney Bench, both good friends and workmates for many years within Southam Works, are shown together in this apparent retirement photograph taken in support of Derek finally calling it a day in 1985.

Shown left to right: Rodney Bench is next to Derek Biddle at the front with Derek "Geordie" Stacy. At the rear are Simon Clifton, Shaun McGee (Chargehand foreman in his dark overalls) and Tony Burgess. A multitude of gifts and presentations, plus lurid messages amongst the cards, pertaining to various sexual practices in bed, bear testimony to this happy occasion. I personally did not know Derek Biddle, although during my eight and a half years at Southam we exchanged pleasantries in the Works' canteen, invariably watched over by Danny Burke. Some other names of people who worked in Southam RPC Works for many years include Ron Lockley, who was the Chief Clerk for more years than even he or anyone else can remember. Very much a person who visited employees who were off sick for long periods, Ron is still remembered for these simple acts of kindness. Margaret Bloxam and Carol White worked in the main office. Carol lived with her mother and brother, he being Mick White who took over as Transport Supervisor when Fred Williams

retired many years back.

Cement production finally finished at Southam Works some time back, with many employees offered redundancy terms. Those who wished to transfer to the new Rugby Works did so. Southam remains open purely for quarry extraction purposes to supply the new cement works, ten miles away. Dust is transported to Southam in covered rigid artic tipper lorries, whilst compressed tyres and clay form the return loads to the kiln at Rugby. In recent years under Cemex ownership 70% of Southam cement works has been demolished, leaving only the chimney and clinker shed remaining.

Shown parked up and loaded for the next day are two separate artic lorries.

These are parked alongside Southam Works' new palletiser shed. The rear of an unidentified loaded flat trailer is on the right hand side. Taking centre stage, with the load covered, is B841 TAC, carrying F/N 240. The front panel of a Seddon Atkinson 8 wheeler bulk tanker is just visible, as is the main office block within Southam Works main yard area. Chris Moon looked after lorries in his care as though they were his own.

F/N 245 is shown above getting ready for carnival duties, certainly after 1988. Because small children would be sitting on the platform trailer bodywork, a set of plates were used to slot into the castellated bodywork to effect a safer flat area. These were then sheeted over to provide a degree of comfort as shown.

It is fair to say, now looking back to the last few years of RPC Transport and the constant 24 hours use to which these articulated lorries were exposed to, their overall day to day mechanical performance never faltered. Years of producing well tried and tested ERF chassis by the manufacturer shone through. Mechanical breakdowns were few and far between, however, one day, whilst returning upon instruction to Rugby Works from the RMC plant at Pershore near Worcester, my artic bulk trailer suffered a double rear wheel puncture on the offside rear axle. This happened whilst I was less than seventy yards from the Northbound service station on the A46 Warwick by pass. After telephoning Southam for assistance, John Avidaeus, the young fitter, came out in one of the transit pick ups with two new tyres. He was absolutely petrified when he knew the job was on the off side, near the passing traffic, so I went and borrowed some traffic cones from the service station. I set them ten yards back from the rear of the lorry to warn passing traffic, and managed to cone off the entire off side of the complete lorry, thereby allowing total safety for us both! To say that John was scared was putting it mildly, he was almost out of his skin, but between our respective energies, we managed to get the job done, and eventually went our separate ways.

Swaley Smith, a showman/dealer, bought C42 VWK initially in chassis cab form, it is shown here at the Beaconsfield Fair in May 1992. All RPC lettering was blacked out before leaving RPC ownership.

Photographed again in the early part of this new century by Rod Jesson at the Mitcham Fair in August 2000, C42 VWK has since undergone quite a bit of improvement as shown in this accompanying photograph.

Seen alongside the other ERFs owned by Robert Birch, compact box bodywork has replaced the original open artic chassis. Painted in a pleasing white and grey combination, the end result is a purposeful showman's tractor. Parked between other family transport, like almost all of these former RPC lorries, I have no doubt that these former ERFs will outlast perhaps some of their owners, and continue to give trouble free service for a good few years.

I was recently informed by John Drayton, the former Raw Materials Co-ordinator and Quarry Manager at the Barrington Cement Works near Cambridge, that he has saved one of these ERF C Series artic units for preservation.

CHAPTER 10

Cement Works, Depots and Crown House Remembered

During my twenty two and a half years as a driver with Rugby Cement I did not manage to visit Barnoldswick, Lancs, which I do believe was a railway bulk site developed to provide service to customers engaged on motorway building. Nor did I visit RPC Norwich Depot, also rail connected, although I was to be involved delivering bag loads ordered through their Sales Depot.

Shown above is a night shot of the newly built bulk and bag loading areas of Rochester Cement Works on the opposite side of the A228 to the main production area. Visible here are loaded ERF bulk and bag 8 wheelers with more bulk lorries on the left hand side. Numerous Dodge Hi Liners, and some Bedford KM 4 wheel platform lorries remain empty, facing centre. This photo was taken from the old silos on the East side of the main road.

By way of a total contrast, and taken during daylight hours, and taking remaining centre stage position in this newly constructed area, is the Transport and Despatch building. Surrounded by a mixed collection of ERF 6 wheeler bulk Dodge Hi Liner platform lorries, plus one tanker version, some Bedford KM flats and a couple of Foden bulk lorries, the amount of visible parking area shown is a vast improvement from cramped conditions in years past within the main Rochester Cement Works production areas.

After 1988, when I qualified on to Artics, I remember loading bulk cement in a covered area, which was both dry and safe. Although this photo finish is suspect the River Medway is shown on the right hand side, and beyond these hills lies the M2 motorway.

I never went to RPC Lewes Cement Works, and so therefore cannot comment on its location, nor the buildings within. Shown here are two Rochester based bulk lorries discharging their loads into storage silos at Lewes.

Bulk lorries and platforms for bags as far I know, but I am not 100% sure, loaded on alternate sides, both completely under cover. Even by the end of the 1970s, the continued use of Lewes was to be in doubt. I am readily assured by Jim Hastings, a former Rochester based bag driver, that if you had to take a load of "stock bulk" to Lewes from Rochester, then blowing into these silos could, and often did, take you a full hour. Nothing has changed, you might say!

A complete new transport storage building incorporating road and rail despatch movements was to be built on the opposite side of the cement works on the A228 Snodland to

Rochester road. This road runs parallel with the main railway line and the alongside the River Medway. A branch line went into this new facility, which allowed for receipt of bulk coal supplies into this area and bulk cement deliveries to be sent out in rail wagons.

Shown here is a closer view of this completely new RPC Transport Despatch area. On the bottom right hand side is the Palletiser building with storage silos connected to the new innovation. All these would be used for bag packing etc. The other silos visible to the left would, I think, be concerned with bulk tanker loading and loading of bulk rail wagon deliveries to depots. The long, low building in the centre of this photograph is Despatch and Transport and the objects behind are a lorry wash and diesel fuel storage tank.

All repairs and servicing for Company lorries remained within the main cement works areas. A mixed cluster of both RPC and contractor's lorries are shown within this complex, which allowed better access in and out of this area on to the main road and elsewhere. Not knowing who took this photo, or from what height, I cannot really comment, but ERF B and C Series lorries are just visible in both rigid and artic form, so maybe 500 – 700 feet would be a fair guess. Grey shadowed cement works exterior surfaces on most silos and support buildings are a part of long lived cement makers architecture.

This aerial view of the South Ferriby Cement Works dates from about 1984. The vast scope of rebuilding and enlargement in all areas of these works is very evident. The work's yard is dotted with numerous orange painted RPC Transport lorries, a large proportion of which are also visible. The new palletiser building dominates the lower right of this fantastic aerial photograph. This in itself is connected by conveyors to the original bag packing shed.

The sheer entirety of South Ferriby cannot be envisaged by the human eye, but it is made apparent when you get down to ground level that the enormity of the place can be appreciated by the individual. The photograph shown overleaf shows these works from the riverside. The main A1077 road passes the cement works, which in later years, certainly under Rugby Cement ownership, experienced an almost complete rebuild. Special cements such as a self-sealing oilwell cement, plus other new products, were produced at these works after the rebuild.

Prominent on the right hand side are the top loading silos, now complete, together with the old bag packing shed completely panelled over. The smaller chimney shown in this photograph has since been dismantled, replaced by the taller chimney version which remains in regular use today.

Two shades of light and dark shadowed cement works structures at South Ferriby Cement Works are portrayed in the above photograph, together with the adjacent picture, taken from the River Anchorholme's edge. This shows the contrasting colours of cement works architecture. Whilst I was never there to see these cement works during daylight hours, the effect, even at night, was even more scary and sinister to the unwary in quiet unattended areas of the works.

Judging by the various types of lorries seen in front of the main bulk loading areas, I would date this photograph certainly from the middle to late 1970s. The Bedford KM 4 wheeler dates from 1972, as does the far right ERF 8 wheeler. The other ERFs shown also come within this category or period. Since this photo was taken, much rebuilding has taken place within the South Ferriby works

and quarry perimeters. Shown far left is a Ford Transit work horse minibus. This would be used for a real variety of duties, ranging from works engineers, shift works or even taking injured people to hospital. We had similar vehicles at Rugby and Southam elsewhere within the group.

Tony Foster, whose own story can be found earlier, spent sixteen years on nights, based at Leeds Depot. Much of his work involved collecting bulk loads from South Ferriby Cement Works and delivering them back to Leeds. Some idea of the immense storage capacity held within the half dozen silos is shown by Tony's own detailed list. On the photograph overleaf it reads as follows left to right:

Silo 1 - 500 ton ordinary Portland cement (opc)
Silo 2 - 500 ton ordinary Portland cement (opc)
Silo 3 - 350 ton ordinary Portland cement (opc)
Silo 4 - 450 ton ordinary Portland cement (opc)
Silo 5 - 100 ton sulphate resisting cement (src)
Silo 6 100 ton rapid hardening cement (rhc)

The photograph shown right dates from the early to middle 1970s. The L/V cabbed 8-wheeler on the left is one of the first thirty ton chassis. The B Series 6-wheeler in the centre came around 1976 onwards, whilst the Foden shown on the far right came in the late 1980s.

The combined OPC storage in the four large silos amounted to eighteen hundred separate tons. This was the most commonly used Rugby product, both in bulk, or indeed in bagged form. Not knowing too much about the then construction industries in Yorkshire when this photo was taken, I make this comment purely because of both the sulphate and rapid silos. I remember delivering seventeen and a half ton of sulphate resisting bags to the former Jowett/Bradford Works in Idle, Bradford, in 1971. Possibly, this came through the sales office at South Ferriby Works. RPC Transport Depots such as Leeds, Gloucester and Greenford opted for a single storey building.

According to Tony, he is shown centre stage checking the water etc before the start of his shift, the B Series ERF 6 wheeler was F/N 361, OHP 291P, which came new in 1976. The drivers' rest room is shown on the right, but this building would also have a depot manager, plus other members of staff also catered for within. The pipes shown on either side of the six separate silos enabled all bulk loads to be blown into storage. All bulk delivery lorries were weighbridge loaded, thereby eliminating overloading. This is an excellent photograph of Leeds Depot, which over very many years played host to visiting drivers at times from both Rugby and Southam Cement Works alike.

Sandiacre Depot – Toton Railway Yard, Sandiacre, Derbyshire

Situated in Nottinghamshire, midway between Long Eaton and the Derbyshire border, the former British Rail owned RPC Sandiacre depot was known locally as Toton Railway Yard. This particular shot of Sandiacre Depot, with the cement silos forming the backdrop, was taken mainly to capture the English Electric Locomotive. The building with a chimney behind the loco was the RPC Transport Office. The stark construction of the silo storage is identical to that of Greenford Depot with weighbridge controlled loading of bulk vehicles ensuring quick turnaround. Stock delivery pipes are visible around both structures.

Sandiacre Depot brings back many Saturday morning memories for me, as all bag drivers like me were required to take their turn with either customer or inter depot bulk deliveries, when the necessity demanded. This particular photo was taken in January 1990. Shortly afterwards, all the buildings and structures were dismantled and the land handed back to British Rail. Two drivers based here at Sandiacre, whose names spring to mind were "Cassius", a large rotundly built driver, and "Dougy", both good friends of mine. When trainloads of bulk cement powder were delivered to Toton Yard from Rugby Works, perhaps two or three bulk rail wagons could be systematically unloaded at the same time. Using the depot's own compressed air suction system, each wagon load was blown into either of these two storage silos shown. This system was useful when larger jobs entailed bulk cement deliveries over a wider area from the main works.

Southampton Depot, Hampshire, was well placed in Southern England. Both bulk and bag deliveries further south could be made by RPC Southampton based vehicles. I made my first visit there in 1978, with bulk tanker transfer loads, but I remember taking a brand new Seddon Atkinson 6 wheeler flat down to Chinnor Works where I loaded lime in bags and garage spares, together with a fitter who was going on detachment. All this took place in the early 1980s.

In this photo the depot offices and the bag storage shed are shown side by side. They were compact in design, but both structures fulfilled daily and nightly procedures for many years before everything disappeared for good after 1988.

Taken from the top of the bulk loading silos, the following photo typifies all the depots operated by Rugby Portland

Cement. ERF, Foden and a loaded Seddon Atkinson 6 wheeler are visible.

Rugby Cement shared the British Rail goods yard premises with Tunnel Cement, whose Bedford KM bulker is shown loading. These scenes now sadly are no more.

Shown right is a daily scene which faced most of the RPC Southampton based drivers, whereby storage silos received their bulk supplies from Rochester, Chinnor and other Rugby Cement Works. As with most rail connected Depots motive power discharged bulk rail wagon loads into storage silos whilst RPC Transport bulk lorries were top loaded on weighbridges. The B Series ERF 8 wheeler dates from 1974, whilst the S10/8 Foden Haulmasters came four years later on in 1978. The walled off enclosure in the centre of the yard contained a storage tank for lorry fuel.

Shown below is Barrington Cement Works near Cambridge when it had more than one production kiln together with two very prominent and recognisable chimneys, visible from quite some distance away. On the middle right of this photo is shown the transport workshop with some orange painted lorries parked in front. Just slightly further down are more orange lorries and trailers. The enormity of the quarry perimeter is shown to good effect, but what is not shown here are the enormous depths within the quarry.

Two further photographs show the entirety of the Southam Cement Works certainly over a period of between ten or twelve years between 1972 and 1984. Each of these aerial pictures shows many changes which were to take place within these works. Taking centre stage is the old RPC Garage, with the attached lorry wash which was built purely for bulk tankers. If you, the driver, didn't get it right, the water jets soaked your ankles and legs before you climbed on to the catwalks. One rather worrying aspect of the two inspection pits next to the lorry wash was when heavy rainwater ran down the factory yard most of the overflow filled these two pits almost to the top, making them totally unusable until such times as the flood levels drained away.

Tim Griffin, together with John Avidaeus and the Indian fitter called Sandhu, decided to wind up Bert Muncey, a Southam bulk driver who can best be described as a bit slow on the uptake. Tim shoved an air-line into the swirling water in no. 3 and 4 pit as John tied a piece of rope to an old bucket, and with enough of the remaining rope he placed the bucket upside-down on the water level. In comes Muncey and he said to Tim "What the hell are you lot doing?". Tim said "We've lost a tool box. It fell down into the water and we've sent the Indian down into the water to find it. His head is under the bucket with the air line to help him breathe". Muncey accepted the story, in his innocence, then went down to the Despatch Office and told all the staff in there what was going on in the garage. Of course it was sheer nonsense, but Bert Muncey was absolutely convinced that what he'd experienced and seen, ten minutes previously, was genuine!

Various Bedford KM 4 wheeler platforms (loaded) are seen parked behind the old garage, along with Ted Shoobridge's ERF L/V 8 wheeler covered box tipper.

A bit further over in the right centre of this picture is the Works' canteen block, where Danny Burke "ruled". The two yellow covered loaded flat trailers belonged to Bellview Transport. Its policy was not to waste time loading up. Consequently, with three trailers always in use, at least two would be loaded at any one time. The old structures around the former

bulk and bag packing shed, plus the silos, are seen in the top centre. These two Commer bulk and platform lorries were later disposed of for scrap. The main cement flow conveyor belt from the mill to the storage silos has been a central structure within the Southam Works yard for many years, as has the dumper shop, easily recognised by its red brick facing wall, top left centre.

The despatch portacabin building is hidden directly beyond the canteen block (centre). This photograph is a superb picture because it shows the observer exactly how daily things were portrayed to everyone, and in particular to the people who worked there.

This second photograph of Southam Cement Works shows the entire cement manufacturing complex after completion of the new clinker shed (seen centre) which, at that particular time, was the biggest single span new building in the United Kingdom. Cement clinker and bulk coal supplies were delivered almost daily by outside contractors. Both materials were stored on site prior to use. Coal from the visible heaps was loaded by a bucket loader on to the conveyors shown, and taken directly into the coal mill areas.

Cement making is a constant process which, unless a kiln is shut down for maintenance, or indeed a breakdown occurs elsewhere within the works, continues on indefinitely. Clay and chalk are excavated from source and transferred to the wash mills for slurry production and screening. Gypsum and sand are delivered into the works along with kiln coal.

These materials are brought in daily by outside haulage contractors. Cement cannot be produced without clinker, and so sufficient supplies of this material must be kept on site. Not knowing too much of what happens to the kiln coal after it reaches the coal mills, I can only presume that this material was used continuously for firing the kiln.

At the bottom of this superb photograph is the new transport garage and workshop. A cluster of RPC lorries is visible amongst the parking areas, and contractors and some RPC loaded trailers are visible parked in the main yard. The former new palletiser building, shown centre left, dwarfs all other buildings in Southam Works' Yard. The single works chimney, like so many others in the Rugby Group, was a landmark, and visible for many miles. Steam emits from the top (not smoke). The absence of employees' cars in the car park, suggests a Saturday afternoon at some point after 1988, or when this photograph was taken, possibly over a weekend. All of the landscaped areas behind the works as shown were presented up to a maintained level of acceptance in view of damage to trees, plant and ordinary buildings caused by cement dust.

The main Coventry to Banbury road, the A423, is shown on the bottom centre. Most of the tree and hedged areas appear to be immaculate in presentation to the reader looking at this photograph. Get up close and it changes dramatically.

The night-time photograph of Crown House, shown overleaf, would probably be regarded by all former Rugby or Southam Cement Works' based transport drivers as being "there but not seen". I myself would tread a well worn path to this imposing building from memory between August 1970/71 when I experienced a spate of "on site" bumps and scrapes with both 4274 MF, my faithful S21 Foden 8 wheeler, and also my brand new replacement, a 1971 Gardner 180 powered ERF 8 wheeler flat DNX 735K. Albert Southam, the Assistant Transport Manager, said to me on more than one occasion "I think that you, Glen, and us, will have to part company if you carry on much longer with these minor accidents!" Needless to say, thankfully, I lost 711 after just ten months, and so I reverted back to a brand new Bedford KM 4 wheeler fleet given to me in October 1972. Crown House was probably better known to all local drivers by other less well-known names such as "The Kremlin", or "Clown House". Drivers from earlier years referred to the building as "The House of Crowns". Numerous other non-polite names and references were used by drivers summoned to report for some misdemeanour or other. Drivers ordered to report to these premises were usually driven there by a colleague. This practice was geared up to put the individual concerned in a state of apprehension as to which Assistant Transport Manager saw you.

This photograph opposite was taken at around 8pm on a winter's night by Robin Palmer, the former Company's official photographer. This project also involved the assistance of the Crown House Commissionaire who, at that time, was none other than Barney Barnacle. This pair endeavoured to switch on all the lights within Head Office, starting at the Top Floor and descending, floor by floor. The only "fly in the ointment" being the 6th window on the top floor, which was Sir Halford Reddish's toilet. Because the bulb was missing, the toilet could not be used. The actual photograph was taken from the Town Hall steps, opposite Crown House, and shows the entire building, floodlit apart from the Chairman's Loo!!

Many drivers, including myself, for reasons of their own, returning to Rugby Works from the Leicester, Coventry Midland areas, and elsewhere, opted to by-pass Crown House by returning via the back entrance on Parkfield Road into the works. Others, coming back from Northampton and Daventry areas followed the A45 to the traffic lights at Dunchurch and turned right, eventually again turning left at the lights by Frosts the Printers (as it was then) and followed straight down to the cement works. By following these preferred routes, which in most cases were the official ways, drivers eliminated having to pass Crown House during daylight hours. Early morning deliveries, before Crown House staff began at 08h30, saw hordes of RPC lorries pass Head Office, but we all reverted back to the routes mentioned earlier on return journeys.

Looking back to these early years at Rugby Cement which, to be perfectly honest, were to take on a completely new meaning for me, simply because I was taught to drive heavy lorries with a degree of professionalism such as I had not experienced before joining the Company. Because of my choice, or option, of asking to go on Bags over the years, I was to drive 4, 6 and 8 wheeler platformed lorries, followed by artics after qualifying to Class 1 in 1988. I managed a total of twenty two and a half years Company service, eighteen of which were spent on regular bag delivery schedules. I never had an accident on the public road.

After I was transferred to Southam Cement Works, along with my platform colleagues, in 1982, Albert Southam and I became good friends, particularly so because he was instrumental in setting up appointments for both myself and Tony Higgins to meet David Lindop, the then Company Secretary, to obtain his permission for us to start collecting material etc. required for preparing Part One of this story.

RPC Greenford Depot, Middlesex.

During my time with the Company, I never visited RPC Greenford Depot. It was to come into its own when the M1 Motorway was extended by a further 17 miles into Central London from the Watford Boundaries in the early 1970s. Supplied with bulk cement stock in railway wagons from Rugby, Barrington and later Rochester Cement Works, I'd almost despaired of ever obtaining visual photographic evidence of Greenford Depot until I was given a colour print by Terry Golder when he was delivering the last bulk load from the Greenford site silos.

Shown here is the full aspect of the twin storage silos at Greenford Depot which are bordered by the railway sidings. Terry Golder was one of two former Chinnor based owner/drivers after RPC Transport was disbanded. This scheme began about 1988/89. Terry's Seddon Atkinson 301 8 wheel bulk tanker is shown in classic pose. The combined storage of these two silos would perhaps be around 800 ton. Delivery pipes, for assisting with bulk stock delivery by road vehicles, are visible on each structure corner. This photograph is the copyright

of Terry Golder, to whom I remain extremely grateful for allowing me to use it.

Shown here is a daily scene at the Exhall/Coventry Plant of Mixconcrete. F/N 439, based at Southam, discharges its load into the silo alongside Volvo/Leyland mixers of the period.

Mixconcrete old Exhall Plant, Coventry.
RPC 439, YWK 552S in action

Bag Palletiser Shed, Newport Depot, Monmouthshire

Newport Depot, Monmouthshire, Bulk Storage Silos.

For me, many superb large and small photos of all transport scenes are included in this second publication, all of which refer to earlier years after I joined the Company in 1968. Shown in all its original splendour is Southam Cement Works Bag Shed, overshadowed by the storage silos, themselves a landmark on the Warwickshire skyline for decades.

The old thatched storage shed for varied bags of lime, masonry and other non-Southam produced items is shown behind the windowed buildings on the immediate left hand side. Original covered and connected structures on top relate back to pre-war manufacture of cement at Southam Cement Works.

Of particular interest to ex-employees, particularly drivers of RPC Transport, the scene above shows a B Series ERF bulk tanker on the bulk weighbridge. One of Toll Bar's red and white ERFs is almost loaded with bags on the old chutes, whilst a Commer Maxi 4 wheeler bulk lorry, plus two other RPC flat lorries and one artic await their turn to load. Another parked up Commer Maxi bulk tanker is visible by the windowed building. This is a daily scene of operation which, during the late 1970s and early 1980s would change completely when ALL of the visible buildings from left of the bulk loading areas, including all of the overhead conveyor housing plus little covered sheds etc. would be completely dismantled. This included both storage buildings already referred to. This photograph was taken from the top of the main kiln shed at Southam Cement Works, and probably dates from around 1977. The Maxiload Commer bulk lorries were shortly to be removed from fleet service, being replaced by Dodge Hi Liner chassis.

Today's generation, together with ordinary people engaged in building and construction projects, such as those planned or executed accordingly, don't appear either to be interested in times past of our industrial history for one reason or another. It is the old story, you can lead a horse to water, but you can't make it drink. Some years back, just after the rebuild of Rochester Cement Works in Kent, over a ten year period 1969 – 1979, many black and white full plate photos were taken at each stage of the construction. I now know that this was asked for by Sir Halford Reddish, our Chairman / Managing Director, so that a record of rebuilding stages etc. would be kept in Company records. The buyout of Rugby Cement by RMC, together with the eventual purchase of all RMC's assets, including Rugby, by Cemex in later years, was followed eventually by the closure of Chinnor, Southam and finally Rochester. These photos, which numbered in their hundreds, were dumped in skips when the Rochester Works was being cleared. Alan Moorey, a good friend of mine for many years through old lorry rallies etc., worked as a driver for EA

Castle, who themselves had delivered cement in sacks for more years than anyone could remember out of Rochester. Consequently Alan, on one of his last visits to these works, saved all of these by then unwanted photos, over three hundred of them, as well as all or any general photos taken both within Rochester and elsewhere within the Rugby Group over its many years of operation. Many of these photos were held in storage at Rochester. A transfer of these photos was arranged by Alan and me at one of the Gaydon Old Lorry events. The total weight of this unique collection of material amounted to almost a quarter of a hundredweight of records and activity going back to Post War years within the Company. I personally was not interested in the construction stage photos involving the Rochester rebuild, and as such willingly passed them all to John Frearson, a gentleman concerned with the study of all earlier years and references to Rugby Portland Cement's years of manufacture, existence and origins.

CHAPTER 11

The Drivers, Supervisors and Reunions (And, the Final Chapter!) RoSPA Safe Driving Chicken Dinners / Medal Presentations

For many years, before and after the Author joined the company, RPC Transport supported safe driving practices by being a member company of RoSPA (Royal Society for the Prevention of Accidents). If any driver had twelve months accident free, a further year of safe driving was therefore necessary, by which time you were then qualified to attend such functions.

These yearly events became universally known as the "Chicken Dinners / RoSPA Presentations".

Southam Drivers, possibly in 1968 shown below:

Left to Right, back row: unknown, Malc Thornton, John Brunt, John Baskot, Mark Shuttleworth, Ted Gaskins, Roy Bate, unknown

Left to Right, front row: John Bousfield, John Isham, Chris Johnson, Ken Harvey (RPC Transport Manager), Lew Smith, Harry Gowlett (Southam Works Manager), John Overton, Fred Williams (Southam Despatch Supervisor).

More Southam based drivers plus familiar faces around 1970s.

Southam Works boasted many different individuals amongst the drivers and transport in general. Here are some of them.

Left to right: Clive Mumford in his early years (Garage Foreman), Jack Reynolds, Fred Williams (Southam Despatch Supervisor), John Baskot, George Trotman, John Brunt, Mark Shuttleworth, Harry Gowlett (Southam Works Manager), Cliff Underhill, John Overton, Oscar Jayes, Frank Linnel, Vic Bourton, Ted Shoobridge.

I knew most of these gentlemen, although Vic Bourton did not stay long at Southam before he died. Ted Shoobridge on the right hand side was full of himself in many ways. John Overton and Frank Linnel were real gentlemen. Ted worked 8 wheel covered tippers taking two trips to Alexandra Stone at Malvern every day, but I have since learned through my research he was also towing cars out of ditches. He along with Chris Johnson plus other characters came to RPC Transport from Midland Red Buses.

Shown below is a collection of both Rugby and Southam Transport drivers taken at a RoSPA dinner, possibly in the late 1970s.

I will attempt to name and describe all the standing drivers *from left to right.*

John Heritage (known as Buddy), Ian Mackie a night driver and loader at Southam, Maurice Goulding better known as Spike, Mr Overton, Oscar Jayes' head in-between Lew Smith with his moustache, Jack Smith, John Brunt, Gilbert Henderson - a bit of a singer apparently, D Seward*, Tony Hall known as Captain Pugwash, Chris Johnson one half of the Union, Bob Reynolds, behind Ken Simpson always laughing, Les Clark later to become an owner operator, Chris Moon my mate and good friend, Trevor Griffin (Southam Despatch Supervisor), John Bousfield, an unknown driver from the Birmingham Depot and Roy Bates.

*Doug Seward was not a driver. Along with other later managers he introduced the Owner Driver Scheme which began initially in 1987 and lasted until mid 2000s.

Seven drivers are shown seated and named *from left to right*

Kevin Billingham a great friend of mine along with Arthur "Fruity" Harris. Kevin was sadly killed on the Rugby Southam road a few years back by a foreign driver on the wrong side of the road. Jock Brown ex para, the other half of the Union, John Gilkes a gentleman made redundant in the middle 1980s. He later drove for Dowdeswells of Stockton, Malcolm Clark, Dave Bishop, unknown, Ray Player, Harry Gowlett (Southam Works Manager).

Some more Long Serving Southam Based Transport Faces

Shown standing left to right: Sammy Gill - golf was his passion, Taffy Davies a real live wire on Bags, Dougie Tomes captain of a tanker and then I/C of the Tyre Depot, Jack Reynolds a nice man, unknown, Fred Williams Transport Supervisor, Cliff Underhill, John Brunt, George Trotman - he was shy about his age, John Isham a good friend of the author.

Shown here is a group of Southam based night drivers who, with the exception of Les Butcher (seated centre) all survived to the early 1980s before redundancy reared its ugly head.

Standing, left to right: Maurice Golding better known as Spike, Ray Player, Ian Mackie, John Bousfield, John Gilks.

Seated, left to right: Bob Mann a former fireman, Les Butcher (this photo was taken at his retirement party) and George Greenaway.

One of the early RPC Transport's Safe Driving Chicken Dinner and Medal Awards occasions, involving drivers from Rugby and Southam Works and Birmingham Depot

Back row standing, left - right
Bill "Happy" Alder, Sid Cave, Alan Cruickshanks, Fred Saunders, not known, Doug Johnson, not known, Peter Bunyard,

Faces and names from memory include the following,

Lower area standing, left - right
Mr Baker (Southam Works Manager), Johnny Cant, unknown, Jack Skelcey, unknown, Ken Whyment behind, Bert Kemp (Birmingham depot, bags), Malc Thornton, Len Watts, Reg Coles, Billie Jenner, Les Timms (behind), John Isham, "Bristol" Smith, in-between, unknown, Alec Watts and Roy Bates behind Ken Harris (Assistant Transport Manager), Dick Smith (Despatch, Rugby Works), Fred Williams (Southam Works Despatch). Fred Seamer, Roger Sanford, Albert Kimberly behind, next to Ken Harvey (RPC Transport Manager), not known, not known, Nobby Clark, Ron Sheasby (behind), Pete Gudgin, Fred Jennaway, Albert Southam far right (Assistant Transport Manager). The date of this gathering is sometime during the middle 1970s.

Rugby Works Transport Drivers, Middle 1970s Onward

Back Row, left to right: Brian Strefford (the youngest driver), Dennis Garlick (choo choo!), Ken Smith, Jack Kenny (always poking about in lay-bys), Fred Seamer, Sid Cave, Fred Saunders (always late in the mornings), Tony Hall (Captain Pugwash), Mr Baker (Works Manager), Chris Moon, Reg Coles, unknown, Bob Reynolds, Roy Bates (Woofer), Alec Watts, Roy Allen (Telegram Sam), Dick Smith (Rugby Despatch Supervisor), Peter Bunyard

Seated, left to right: Peter Gudgin (known as Branch), Bill Jenner, John Heritage (Buddy), Johnny Cant, Dave (Nobby) Clark, Gwynn (Taff) Roberts, Ken Wright (never off work), Bill (Cassius) Clark.

RPC Rochester Based - 826 Onwards – renumbered fleet from 1976
Bulk Drivers

*	Fleet Number	Name	Reg	Truck Type
*	729	Maurice Barton (Dick)	HUE 729L	ERF A Series 8 Wheel
*	826	Alan Segar	TAC 152N	ERF A Series 6 Wheel
	837	Kevin Parry	GKV 469N	ERF A Series 6 Wheel
	838	Dave Hallums	GKV 470N	ERF A Series 6 Wheel
	840	Vic Dallas	GKV 472N	ERF A Series 6 Wheel
	851	Jimmy Deville	HKV 981N	ERF A Series 8 Wheel
	418	Tony Keeley	WWK 620S	ERF B 8 Wheel
	424	Joe Taylor	WWK 621S	Foden
	420	Owen Jarrett (Love)	WWK 622S	ERF B 8 Wheel
	430	Bob Cook (Scootabout)	EDU 537T	Foden
	431	Roy Gladish	EDU 538T	Foden
	434	Vern Hodge	YVC 253S	ERF B 8 Wheel
	438	Syd Kelvie	YWK 551S	ERF B 8 Wheel
*	462	Cyril Weeks	BHP 478T	ERF B Series 6 Wheel
	437	Ian Crombie (Duckie)	BHP 502T	ERF B 8 Wheel
	440	Arthur Jarrett	BHP 503T	ERF B 8 Wheel
	443	Frank Kennard	BHP 510T	ERF B 8 Wheel
	460	Ron Austin	BHP 511T	ERF B 6 Wheel
	464	Brian Newman (Bootsie)	CVC 185T	ERF B Wheel
	494	Kenny Smith	EKV 980T	Foden Haulmaster
	657	Dave Stockbridge	AAC 455X	ERF C Series
	658	Fred Cambell (Harry Worth)	BAC 621Y	ERF C Series
	659	Ronnie Ring	BAC 622Y	ERF C Series
*	660	Rod Davis	BWK 200Y	ERF C Series
	669	Taffy Nash	DKV 868Y	SA 2008W
	214	Syd Brown	A30 LKV	Foden
*	201	Peter Manson (Fanjo)	A32 KWK	Foden
	202	Jack Steven	A33 KWK	Foden
	205	Kenny Pearce	A36 KWK	Foden
	206	Derek George	A37 KWK	Foden
*	215	Dave Ingram	A601 LWK	Foden
*	226	Kenny Norwood	A998 MHP	Foden
	227	Tony Baldcock	A999 MHP	Foden
	229	Brian Ballard	B782 OKV	Foden
	230	Stan Fryer	B783 OKV	Foden
*	236	Dave French	B842 TAC	ERF C Series 8 Wheel
*	237	Mickey West	C706 URW	ERF C Series 8 Wheel
*	238	Terry Jafferies	C707 URW	ERF C Series 8 Wheel

*Denotes driver that came off Bags and went onto Bulk when their Bag Lorries went back.
Dodge Hi-Lines and Bedford KMs.

RPC Rochester Based Bags

10 tone Dodge Hi-Line

Fleet Number	Name	Reg
517	Brian Woodhouse	EWK 850T
519	Dickie Masters (Sicknote)	EDU 450T
525	Murdoch McPherson	EWK 858T

Seddon Atkinson 300

Fleet Number	Name	Reg
559	Brain Haslewood	SRW 703W
569	Ted Hacker (Concorde)	WVC 627X
570	Roy Jewiss	WVC 628X
584	Jim Hastings	YVC 446X
590	Chris Oliver (Happy)	BAC 617Y

ERF C Series Blue Cab

Fleet Number	Name	Reg
873	Brian Tallon (The Claw)	EHP 941Y
874	Johnny Prout	EHP 942Y
875	Mick Bonniface (Overload)	EHP 943Y
876	Bill Horsham	ERW 696Y

ERF C Series Brown Cab

Fleet Number	Name	Reg
897	Allan Chalklin (GNU)	A532 HAC
898	Jeff Powsey (Puzzle)	A533 AC
899	Malcolm Gambrill	A534 HAC

897 / 898 / 899 were Chinnor Swaps for 556 / 548 / 550 / Flat Beds 6/8 Wheelers for Castellated bodies.

Night Drivers

Martin Whipee – Bob Norris – Later, Kenny Norwood.
Then Martin Whipee swapped with Malcolm Gambrill. Bill Horsham then went into the office as Transport Clerk – Despatch. Later, Malcolm Gambrill came back on to days on 876 – Chris Fry.

Dave Hallums (Days), had one of the 6-wheeler K Type Dodge Tank/Flats 751 and could not operate the Eaton and 2 speed axle. It used a full tank of diesel to get down to Southampton and it needed filling up to get back to Rochester.

When he got 838, a square fronted ERF tank, he complained about the noise of the engine (a 150 Gardner) saying that it was too noisy and way above the decibel level, edging to get a new motor, so he was given a pair of ear defenders.

Rochester based drivers. None are known to me personally.

Standing left to right: not known, Nigel Cook (workshop foreman), Ronnie Ring, Jack Starkey, Wally Brenham, Ron Young, George Elson, Ron Austin, John Kersey, Eric Hicks, Arthur Jarret, Bob Cook, Alan Chalklin, Bill Houghton, Joe Taylor, Charlie Hawkes (Transport Despatch Clerk), Harrold Tregg, George Fowler (Transport Supervisor).

Seated, left to right: Fred Campbell, Fred Pellett, Con Eatwell, Tony Cass, Vernon Hodge, Eric Perkins, not known.

More Rochester Transport Driver Faces

Standing, left to right: Alan Chalklin, Bob Ralph, not known, Harold Trigg, Fred Pellett, Ronnie Ring, Ernie Perkins, Harry Ballard, Frank Gladdish, John Kersey, Ron Hadlow, Brian Newman, Bob Cook, George Elson, Bob Olds.

Seated, left to right: Jack Starkey, Con Eatwell, Joe Taylor, Cyril Weekes, Sid Brown, Eric Hicks.

All information on former Rochester drivers supplied by both Jim and Steve Hastings. Steve also supplied all the vehicle/driver details, so to these two long term friends I offer my sincere thanks.

RPC Transport, South Ferriby RoSPA Drivers Groups.

Back row, left to right: John Todd, Cedric Reynolds, Ray Barley, Dennis Lawtey, Brian Scott, Graham Lewis, Byron Bennett (Assistant Transport Manager), Brian Gravell, Keith Lacey, unknown, Alan Fowles, Pete Bullivant (Garage Foreman), Mick Briggs, Brian Pearson, Aubrey Wattam, Eddie Holtby, John Denton.

Middle row, left to right: Geoff Clark, Dave Peacock

Front row, left to right: Gordon Avell, John Clipson, Keith Shaw, Les Miller, John Westfield, Ray Lawtey, Trevor Richardson, Dave Stanley.

Back row, left to right: Trevor Richardson, Brian Gravell, Brian Scott, Alan Peal, John Clipson, Dave Peacock, Brian Pearson, Keith Lacey, Cedric Reynolds, Pete Bullivant (Garage Foreman), Byron Bennett (Assistant Transport Manager), John Todd, John Hodson (Works Manager), Geoff Clarke, Aubrey Watton, Eric Longbottom, Geoff Clark.

Front row, left to right: Les Miller, Bruce Barker, Mick Briggs, Alan Fowler, Ray Lawtey, Charlie Spencer.

Back row, left to right: Brian Gravell, John Baxter, Murwood Foster, John Westfield, Charlie Spencer, John Catline, Keith Shaw, Keith Lacey, Byron Bennett, Normal Wright, Fred Molds, Pete Bacon, Gordon Wallace, John Denton, Mervyn Smith (Transport Manager).

Front row, left to right: John Todd, Ron Thornton, Ray Barley, Alan Peal, Ray Barley, Jack Howell, Jim Burt, Pete Bullivant (Garage Foreman).

I am indebted to John Todd, who took time and trouble to list all the names of his former South Ferriby driver colleagues. Also, sincere thanks are due to Brian Peeps who, during his service with both Eastwoods and Rugby Cement, captured his days on film. His kindness in allowing me to use many of his photos rates a superb thank you.

Barrington Works Transport Drivers 1970s onwards.

This detailed information on all Barrington drivers was kindly supplied by Peter Dimes to whom I offer my sincere thanks for his time and kindness.

Back row, left to right: Ray Cole, Roy Chiswell, John Charlton, Ken Bullpen, Derek Nomads, Stan Pearce, Don Reddick.

Middle row, left to right: Alistair Reed, Vic Pope, Ernie Collier, Norman Morsel, Bill Covington, Pat Bushnell, Harold Thomas.

Front row, left to right: Keith Rule, Ray Shin, Len Welch, Charlie Field and Arthur Page.

Author's Note – Ernie Collins was later promoted to second in command at the Central Garage. His parting words to everyone, "Yes Mate", became his nickname.

More Barrington Works Transport Drivers, 1970s onwards

Back row, left to right: Ray Cole, Peter Dunes, Stan Pearce, unknown, John Thompson, Terry Forget, Norman Clarke, Roy Chiswell.

Middle row, left to right: Bill Slater, Melvin Elson, Alan Hughes, Phil Chamberlain, Keith Jarman

Front row, left to right: Pat Flynn, Terry Blanchester, Ken Bullpen, Walter Shaw (Works Manager), Pop Randall, Derek Wayland, Peter Ticker

Author's Note – I knew Derek Wayland from 8 wheeler bags days, and Keith Jarman in later years when he became the Transport Supervisor before he finally retired.

RPC Transport RoSPA Safe Driving Chinnor Works Drivers Groups October 1976

Back row, left to right: Tommy Wait, Ivan Butcher, John Preece (Twinkle), Terry Golder, Len House, Ken Austin, Ron Berry, Peter Bilson (Works Manager), Trevor Griffin (Despatch Manager)

Front row, left to right: Len Walton, Frank Faulkener (Uncle), Bill Ayres, Claude Honour, Len Read (Big Daddy), John Ayres, John Rampton, Bill Messenger.

More Chinnor Drivers Groups RoSPA Safe Driving Dinner Awards 1977

Back row, left to right: Ivan Butcher, Terry Golder, Ron Berry, Len House (Buff), Martin Witcher, Mr Neaves (Works Manager)

Front row, left to right: Trevor Griffin (Transport Supervisor), Bill Ayres, Tommy Wait, Bill Messenger, Ken Austin.

Mr Neaves was ex RPC Trinidad who along with a chief engineer were transferred to Chinnor Cement Works after Trinidad became independent.

Mr Neaves worked alongside Peter Bilson for a period of time.

RPC Transport Chinnor Works Drivers Groups RoSPA Safe Driving Awards 1983

Back row, left to right: Fred Amer, Ken Austin, Dick Craiker, Bill Morgan, Peter Bilson, John Martin, Terry Golder

Front row, left to right: Chris Sandford, Fred Rymer, Bill Messenger, Tommy Wait, Allen Nunn

RPC Transport Chinnor Works, RoSPA Safe Driving Awards, Driver's Groups 1984

Back row, left to right: Fred Ryner. Ken Austin, Ron Berry, Brian Stopp, Peter Bilson (Works Manager), John Johnson, Bill Morgan (Head of Sales), Chris Sandford

Front row, left to right: John Preece (Twinkle), Bill Ayres, Tommy Wait, Bill Messenger, John Martin (Supervisor), Len Read (Big Daddy)

Author's Note: I am indebted to Terry Golder for his help and assistance in the preparation of each of these four photographs of former Chinnor Works Drivers.

Rugby Cement Chinnor Works Christmas Dinner 1989

Left to right: A driver from Crown House, Ron Ludlow (driver of 850), Bob Westall (Chinnor Garage Fitter), Graham Munday (Garage Chargehand), Charlie Greig (Garage Foreman).

In the back view is Mark Couchman (Garage Fitter).

Almost nine years were to pass before all daily and nightly operations came to a final stop in 1999 at Chinnor Works. Graham Munday and Charlie Greig were redundant on August Bank Holiday of that year. It's interesting to note from this happy photograph that Graham Munday sports a beard and hair ON TOP of his head. Like us all in this New Century, he is now going a bit thin on top!

Whilst deeply involved in preparing RPC Part One, I decided to organise the first of what would eventually turn out to be four separate reunions of RPC Transport staff, together with members of the various works sections who wished to attend. Looking back to the 1993 first ever gathering, now more than twenty years ago, it is very hard to realise how many former colleagues who attended that initial event have now since passed away. Shown below is the invitation and photograph which I used in the Crown House Magazine "Topic" to advertise the event.

As the caption says, we had the initial one in 1993. Alan Cruickshank was a retired Rugby Works driver, and his daughter Denise ran the Green Man Public House in Dunchurch. We had that venue for two reasons - one was that there was no charge on account of RPC involvement, and the second is that it had a large car park and was known by everyone who attended. But in the event, a spiralling staircase to the first floor made things difficult for handicapped guests. Nevertheless, it was a resounding success for everyone who came. Again, this advertisement / photo invitation says we were to hold two further gatherings at the Royal British Legion Club in Hillmorton, one

Advertising leaflet using one of Tony Higgins excellent photos for RPC Transport No.1 Reunion

in October 1996 and a second one, from memory, in or around 1999.

Chris Moon, my colleague on Bags at both Rugby and Southam, organised both these reunions as he was a regular member at the Legion. The car parking here was limited, space wise, and many cars were to be parked on the roadside verges, which to me suggested that any future venues had to offer more secure arrangements.

Two photos taken at the 1999 event show some of the smiling faces.

Both pictures are full of characters known to me during my time with RPC. Shown left to right in the top photo are George Foot (one of Rugby's finest and a Night Driver), then with his face to the camera is Stan Reader (a Southam Bag Man), the lady next to him is unknown to me. Stan's wife is next, looking at the nonsense letters held by John Hancox, a former Southam bag contractor. Mick Tuffrey is shown next with Johnny Brunt, a Southam bulk driver.

The second photo shows many years of experience with RPC Transport. Left to right are Freddy Hack (Chief of the night

drivers), Stan Hibberd (a driver from many years back), stood next to him is his long term friend and colleague, John McDonnell, better known to everyone as Big Mac. The smaller figure is Derek "Geordie" Stacey, one of Rugby's Central Garage's finest. Next to him is Clive Mumford, the former Southam Garage Foreman, who appeared to be maturing nicely in his pensionable years. Clive has his left hand on the shoulder of Peter Banyard, one of Rugby Works' best known and respected bulk drivers.

This third photo is from one of the Legion reunion gatherings and shows in the foreground more ex senior style RPC drivers plus two members of Rugby despatch office. Seen sitting on the immediate left hand side is Dave "Nobby" Clark, one of Rugby's best known characters. Standing next to him is a former RPC driver who migrated some years ago down to the Southampton area. Just his name invokes laughter! This being Peter Wiltshire. On the right hand side in the blue jacket and tie is Jack Parton sitting next to Dick Smith, the former Despatch Supervisor at Rugby before he retired some years back. In the background, no doubt reminiscing about happier times, are Dave Bishop on the right with Les Clark in the centre, and his lady Carol. All three were employed at Southam Works on contractor's transport. When I think back to the middle of 1968 when I started with RPC Transport in amongst almost sixty different individuals who I didn't know, I now look back over these wonderful years and reflect on what has happened since. Many of the friendships made in the early days are just as good as ever. As with every large road transport company of years back, you were bound to come up against some individuals

who did not take kindly to the regimentation of daily life at RPC Transport. They did not last long, and for reasons of their own, left the company for good.

Others by way of their own folly, broke rules either by fiddling or stealing or other misdemeanours, and were sacked outright, but the large majority of drivers, including ex-servicemen, settled down and chalked up many years of loyal service before it all came to an abrupt end through no fault of their own.

Some more former Rugby Works characters are shown looking to the lens.

The head of Fred Saunders on the previous page is shown on the left. Next is Brian Chater, now a recognised local windows and doors manufacturer. Sitting directly opposite him are three former members of Rugby's notorious drivers. Seen on the right hand side is Albert Kimberley, known to his colleagues as The Fugitive. Norman "Brummy" Marshall is shown centre with Johnny Douglas, wearing his best blue jersey. Next to him are Dougie Cleaver and his wife Doris. Bryn Roberts, one of three Taffies employed at that time as drivers is seen sitting in the centre of their photo. He was later to transfer into the Works Laboratory.

We must jump on several years now to the fourth and final RPC Transport reunion which took place on 23rd December 2004. With a completely new venue, less than half a mile from Crown House, the Indian Club in Edward Street, Rugby offered a huge hard standing car park with security cameras and wheelchair access. Because this was going to be the last event it was thrown open to whoever wanted to come, consequently, because of the number of people expected I needed assistance, and so two former colleagues from Rugby, Roy Allen and Mick Shepherd, together with their wives, Rosemary and Betty, looked after the catering. Arthur and Rene Harris concentrated their efforts on Southam Cement Works employees and drivers alike, whilst Isobel Watson looked after Crown House enquiries, plus those of RPC pensioners. One former Chinnor Works driver, Len House, journeyed all the way from Cornwall and was determined to attend by catching the Southam Works coach. His intention was to stop with relatives at Bicester but hospitality was offered to him by Arthur and Rene Harris, so he stayed the night because of the lateness of the event finishing and he returned to Cornwall the next morning. Shown below are four familiar faces representing Chinnor Cement Transport at the 2004 event. Shown left to right are Bill and John Ayres, fondly remembered as "the Twins" by

all those who worked alongside and knew them. Len House, the long distance traveller from Cornwall sits next to Charlie Grieg, the later Chinnor Garage foreman.

Shown below is another general photograph of the happy guests during that memorable evening. Drivers with their wives or partners mingle with others from the works and garage. Neville Walker shown on the left, grinning like a Cheshire Cat, is going thin on top. He notched up almost thirty nine years' service with RPC Transport. Colin Smith on the right went to RPC Transport's garage straight from school and was still with the Company in 1989 with an equally long service period under his belt. Shown with his back to the camera is by far the most successful ex RPC owner driver Charlie Jones. On his right is Barney Barnacle, a former Crown House commissionaire, and ex Rugby Works crane driver whose story in this second book deserves exceptional credit.

Peter Jackson, former Head Chemist, and David Holton, ex Crown House payroll manager, discuss tactics whilst Len House's back separates the reunion organiser in shirt and tie, yours truly, Glen McBirnie.

During this last enjoyable gathering, it was voiced by certain long serving drivers and RPC pensioners that some form of gift should be made to Isobel Watson in lieu of her energies. This was duly achieved by the people concerned and the organisers.

The head of Ken Tansley, the former Rugby Works carpenter and ex RPC driver from years' back, is just above Colin Smith, looking decidedly serious. Charlie Jones and Barney, mentioned earlier, are shown talking to Isobel Watson whose head is just visible on Charlie's left.

Shown above are ex Rugby Drivers and Garage Fitters at the last reunion.

Back row, left to right: Tony Burgess, Ken Le Kleux, unknown, Simon Clifton, Charlie, John McDonald, unknown, Chris Moon, Ken Tansley, Dougie Cleaver, unknown, unknown, Roy Allen and Freddie Hack (night driver).

Middle row, left to right: Derek Stacey, Mr French, Dick Smith (Transport Supervisor), Ray Cheatle (night driver), Mick Shepherd, Dennis Garlick, Ken Wright, unknown, Colin Smith, Fred Seamer, Unknown, John Douglas.

Front row, left to right: Neville Walker (standing), unknown, unknown, Jim Law, Charlie Jones, Dave Cooksey, Billie Jenner, John Heritage, unknown.

CHAPTER 12

The Conclusion. Crown Won't Let You Down

How do you begin to tell the ordinary person what it was like to work for RPC Transport? Remembering my own early days at Rugby Works in 1968 really sums it up. 6am starts and learning how to blow (discharge) the many different types of cement tanker lorries under instruction.

As the days and weeks went by the individuals soon fitted into working alongside so many different characters and temperaments. Working at "The Portland" as it was known locally here in the Rugby area, people in general were, I think, slightly jealous because weekly pay and conditions were way above anything else other than what the car factories offered in the 1960s and 1970s.

Drivers were expected to drive and deliver. You were paid for all hours worked. In the event of punctures, accidents or breakdowns (which themselves were few), you got on the telephone, and other people came out to your assistance. There appeared to be a lot of regimentation in the rules and regulations. This did not find favour with some drivers who soon left, but for the vast majority of drivers right across the Rugby Group many were to achieve long periods of loyal service.

Equally so, generations of ordinary families were to spend their entire working lives working for the parent company, Rugby Cement, either in the quarries, cement mills or indeed elsewhere within the Company, in works and depots situated across the country.

Colin Smith left school and went straight into the old Parkfield Road garage at Rugby. He would go on to achieve forty one years' service, much of it later on at Central Garage, and would end up a chargehand foreman. His father before him, Ron, A former driver, was semi-retired when I started. He was employed filling up lorries and doing other jobs. Les Smith, an uncle, was a driver at Rugby, known to everyone by another unmentionable name, whilst Derek Smith began at Crown House, but was later to be transferred into Southam Works Despatch Office. Albert Bunyard started as a driver in the late 1940s and 1950s, but a combination of ill health and hospitalisation saw him transfer to the garage. Three of his sons were to become drivers initially; Alan, only stayed for a short period, but Peter and Barry were to contribute many loyal years of service.

Ray Lowe came out of the army and joined RPC Transport. He would go on to achieve 30 years or more, whilst his wife Anne would spend some years at Crown House. His son Ashley started in Central Garage in the 1970s. Bob "Snowy" Caldwell had been an RPC Transport driver for many years when I started. His son Alan stayed with us for a short period of time. Peter Dimes followed his father into the Eastwoods Cement Fleet as a driver at Barrington Cement Works near Cambridge. He would go on to achieve nearly 36 years working for two separate companies at Barrington (Eastwoods and Rugby). Jack Howell was a bulk driver at South Ferriby

Cement Works in Humberside for quite some time. His son John started as a bulk loader, and was still there in this new Century, working for Cemex. John finally called it a day in 2013 as retirement loomed.

Who can forget "the Twins" at Chinnor Cement Works near Oxford, John and Bill Ayre, both of whom were to spend a large part of their driving life there? Other names from Chinnor include Frank Faulkener (Uncle), whose son became a supervisor and engineer, and Horace Carter along with his son Dave who both served at Chinnor in different capacities. Dave Carter still works at Cemex, Rugby, in the Laboratory.

The wellbeing of all employees was foremost in the mind of the former Chairman / Managing Director of Rugby Cement, the late Sir Halford Reddish, whose policies of looking after his employees were well known. His views on managing his company, together with the workforce over many years, are themselves documented in detail earlier in this second story.

RPC Transport survived a 61 year period of serving their customers. Rugby Group was the parent company taken over by RMC in 2000 but the Rugby Cement name continued until 2005 when Cemex arrived.

Rugby Cement will be remembered for many things, but above all else it will be these big orange bulk tanker lorries which were to capture the general public's interest and admiration.

Shown below is BUE 331J F/N 699 parked in Rugby's yard. This photograph, as well as our own dear memories, represents the epitome of why being a Rugby Cement driver was the best job in the world to all of us who were lucky enough to do it.

Never forgotten, always remembered.

Glen Mc Burnie